Advance Praise F~~or Stage Climbing~~

"*Stage Climbing* brilliantly tr~~...~~ for reaching your potential into t~~...~~ ec-tive action steps that anyone ~~can apply to quickly make desired~~ life changes."
—Stephen R. Covey, author of *The 7 Habits of Highly Effective People* and *The Leader in Me*

"In *Stage Climbing*, Dr. Broder eloquently shares his powerful strategies to reach the highest potential in every area of your life. An easy and simple guide to fulfillment."
— Deepak Chopra, author of *The Seven Spiritual Laws of Success*

"It is time to release *your full potential in all your dimensions* and this book will inspire you to your highest stage!! Happy reading!"
— Mark Victor Hansen, Co-creator of the #1 *New York Times* bestselling series, *Chicken Soup for the Soul*

"I highly recommend *Stage Climbing* for anyone who would like to understand, accept or change an aspect of his or her life. *Dr. Broder offers a brand-new approach that will get you the results you want for your career, relationships, spirituality or any part of your life where you apply it.*"
— Peggy McColl, *New York Times* bestselling author of *Your Destiny Switch*

"*Stage Climbing* is one of the most innovative and brilliant models for helping people to change at the deepest levels. *I have suc-cessfully used it on myself* as well as with the clients I counsel, and strongly recommend it to anyone seriously seeking to gain a better understanding of themselves and take control of their lives very quickly."
— Karyne B. Wilner, PsyD., Clinical Psychologist and Director, Profes-sional Program in Core Living Therapy

~ **"*Stage Climbing* represents a breakthrough.** It is a completely new career and personal development tool that takes a jumble of feelings and descriptions and drills them down into discreet categories that anyone can understand. **It concisely let me see where I was in my career and personal development and it gave me the tools I needed to achieve greater development and more fulfillment."**
— Sharon P. Stein, Health Care and Medical Sales Professional representing Fortune 50 firms and the American Red Cross

~ "When I read Dr Michael Broder's latest book, *Stage Climbing*, I realized why I firmly believe that this book will help you uniquely transform your life. Broder's three "Es" of Experience, Expertise, and Eclecticism were applied to this book. Broder's new ***Stage Climbing* theory synthesizes some of the greatest thinking of modern psychology while creatively adding an easy to use practical ("simple but not simplistic"...) approach toward reaching your highest potential with remarkable efficiency."**
— Richard A. Lippin MD, Chief Medical Officer, Tobyhanna Army Depot Occupational Health Clinic, and Former Chair, Mental Health Committee-American College of Occupational and Environmental Medicine

~ "With precision, clarity, wisdom and heart; Michael Broder takes the reader through the process of *Stage Climbing* towards the task of greater knowledge and awareness about one's highest potential. **This is an extremely well written and magical book."**
— Murray Needleman, Ph.D., Clinical and Media Psychologist

~ "I fully recommended *Stage Climbing*, by Dr. Michael Broder. **He has a special way of engaging the reader and his compassion shines through.** If you follow his ideas you will ascend to good mental health."
— Windy Dryden, Ph.D., Professor of Psychotherapeutic Studies, Goldsmiths University of London

~ **"*Stage Climbing* could be a life-changing event for anyone who reads it and applies the strategies to their unique situation. It is also an excellent read."**
— Antoinette Champclos, French author of *Méthode infaillible pour réussir vos études*

~ Dr. Broder ties in the old classical concepts of psychology with the new approaches to self-healing, personal growth and empowerment in a way that's never been done before. **The tools Stage Climbing provide are key.** No book in this area has provided them so comprehensively and in a way that **speaks directly to each reader. All of the ingredients for lasting change are there for any reader who wishes to make use of them."**

— Andrea Vlacho-Christos, author of *Healing Our Animal Friends With EFT*

~ **"Stage Climbing is so illuminating.** It has helped me understand not only when I developed certain behaviors but also why and what needs each one was originally intended to address, and this insight **has increased my acceptance of myself and others and provided me with a path to greater purpose and meaning in my life."**

— Carol Noblitt, Director of Development for the Real World Foundation

~ **"Stage Climbing** is a welcome landmark in the field of human development and personal growth. It is profound in its theoretical framework and practical in its self-help applicability. Its original seven stages of maturity are intellectually rigorous and its methods for advancing to higher stages are sound and specific enough to be life changing. **It has been said that we come into this life with no manual to guide us. Well, Dr. Broder seems to have provided a highly credible, amazingly accessible and positively actionable manual for living life fully.** Knowing his previous self-help books, **Stage Climbing** can be considered his **magnum opus,** a remarkable work of psychological innovation and for consciousness evolution. This book offers solid and creative ways to step up to the next highest stage of life potential and fulfillment."

— Larry J. Rosenberg, Ph.D., Life Transformation Consultant, Sedona, AZ

~ "Dr. Broder has distilled a lifetime of professional service into a unique set of perspectives... and a set of highly effective strategies for transforming this clarity into meaningful change within our everyday lives. **With practical guidelines for enhancing parenting, career selection, and love relationships; Stage Climbing is a "must read" for human service professionals, as well as anyone seeking a wonderful 'road map' for more successful living."**

— Bruce Coopersmith, Ph.D., Clinical Psychologist, Philadelphia, PA

~ "*Stage Climbing* **offers a masterful integration of cognitive therapy tools** across the developmental life span. It encourages self-acceptance and honest self-assessment. **With amazing detail, Dr. Broder prescribes activities and tools to cognitively dispute limiting beliefs at each stage, leading the reader to pursue desired incremental behavioral changes towards living one's fullest potential.**"
   — Barbara Lyn Grinnell, Ph.D. Licensed Psychologist, Wynnewood, PA

~ "*Stage Climbing* **provides me with an intelligent framework for organizing my thoughts and deciding the most efficient place to intervene when I'm working with a client.**"
   — Arlene Foreman, Licensed Professional Counselor, A Center for Marriage Counseling

~ "Michael Broder's *Stage Climbing* is a thoughtful, manageable, and elegant approach to our important therapeutic work. **It provides a brilliantly useful and succinct paradigm for understanding and promoting clients' resources, development, and growth ... Michael, you did it again!**"
   — Elaine R Axelrod, PhD., Psychologist and Shamanic Practitioner

~ "Having just finished *Stage Climbing*, **I found it to be a page-turner** which is already conditioning my reactions to life's opportunities/challenges. **It gave me some easy-to-understand goals that are helping me to become the person I most want to be.**"
   — Harvard Ayers, Professor Emeritus of Anthropology, Appalachian State University, author of *Arctic Gardens: Voices from an Abundant Land*

~ "*Stage Climbing* **introduces a new, simple, yet powerful tool.** It cuts to the chase in helping you understand your life as well as taking it to the next level with the many effective strategies offered. **I highly recommend it to anyone who wants to see immediate results!**"
   — Fran Grabosky, Licensed Psychologist, Tampa, Florida

~ "*Stage Climbing* **is such a wonderfully helpful guide to getting the most out of life and bettering ourselves along the way.**"
   — BJ Rosenfeld, author of *The Chameleon in the Closet*

~ "*Stage Climbing* is insightful, informative and well written. It can show anyone the Shortest Path to their Highest Potential."
— Hemant Gupta, Ph.D., author of *Road to Digital Divine* and *Joy from Deep Within*

~ "**Dr. Broder has written an important and thoughtful book, one which is indispensable to mental health professionals but also accessible to anyone valuing psychological well-being.** Although based on complex psychological theories and on the shoulders of such greats as Maslow and Erickson, Dr. Broder has created yet another system to facilitate psychological growth and enable readers to be more impactful in their lives. He has formulated a well-organized, clear, concise method for exploring deep psychological processes. In that process, he has revealed himself to be an important theorist in the field of psychology. **What also comes through is Dr. Broder's respect and passion for his profession and its powerful potential to not only heal, but to enable one to live a more fulfilling and meaningful life.**"
— Dr. Marion Rudin Frank, President, Professional Psychology Services, PC; Founder and Coordinator, Philadelphia Jungian Professional Club

~ "The concepts in *Stage Climbing* integrated a variety of developmental and therapeutic psychological theories in a well organized and practical manner; the concepts were worded in a way to be useful to practitioners and laypeople alike. **In reading about careers, romantic relationships, family relationships, altruistic endeavors, and other facets of life, I thought of scenarios in my own life, the lives of friends and loved ones, and my patients. Personally, the concepts gave me courage to enact behavior change** by addressing a professional issue with an authority figure; I felt empowered for having stood up for myself! I have no doubt this book would be useful in helping others in understanding and changing their own behavior by realizing the areas in their own life that could benefit from growth and change."
— Alicia T. Rozycki Lozano, Ph.D., Clinical and Counseling Psychologist, San Angelo, TX

~ "Michael Broder has done it again! **His innovative way of categorizing behavior according to a person's level of maturity helps my clients to move towards their goals in the most efficient manner.**"
— Jacqueline Summers, Licensed Psychologist

STAGE CLIMBING™

THE SHORTEST PATH TO YOUR HIGHEST POTENTIAL

Michael S. Broder, Ph.D.

MPA
PUBLICATIONS

Stage Climbing™: The Shortest Path to Your Highest Potential
Copyright © 2012 by Michael S. Broder

Published by:
MPA PUBLICATIONS
255 South 17th Street, Suite 2900
Philadelphia, PA 19103
Phone (800) 434-8255, (215) 545-7000
Fax (215) 545-7011

For information or to place an order: orders@stageclimbing.com
To contact the author: mb@michaelbroder.com
Web sites: www.DrMichaelBroder.com; www.StageClimbing.com

ISBN: 978-188957739-5
Library of Congress Number: 2011930965
1. Self-help, 2. Psychology, 3. Spirituality, 4. Motivation

This publication is designed to provide accurate and authoritative information in regard to the subject matter covered. It is sold with the understanding that the publisher is not rendering psychological, medical, or other professional services. If expert assistance or counseling is needed, the services of a competent professional should be sought.

To my beloved grandsons
Adam and Kyle

CONTENTS

Part I: The Seven Stages:
What They Are and How to Climb Them

Part II: Calibrating Your Stage Climb: The Shortest Path from Where You Are Now to Where You Want to Be

Chapter 13: Organizations and Institutions

Chapter 14: *Stage Climbing* in Action
Reach Your Target Stage in Any Chosen Area of Your Life and

ACKNOWLEDGEMENTS

The concept of *Stage Climbing* that has come together in this book could only be the result of the inspiration, influence, and help of many extraordinary people whom I have been fortunate to have had close to me throughout my career.

First and foremost, let me thank the two psychologist colleagues I am most proud of for their constant support, wisdom, and hands-on help with designing and shaping both the *Stage Climbing* concept and producing this manuscript: My wife and partner, Dr. Arlene Goldman, who believed in *Stage Climbing* from the very beginning, has been involved in every aspect of bringing this book to fruition. She continues to be an extraordinary resource for helping to shape the *Stage Climbing* vision and expand its applications.

My daughter, Dr. Joanne Broder Sumerson, a research psychologist, was not only of tremendous help with many of the technical aspects of *Stage Climbing*, but actually began being a resource for it the day she was born. Joanne, this book contains many of the principles by which I raised you, and it is my deepest hope that you pass it on to your own children as well as the many students and professionals you will teach, mentor, and influence throughout your career.

I am very indebted to my team whose hands-on work with such tasks as editing, formatting, cover design, Web design, gathering of resources, and promotion brought *Stage Climbing* to reality. They include Sandra Batten, Jenn Gibson, Josh Johnson, Frank LoRiggio, Meg McAllister, Judy O'Hearn, Mark Pitzele, Christine Retz, and Layla Smith.

My gratitude goes out to those who were important advisors on various aspects of this project. They include Jay Abraham, Tom Antion, Jacques

Bazinet, Matthew Bennett, Geoffrey Berwind, Martha Bullen, Arielle Ford, Rick Frishman, Bill Harrison, Steve Harrison, Mark Levy, and David Riklan.

Unlike my other books, *Stage Climbing* introduces a brand-new concept that I felt needed to be vetted thoroughly before this book could be published. Some of the many trusted colleagues and friends who reviewed various drafts of the manuscript and whose feedback was crucial to this book include: Harvard Ayres, Sara Baldry, Dale Blair, Dr.Tom Blash, Sandra Brownell, Andrea V. Christos, Dr. Helen Coons, Dr. Bruce Coopersmith, Paul Divas, Deborah Donze, Dr. Marion Frank, Fran Grabosky, Dr. Barbara Grinnell, Dr. Arlyn Miller, Dr. Jim McMahon, Bill Murphy, Dr. Murray Needleman, Diane O'Connell, Dr. Cheryl Patchin, Lynn Roberts, Dr. Larry Rosenberg, B.J. Rosenfeld, Chris Smedley, Sharon Stein, Jacqueline Summers, Conrad Toner, Dr. Karyne Wilner, and Jamie Wolf. Thank you all for your invaluable input!

Finally, let me express my everlasting gratitude to the many thousands of clients I've seen in psychotherapy and that I have coached; the many thousands more mental health professionals I've trained; and the millions I've reached through my talks, radio shows, audio programs, previous books and articles, TV and other media appearances over a career spanning almost four decades. I have learned something from every one of you that hopefully has found its way into these pages!

TO THE READER

*"What lies before us and what lies behind us
are tiny matters compared to what lies within us."*

—Ralph Waldo Emerson

Welcome to what I hope for you is a life-changing journey, designed to put at your disposal the tools you need to reach your highest potential in virtually any and every area of your life!

If this seems like a daunting task or a promise that is too good to be true, let's begin with the good news: **Within you resides everything you will ever need to get there in the shortest time possible.** *Stage Climbing* will show you the way. All you need to do is to make the commitment to yourself to get on board by learning the process and then applying the strategies you are about to learn that speak to where you want to take your life.

One of the subtitles I considered for *Stage Climbing* was "An Adult's Guide to Help You Get Motivated and Grow Up—Wherever You May Have Stayed Behind," because yes, this may indeed be the very first self-help book ever to teach adults *exactly* how to achieve optimal maturity wherever you believe you may be lacking. **However, "getting motivated" and "growing up" are merely important steps toward the real goal of this process, which is to be operating from what I call "your highest potential"— wherever you are not already.** You might also think of this as your best life, as life rarely gets better.

The main premise of *Stage Climbing* is simple: Inner peace, optimal motivation, passion, and a life determined by your unique purpose and

characterized by excellence—all staples of those parts of you that are being lived at your highest potential. You will soon see how all of this is firmly and naturally within your grasp, once you learn how you are holding yourself back in a certain area (or areas) of your life—and we all have them—and **how to "grow up"** (as I often refer to it metaphorically) **to your highest potential.**

Stage Climbing is about you and your life as well as how to take immediate control of it along with the process by which you reach your potential. It's also about how and why you think and act as you do, how you once were, and how you could be. *Stage Climbing* will teach you a set of principles that will also help you deal with anyone who has ever crossed your path or who ever will.

My primary mission is to present you with a concept that is so powerful that it can enable you to understand and then choose to accept or change virtually every area of your life. My secondary mission is equally important: that this concept I call *Stage Climbing* be an extremely simple one to grasp, very easy to use, and one that puts many things that you might already be familiar with—whatever you define for yourself as personal fulfillment, for example—into a new perspective. It's possible then that you will find countless ways to use it to enrich your life and the lives of those you care about. At the very least, you will find numerous ways to enhance and clarify the way you view yourself and others. *Stage Climbing* transforms a holistic overview of how you operate into easy-to-understand action steps you can use anytime you choose. It even bridges the often murky gaps between self-help, psychology, and spirituality.

Let me begin by asking you a few questions: What part of your life could be better? Where could you feel happier? How can you operate with a greater level of fulfillment or maturity? Be more motivated? Feel more at peace? Function in a way that's more on target or where you feel more satisfied with your life as it is today? Where do you wish that your contribution to those around you— your family and friends, your community, your profession, or the world—could be greater? Where could you be or at least *feel* more successful? Take note of anything that may come to mind as you ponder these questions. Throughout *Stage Climbing*, you will find many opportunities to address them all.

Stage Climbing is a new way of thinking that can help you to do many things if you let it. For example, you can think of it as a simple system for understanding exactly how complex you are. It's also a formula to give you insight into where and how you may be stuck in a specific aspect of your life; such as relationships, your career, your self-esteem, or your life's calling, mission, or purpose. *Stage Climbing* will also give you powerful strategies for moving forward in those areas. Not only will it help you to find the fulfillment you want, but will help you go beyond that level of fulfillment and onward to a new plateau that until now perhaps you may not even have thought possible. Again, **you need only pursue and make optimal use of the ideas and strategies in this book that speak to you. They all point toward an aspect of your highest potential.**

Stage Climbing introduces you to a user-friendly system that can give you a fresh and clear perspective on practically any issue, dilemma, or personal conflict that you are trying to understand that involves you or someone in your life. It's then your choice either to change or accept certain things that may have been a source of difficulty until now.

If you compare yourself to others, this book will help you to stop doing that. Instead, you will clearly see how to make **the only comparison that is truly valid: the one between *your life as it is now* in one or more areas, and *what it could be.*** The latter can be thought of as your full or highest potential, as you now see it. By using merely the resources that exist within—resources readily available to you at this moment that are just waiting to be recognized and activated—you are free to reach or get as close to that potential as you are willing to go. For over thirty years, I have used evolving versions of this concept as a clinical tool in my practice as a psychologist to help bring about change for thousands of clients who have represented almost every conceivable population or walk of life.

One of the great mysteries of the mind is something I call *psychological farsightedness*. So often, we cannot see that to which we are too close. Therefore, I hope you will also consider this book to be a set of psychological "reading glasses." *Stage Climbing* provides you with seven distinct and ascending views or stages that you can apply to any facet of your life. You then have the power to choose to stay where you are or move on to the target stage *you select*. In the process, you may even find yourself raising the bar on how you define your best or optimal life.

Stage Climbing is a different kind of book. It's about your life in "seven chapters." And since it's about you, **I offer you many examples, but deliberately avoid case studies that would take you away from focusing on**

your own life story or the story of whomever in your life you may be thinking about.

Since as humans we are each a unique work in progress, not only will this book have a different meaning for each person who reads it, but it will also offer you benchmarks to help you see clearly how you have advanced through this process each time you reread or come back to it as a reference. The kaleidoscope is a wonderful metaphor for how the human mind works—the components of a kaleidoscope remain indisputably constant, yet what you see never looks the same way twice. *Stage Climbing* unleashes this phenomenon with all the components of your life.

How we each develop to become the unique individuals we are is the area of psychology I have always found to be most fascinating. **My life's work has been to help people—often very high achievers—identify what they see as their potential in one or more areas of their lives; and then do what it takes to make the life changes they've chosen in order to get there as rapidly and effectively as possible.**

In the very earliest part of my training and career as a psychologist, I first became interested in answering for myself the questions *Stage Climbing* addresses. In addition to my professional curiosities, when my daughter was born, like most new parents, I found myself mesmerized by watching her very early development. Thus, in graduate school, I studied virtually everything I could find on the subject of human development, especially the top theorists and their trademark theories. For example, Sigmund Freud's *Psychosexual Development* (Strachey, E., & Freud, A., 1953), Erik Erikson's *Psychosocial Development* (1963), Lawrence Kohlberg's *Moral Development* (1987), Abraham Maslow's *Self-Actualization* (1987) and many others who in some way attempted to explain adult behavior based on how we develop. The problem was that as brilliant and groundbreaking as these concepts were—especially in their heyday—there were many gaps and missing pieces of the puzzle that for me left major questions unanswered. In the end, I was quite disappointed as to how dry developmental psychology could sometimes be, and how unrelated it generally seemed to my interest in creating and mastering the most effective clinical techniques to bring about lasting change in adults. The field of human psychological development seemed to be much too oriented toward *defining problems* while hardly at all focusing on *solutions*.

An early and very influential mentor of mine, the late Dr. William Swartley, introduced me to an obscure article written in the 1950s by Clyde Sullivan, Marguerite Q. Grant, and J. Douglas Grant: "The Development of Interpersonal Maturity" (1957). Their model was to become an important part of the seed from which *Stage Climbing* was to grow. However, like all the others, it had gaps that left major questions unanswered. Another early mentor, Dr. Albert Ellis, the originator of Rational Emotive Behavior Therapy— the original and still a leading cognitive behavioral approach—filled in some of those gaps with his empirically based emphasis on finding solutions by changing beliefs and attitudes directly (1962). Other approaches, such as Dr. Aaron Beck's *Cognitive Therapy* (1976) and Dr. Arnold Lazarus's *Multimodal Therapy* (1981) have made the cognitive behavioral approach the most state-of- the-art form of psychotherapy practiced today. These brilliant pioneers continue to be major influences on the work I do every day. Once again, however, many gaps became more and more evident to me as I used their ideas when treating patients/clients in the real world. So my mission became twofold: to take as long as necessary to fill in those gaps, and then to keep refining my own model called *Stage Climbing.* I decided I would not be happy until it became as useful a tool for you the reader to bring about rapid and lasting change as it has been to me and those I have helped with early versions of its concepts. In the process, I hope you also will find that (at last) it makes the understanding of human behavior, development, maturity, motivation, and how to reach your potential easy and enjoyable.

Before writing *Stage Climbing,* I also needed to satisfy myself that I could explain just about any aspect of my own life by using the *Stage Climbing* model**. My life has been one of many twists and turns. Indeed, *Stage Climbing* meets this challenge and continues to help me understand and navigate the flow of my own life as nothing else ever has; and once you learn the premise and the formula, it will do the same for you.**

I started my very early career as an accountant. Within a few short years and still in my early twenties, I began my own accounting firm, which quickly became successful and lucrative. Around the same time I also married, became a father, and seemed to have it all. However, by my mid-twenties, I became very bored with my career. It no longer had passion or challenge in it. Our marriage wasn't working either. After much contemplation, one-by-one I began making a series of major changes in all areas of my life. Over a period of several years, I sold the firm, got divorced, went to graduate school, got a master's degree and doctorate and changed my career to psychology—the field I loved as a hobby, but had never even thought of as a career.

My two careers have very little in common. In fact, that they couldn't be more different. As an accountant, I often became frustrated by the fact that there usually seemed to be only one view and acceptable protocol for doing most things. To me, there was little room or incentive for innovation and creativity. Although that's certainly not how every accountant experiences his or her profession, that's how I did. As a psychologist, I found that the climate was the exact opposite. I quickly discovered that the psychology profession had much to offer to fulfill what up until then had been missing in my career. It was impossible for me not to be challenged and fascinated by the complexity of each individual I worked with as well as the vast and continuously expanding body of knowledge that I could both learn from and contribute to.

The practice of psychology is really about teaching people to help themselves; and I have been fortunate enough to have the privilege to achieve this with an extraordinarily wide range of people and settings. I have had major contracts to work with both criminals and the police. In my private practice, I have treated patients with severe mental impairments; worked with college students; and with extremely well functioning, upscale and highly accomplished clients. I also have been a consultant to many business, government, and educational organizations and executives, written several popular books, and created many audio programs with major publishers for couples, singles, and those in relationship transitions. My audio self-help programs on numerous personal and relationship topics are used globally by lay people and mental health professionals alike. I have taught graduate students, trained mental health professionals extensively and have run an internationally acclaimed training institute. My radio programs have been broadcast locally and nationally. I have appeared on *Oprah* and *The Today Show* as well as in scores of other print and electronic media. Most of all—and I say this with an immeasurable degree of gratitude to all of my patient/clients, readers, trainees, and colleagues who made it possible—I have enjoyed almost every minute of it!

All the while, I have been working behind the scenes on the concept of *Stage Climbing*. **I decided long ago that I would not write this book until**

I could definitively say that the theory and practice I espouse holds up to virtually any segment of the population or application to which it is applied. For me, this includes my roles as a husband (in a very successful second marriage), father, and grandfather, as well as every type of personal or business relationship in which I am involved.

As a strong proponent and author of self-help books and audio programs, I am sadly aware that many people discount self-help psychology as irrelevant. One reason for this is that it is so often contradictory. Do you deal with life circumstances in the "here and now" (i.e., your present life), or do you go back to your childhood? Is the answer to be found by shedding light on a problem or by somehow delving further into your darkness? When is psychotherapy the best approach versus, for example, medication, meditation, yoga, or some other spiritual practices? *Stage Climbing* **honors it all and demonstrates that practically any approach to understanding human behavior and making your life work better for you has both pluses and minuses. However, there needs to be clear criteria for when, how, and why each approach is effective.** *Stage Climbing* **provides you with a simple model for sorting this out.**

Stage Climbing will also offer you a very handy and more importantly, a *non-dogmatic* way to understand and help you choose the best path for you with regard to any given issue. **You may also find it useful to consider** *Stage Climbing* **an encyclopedia of choices. In addition to providing you the proverbial "meal" as do most self-help books, it teaches you "how to fish."**

Everything you might have been exposed to until now has its place in the *Stage Climbing* process. For that reason, don't discard any favorite self-help books or audios, even those that may not have yet produced lasting results. You may find a new level of meaning and application for them once you see, via the principles of *Stage Climbing,* how they fit into your life.

If you have been overwhelmed, confused, or disappointed until now by the sheer number of approaches there are to changing your life or how effective they've been for you, please read on, and be open to the possibility that once you understand *your Stage Climbing* process, they will deliver those results.

Because the concept of *Stage Climbing* is so simple (as opposed to simplistic), you may find yourself challenging it. I both welcome and honor that. I was so concerned that its simplicity was too good to be true that I consulted many friends and colleagues who are mental health professionals. I asked them to look at outlines and early drafts of this book to get their views on the soundness of *Stage Climbing* from their perspective and to help me detect any inconsistencies within its principles. Their feedback continues to be extremely important to me. **I am now able to say that once you see how *Stage Climbing* works, it will become an invaluable tool not only for you personally, but also for helping or understanding all of those around you, and without labels or blame. This is regardless of your lifestyle, gender, race, ethnicity, demographics, or life experiences**. Of course, this is only to the extent to which you put it to work for you. Despite the claims of so many originators or promoters, there has never been any one approach that flawlessly provides the answer to *every* possible question or dilemma you may have. *Stage Climbing* certainly doesn't claim to achieve that impossible standard, however, it does fill in many glaring gaps that been left unaddressed until now.

In addition, this book will give you a fresh perspective on some issues that may touch any or every important aspect of your life:

❖ Why are we so often conflicted about the things that make us feel happy, successful, motivated, and fulfilled? (Short answer: The seven stages present us with seven levels of happiness, fulfillment, success, motivation, and spirituality from which to choose. Each comes with a different vision; and often they clash. However, by understanding them, you will see them as an enormous and wonderful set of choices, rather than conflicts.)

❖ What do the most successful, accomplished, happiest, or seemingly most fulfilled people have that you don't? This includes not only our contemporaries but the truly great men and women who've managed to most change the world throughout history. (Short answer: Very little that you cannot also choose to develop and learn to access in *your* own unique way, just as they have. One mission of this book is to teach you many of the strategies and ways of thinking that can help you integrate into your life the highest qualities of functioning and self-perception that you might associate with those icons. You can apply it all to your own life immediately. *Stage Climbing* gives you the action steps you need to do this.)

❖ What keeps us in unfulfilling relationships, jobs, or lifestyles? (Short answer: The problematic hooks to our lower stages that you will now learn to dismantle and bring under your control.)

❖ How do I know my mission or purpose in life, and what is the role of spirituality in making that determination? (Short answer: Purpose and spirituality are different at each stage. This is what can make it seem so confusing! *Stage Climbing* sorts this all out. Consider it a tool that teaches you the options, and then shows you how to fine-tune and navigate them. Along the way, you will access inner resources that may have been dormant up until now that will clarify this. Then, simply commit yourself to honor and pursue the choices you make.)

Whether you are sitting high atop the pinnacle of success and affluence trying to make a blessed life even better, in a jail cell where you believe you have little or no control over your life, or anywhere in between, the principles of *Stage Climbing* are waiting for you to put them into action and change your life. **I believe that boundless fulfillment, exceptional happiness, and even personal greatness are within everyone's reach.** *Stage Climbing* will give you a formula to define those virtues, along with strategies to raise the bar higher and higher for what you think of as your best.

We have all had to rise to some occasion, even if simply to deal with a crisis or to help someone else. *Stage Climbing* will show you how to access those inner resources to face the situation practically every time. In the pages ahead, *Stage Climbing* introduces to you this model of seven-stages or visions of yourself and just about everything that's important to you. **The stages span from infancy to beyond even what you may now imagine could ever be your optimal existence.**

Emerson said, "We are wiser than we know." Tapping into your own wisdom and ending all forms of self-sabotage is the essence of *Stage Climbing*. Then watch miracles happen!

HOW TO USE THIS BOOK:
A QUICK-START GUIDE

There are several ways to get the most out of this book. One, of course, is to read *Stage Climbing* straight through as you would any book. That's the best way to gain maximum understanding of yourself via the *Stage Climbing* process and all of its applications to virtually any part of your life. I also suggest that you read one chapter at a time and let the material "sink in," before going to the next chapter. **This Quick-Start Guide will then give you a "cheat sheet" overview of what *Stage Climbing* is about and the terms unique to it.**

Another way is to **follow this Quick-Start Guide for the "short version" of the book and then *skim the book by reading the bold print, charts, boxes, and strategies in Part I*. This way, you will find the book to be a very quick read.** Of course, I also strongly recommend that you refer to the full text for any elaboration you might need as you go along. **Then use the pages and strategies in Part II that apply to what you are interested in learning about yourself and those around you, and to carry out your unique *Stage Climbing* process.** This can be an effective way to both get the gist and to use the *Stage Climbing* process and the specific strategies most applicable to you in order to understand and resolve a specific issue or to learn specific applications. The detailed Table of Contents starting on page v will point you to the application(s) in Part II most relevant to you whenever you need them.

To get the maximum benefit when reading Part I, think of *Stage Climbing* as reading a book about your life in seven chapters. Expect to read many things about yourself. Some things may seem exhilarating, others might be quite painful and difficult to read (especially in Chapters 1 to 4) and still others will put you in touch with new possibilities you may eagerly wish to explore. Every reader will experience Part I differently. Many things in your life will come together more and more as you read. So please remember—if you stay with the difficult parts; be assured that the good stuff will follow. Your past will become clearer, and in reading about the target stages (Chapters 6 and 7), you will get a glimpse into what I refer to as "your highest potential," along with the strategies to get there. **The action steps at the end of each chapter can be taken before going to the next chapter, or you can come back to them later.** Just be sure that at some point you make optimal use of those strategies that speak to you. **The exercises and strategies are what hold the key to lasting change.** Reread Part I or the relevant chapter(s) any time you want to understand a particular era or another aspect of your life (or even when you are trying to gain some insight about someone else).

Part II gives you a look at many of the *Stage Climbing* applications by calibrating numerous categories of life by the stages. For this reason, I even call them "**calibrations.**" **Consider Part II to be an encyclopedia of choices, along with special strategies for many of the categories included.** You will find reproducible worksheets to make your own custom calibrations at the end of each chapter in Part II. **Use the calibrations in Part II along with those you have created for yourself as specific points of reference to help you maximize those applications that most resonate with you.** Chapter 14, the final chapter of *Stage Climbing,* contains strategies for resolving problems, making decisions and bringing many aspects of your *Stage Climbing* process together. **All of the strategies in this book are timeless.** They can be revisited anytime you determine that your *Stage Climbing* process is in need of a major overhaul, a minor tweaking in one stage, or anything in between. *Stage Climbing* is a book you will want to come back to often or whenever you are facing a new challenge.

What follows is a five-step protocol you can use to become familiar with *Stage Climbing* and quickly begin your process:

STEP 1—LEARN THE LANGUAGE OF *STAGE CLIMBING* THROUGH THIS GLOSSARY

Here are the important terms you need to know:

Stage:

Stages are simply levels of maturity that pinpoint the degree to which you have evolved *in a given life area.* **Think of your stages as benchmarks or plateaus. They can explain practically any aspect of who you are or why you do what you do in that part of your life.** There are seven possible stages in any life category, numbered from one to seven. (They are summarized in Step 2 below.) You probably will identify various parts of yourself in each stage. For example, you could be operating at different stages with respect to your career, love relationship(s), etc. as a parent, socially, spiritually, and/or sexually. Our complexity as human beings makes this possible at any given time. These ascending stages are in reality the lenses through which you see your life and all of its challenges.

Default Stage:

The stage that defines how you *typically*—but *not always*—function with respect to a given aspect of your life. Consider this as a rough measure of your actual degree of maturity in any given life area. Your default stage may or may not be the same as your chronological age would indicate. If your default stage is lower than what is age appropriate, it can explain much about your patterns and where you may be stuck. Thus, **your level of maturity** (for that area of life, of course) is simply what you recognize as your default stage as compared to your actual age. **Generally speaking, the higher the default stage in an area of life, the better.**

Target Stage: This is the stage from which you would most like to operate. **Think of it as a goal.** Your target stage in any life area is **the zone in which you are most likely to be living life at your *highest potential*.** When you are operating out of your target stages, **you are using the best parts of yourself to accomplish almost anything!** (See also Life at the Target Stages at the end of this Quick-Start Guide as well as Chapters 6 and 7 for a complete perspective on target stages.)

Hook: **Any part of you that is *uncharacteristically* in a stage higher *or* lower than what your default stage would indicate.** Some hooks can be highly beneficial, while others extremely counterproductive. Thus, hooks can propel you forward or hold you back. **Think of your hooks as things you *sometimes* do, feel, or believe that are anomalies or exceptions to how you normally operate via your default stage.**

***Stage Climbing*:** **A simple system for understanding just how complex you are**. *Stage Climbing* uses deliberate strategies to help you develop new attitudes, beliefs and behaviors to move forward to the higher, or target, stage, which you have chosen for one or more aspect(s) of your life. **Ideally, your target stage then becomes your default stage. This is the very definition of operating at what is now your highest potential.** The goal of *Stage Climbing* is literally to help you to "grow up" (or operate as a grown-up) and in the shortest time possible, in those specific areas of your life where *you* believe you may have fallen behind. ***Maturation to the point where you are operating at your highest potential is a natural process* that often becomes stuck for various reasons.** *Stage Climbing* restores that natural process and brings it firmly under your control. By removing the hooks that block it, you can quickly advance to your **chosen** target stage. This book will offer you numerous strategies to do this.

Calibration: A customized breakdown of the seven stages, each offering a different view or perspective for a specific issue or aspect of your life. Calibrations define each stage and help you pinpoint such things as **where you are now** (your default stage) versus **where you want to be** (your target stage). The chapters in Part II offer you many calibrations for virtually every area of life.

STEP 2—LEARN THE BASICS OF THE SEVEN STAGES BELOW

Stages One through Four are our *normal* (or typical) **default stages from birth through late adolescence**. However, these first four stages are the ones you as an adult will most want to get beyond. Your hooks there—and we all have some—can be troublesome to any aspect of your life. However, as you learn more about the stages, you will find ways that certain lower-stage hooks can actually serve you well and even be great resources and sources of enjoyment. *Thus, there will be times when you will choose lower-stage hooks for temporary and/or specific situations*.

Stage One: Only possible stage during **infancy**; later can potentially render one profoundly **dependent** upon others and result in feelings of inadequacy and victimhood.

Stage Two: Typical stage for **toddlers**; thereafter, a life without internalized limits can result in **primitive** and **undisciplined** behavior, extreme self-centeredness, the tendency to act out and create much chaos for yourself and others.

Stage Three: Usual stage through **late childhood**; thereafter can morph into various degrees of an authoritarian personality and/or **rigid rule abider** who is extremely inflexible regarding rules and ideas.

Stage Four: Typical stage throughout **adolescence**; as an adult, can result in anxiety, depression, self-doubt, alienation, shame, and a wide variety of neurotic and **approval-seeking** behaviors.

Stage Five: Typical stage for an **adult** in our society, where you often think of yourself as a **role juggler,** or the sum of all your life roles**.** Your characteristic view of life at this stage is often **comfortable, dispassionate,** or **neutral**. This stage offers the ideal attitudes and frame of mind to function best, while doing what is merely necessary to keep your life together and functioning in order to live in the higher stages. While a Stage Five frame of mind is important to have at times with respect to certain relationships and activities, it often results in disappointment when you expect higher degrees of fulfillment than this stage can deliver.

Stages Six and Seven are the **target stages** that most people aspire to. As you understand Stages Six and Seven, it will become clear that by removing anything that blocks that natural drive to be your best, you will quickly get to the zone in which you can naturally and effortlessly operate at your **highest potential.** Most people view life at the target stages as life at its very best. **It is at the target stages that you feel the very best about yourself.** The target stages represent what you are here for, or from a spiritual perspective, your life's purpose.

Stage Six: **Mature adult** (determined not by chronological age but by the way you conduct your life) with a strong integrity and sense of self. At Stage Six, you rise *above* your roles; and operate according to your own **unique internally generated values and passions**. To the extent that these become your driving forces; genuine spirituality, fulfillment, and happiness result. This is the stage in which you love, enjoy, excel, and create in your own distinctive way.

Stage Seven: **The highest stage attainable.** You are beyond *needing* self-gratification, and find fulfillment as a result of your **benevolence** and your unique contribution to others, to the world, and to how you can be an agent of change in some large *or* small way. At Stage Seven, your purpose outside of yourself has more importance to you than what is purely in your own self-interest.

STEP 3—UNDERSTAND THE BASIC *STAGE CLIMBING* DRILL

Identify a hook, issue, or an area of your life in which you believe you are not functioning optimally:

_____

Identify the **stage from which you are currently operating** with regard to the above issue, hook, or aspect of your life:

Stage 1_____2_____3_____4_____5_____6_____7_____

Choose your **target stage** (consider this your goal) from which you would like to be operating when addressing this issue, hook, or in this area of your life.

Stage 1_____2_____3_____4_____5_____6_____7_____

Looking at this issue **through the lens of your target stage,** how do you now see it?

By using both the calibrations that appear in Part II and any variations of those that you customize to your own unique situation, **identify the attitudes, beliefs, and behaviors that characterize your chosen target stage in the specific situation you have identified**. Sometimes, that's all you need to do. However, in other situations, more of the strategies in Parts I and II are needed to "hardwire" aspects of your target stage.

Apply whatever strategies and action steps at the end of each chapter in Part I may be needed to **lock in your target stage** in order to make it your default stage with respect to that hook, issue, or aspect of life. The purpose of almost all the strategies throughout this book is to help you do this. With some practice and what you will learn as you read *Stage Climbing*, this will soon become second nature.

Chapter 14 has the complete strategies for breakthroughs in managing your hooks, making your target stage your default stage, and much more, using variations of this basic *Stage Climbing* drill.

STEP 4—READ THE BOLD PRINT AND BOXES IN EACH CHAPTER OF PART I

However, be sure to refer to the text wherever you can use more clarification. Then read about and **apply the strategies at the end of each chapter that can be of any help to you with your unique challenges.**

STEP 5—READ THE INTRODUCTION TO PART II: CALIBRATING YOUR STAGE CLIMB—"WHERE YOU ARE NOW VERSUS WHERE YOU WANT TO BE"

Then refer to the calibrations for the issue(s) you are trying to resolve and/or the aspect(s) of your life you would like to understand. These calibrations are the direct applications of *Stage Climbing* to your life. They each offer you a glimpse of what life looks like at every one of the seven stages in the areas that are important to you. In Part II, there is a reproducible worksheet for making your own custom calibrations at the end of each chapter (all worksheets can be downloaded at www.StageClimbing.com/ worksheets). In addition, there are several worksheets in Chapter 14 to help you pick your target stages and further facilitate your *Stage Climbing* process. Note: To enter the "Members" section of StageClimbing.com, enter your email address (this is your user ID) and the Password: MyStageClimb.

LIFE AT THE TARGET STAGES: HOW GOOD CAN IT BE?

I include this perspective in the quick-start guide in order to give you a glimpse of **what's in it for you** to work on your *Stage Climbing* process. The mission of *Stage Climbing* is simple: **To help you live any aspect of your life at the target stage(s) you have chosen.** Your target stages represent the optimal life that you either are living already or can be living very soon. **You are in the target stage zone whenever you are operating at your highest potential.** For most aspects of life, you will most likely aspire to Stages Six and Seven. Those stages also represent your unique and most authentic self. They are you at your best and happiest, because at Stages Six and Seven, you are guided by your passions, living beyond your ego, and solidly aligned with your purpose. **Your target stages define you as a "grown-up."** They are where your heart *is*, as opposed to where you or someone else thinks it *should* be. In that sense, your target stages can even define why you are here.

Any success, victory, or windfall can trigger great feelings in you—temporarily. However, as you have probably noticed many times, a frame of mind that depends on external factors does not last since you are always subject to the next life event or occurrence, and then the next one, and the one after that. The good news: As humans, that state of fulfillment characterized by your target stages is in fact part of your *natural state of being*—a state that will not fluctuate with external events. In other words, you have inside of you all you will ever need to live a gloriously fulfilling life right now... No batteries are required. Getting there is where *Stage Climbing* fits into your life.

To the extent that you commit to living your life at the target stages, this could be a laundry list that defines your state of mind. Some of these items may not resonate with you but chances are that most of them will. Therefore, the first step is to decide if you are you ready to:

❖ Never again allow the expectations of others to govern you, except when they truly match those you have for yourself—in the privacy of your own mind.

❖ Have a strong and certain sense of self that allows you to overcome (and not be governed by) your confusion, self-doubts, fears, anxiety about the approval of others, depression, and frustrations. Your own judgment and sense of what is right is no longer undermined or overpowered by the judgments of others. You no longer fear the future or death and you have a layer of emotional muscle that insulates you from the pain of feeling the negativity of others, even when it is aimed directly at you. You accept and never berate yourself. You are at peace, free of inner conflicts, and *feel best about yourself*. Thus, self-defeating behavior is an unnecessary thing of the past. It simply no longer serves a purpose.

❖ No longer *blame* your parents, former love relationships, bosses, work associates, or anyone else, including yourself, for the state of your life; are not troubled by the past or hung up on expecting things from people that they will not or cannot deliver. Forgive all of those toward whom you still have anger or other negative feelings—including, and perhaps most importantly, yourself.

❖ View your self-confidence/self-esteem separately from your achievements. That is, think of them as two parallel lines that do not meet and are never dependent on each other. Thus, your successes and failures no longer influence your opinion of yourself in any way.

❖ Be aware of the infinite number of life choices available to you. Feel empowered to make them and have an almost *childlike* openness to new experience.

❖ Live by your passions, desires, purpose, and strong determination. Recognize that your will and inner wisdom are the forces or engines that drive and motivate your life. Be passionate about your chosen activities and allow work and play to be equally joyous. *Your motivation now comes from within yourself*. External rewards are still nice, but secondary.

❖ Experience life as easier and not a struggle. With much less effort than you may ever have imagined, be able to find a way to manifest almost anything you truly need.

❖ Understand just how to relate to almost anyone you encounter, no matter how wise or wisdom-free he or she may be. Be able to accept the right of someone else to have an alternative viewpoint, no matter how much you may disagree with it. At the same time, however, allow yourself to automatically and effortlessly discontinue or emotionally downgrade relationships with other people that are not harmonious and fulfilling. Attract—but never, need to *demand*—the love and/or support you want from those who matter most in almost any situation.

❖ Have a deep and cherished internal commitment to use your natural gifts to the fullest. Know what your assets are and know how to maximize them; understand too your areas of weakness—accept them and no longer allow them to lead you in the direction of failure. Thus, you can make the most of all you have.

❖ Watch your potential keep rising higher and higher and your best keeps getting better and better with only you determining the limits.

❖ Connect to and leave your footprint on things much bigger and more important than yourself.

❖ Be open on a spiritual level with purpose and gratitude your guiding forces providing direction whenever you need it. Connect directly with God, your Higher Self, or whatever you may call your source of higher power—perhaps, *but not necessarily* through religion. However, know that you have the ability to bypass religion and go directly to that source.

❖ Be uniquely your own person and realize that your own happiness and destiny are in your hands exclusively.

If these characteristics seem farfetched or grandiose, remember that they all have one thing in common. **They are each traits that you are free to develop all by yourself, within yourself** regardless of your status or station in life, how others see or approve of you, your standing in the community, your annual income or net worth, who you know, your educational status, or anything else out of your ultimate control at this moment. That is how good your life *can be* at the target Stages Six and Seven. **You can choose to own any or all of these traits and keep them forever, beginning now.**

So how do you get there? Remember, it's a **natural phenomenon** to have that very state of mind you've been reading about. However, if you've become stuck along the way, the *Stage Climbing* process you are about to undertake could be the most important step in your journey to those target stages. In some or perhaps even most areas of your life, you may already be there. Yet, in other life areas, you—as do most of us—may need to help the process along by learning about and clearing away the obstacles that block access to your target stages. While doing that, you will master a new tool for understanding yourself and others, making life changes, managing your emotions, motivating people, and much more.

Page 125 picks up the discussion of the target stages and leads you to those strategies for getting there. However, **I urge you to keep these highly accessible and beneficial goals in mind** as we focus first on the stages that you may need to climb in order to gain full access to the great things that await you at those coveted target stages.

PART I

THE SEVEN STAGES

What They Are and
How to Climb Them

*"One can never consent to creep
when one feels an impulse to soar."*

— Helen Keller

INTRODUCTION
TO THE SEVEN STAGES

I am extremely grateful to the many patients/clients and readers of my pre-vious books: *The Art of Living Single* (1988), *The Art of Staying Together* (1993), *Can Your Relationship Be Saved?* (2002*),* and *The Secrets of Sexual Ecstasy* (2004) who have helped *Stage Climbing* to evolve! In my psychol-ogy practice, couples and adults have always been my specialty. The issues of adults have been the focus of my many articles and audio programs on such topics as anger, anxiety, depression, stress management, self-confidence, making major life changes, and self-actualization. Thus, whenever someone would ask me if I see children in treatment, I would politely decline and offer to refer the child elsewhere to a colleague with that specialty. However, the land-scape of *Stage Climbing* could prompt my response to that question to be a bit more tongue-in-cheek: **I treat children, but only those in adult bodies.** The serious side of that statement reflects the reality of why people seek help from someone in my field.

Many come to see me because they cannot seem to find a suitable love relationship—yet I am not a matchmaker. Others seek my help because their marriages are breaking up—yet I am not a divorce lawyer. I dispense no medi-cation for people who are anxious or depressed; and I have no magical answers for those who consult me about the self-confidence issues that undermine their ability to pursue a dream or maximize whatever is most important in their lives.

What I do have to offer them is help in consciously and mindfully seeing their problems through the eyes of the adults they are, and adopting the atti-tudes and beliefs that empower them to cope with and handle their lives optimally. Almost without exception, what brings people to my office is what turns out to be the inability to call up those well developed, yet seemingly out-of-reach inner resources they often seemingly have no difficulty using in other situations. Instead, they are in some way sending in a child to do the work of an adult, such as becoming too dependent on non-empathetic people while going through a divorce, surrendering to feelings of helplessness that lead to depression, or being too passive and approval seeking rather than assertive with a colleague or boss.

> The principles of *Stage Climbing* teach you how to choose and then consciously send in the best part of yourself to handle any given situation.

In my field, the closest thing we have to a "cure" is simply to be in charge of all your choices. **To the extent that you are the master of your choices, you are free to take whatever action is in your best interest—when possible and appropriate—as well as find peace within yourself when accepting a situation that you don't like is your only real option.** This power is perhaps the greatest gift you can ever give yourself!

Think of each of the seven stages that I am about to describe as distinct views of life, then realize how each of us is a unique blend of up to all seven of them in every aspect of our lives. When you keep this in mind, you will appreciate just how complex you and I—as well as each person you have ever met or ever will meet—really are. **Your challenge is to understand each stage and then choose the stage(s) from which you want to operate in any given situation or part of your life.** The strategies in this book are designed to help you make and optimize those choices.

It is never the purpose of *Stage Climbing* to judge you or your values, or whatever stage with which you identify. However, I will emphatically present the downside as well as the upside of all the seven stages. At times, certain aspects of the first four stages (Chapters 1 to 4) may sometimes be especially painful to read. But I can assure you that it will all come together by the end of Part I. So as you read about the

stages, simply be aware of what's possible for you. Then honor where you are in a given area of your life. Once you do that, you will find that you're free to recognize and then operate via the stage where you most want to be. *Stage Climbing* **will indeed define many issues for you, but will also offer you strategies and solutions for each one. In addition, there is a wide array of resources available to you (at StageClimbing. com) for virtually anything you cannot resolve by using the many strategies in this book. This is important to keep in mind as you read.**

To stage climb is natural. You have been doing it since you were an infant. However, if the world is a classroom, as I believe it is, and living in that classroom is how you learn about life, you may sometimes need a bit of tutoring to help you when your organic or *natural process* becomes stuck or you are trying to make a change. **I have yet to meet the person who—in at least one area of life and to some extent—does not have to help their natural maturation process along in some way in order to reach their potential.** Virtually everyone has difficulty with something that *to them* may seem so easy for everybody else. For example, some people are generally happy and fulfilled careerwise, while leaving much to be desired with respect to their role in love relationships or their degree of self-confidence. Perhaps these things are okay in your case, but you often find yourself worried about how others perceive you, you feel disconnected spiritually, or you are now bored with avocations you once considered fun. If there are people you *look up to* for what you perceive as their ability to master an aspect of life that's difficult for you, chances are you merely perceive them—whether or not with accuracy—as operating from a higher stage than you are. The same can be said for those you may *look down upon* as being representative of a lower stage in some life area or issue(s).

Why is it that most of us have experienced the notions of success, happiness, fulfillment, and even spirituality as paradoxical and confusing? One major reason is that our capacity for those things develops within us—or matures—in stages, very much the way we physically mature in stages. Newborn babies weighing eight pounds or less possess the seeds of everything that they need to become full-grown adults. As babies grow, genetic predisposition will play a major role in their physical development and health. Of course, environmental factors, as well as simply how they choose to live their lives and care for themselves physically, will become additional, crucial, long-term factors in physical health. The same is true of the ingredients for *maturity and mental health.* **Each of us is born with certain seeds that give us an innately unique potential, along with talents and such things as emotional, spiritual, and even creative parameters.** As we evolve through our interaction with the world, it becomes our nature to find and then manifest all of our distinct preferences. This process is what Erik Erickson (1963) called "finding ourselves"; and it is the essence of maturity.

Just as optimal body maintenance—barring death, disease, or accident—will ensure physical maturity, and learning will promote intellectual maturity, the psyche has definite needs in order to mature as well. However, as we grow, certain parts of us are slower to develop than are others. *Stage Climbing* is about recognizing those less-developed parts of you, while optimizing your natural process so that you can reach your highest potential in each and every life area that you choose to pursue. In a sense, it's like going from some form of repression in your life to freedom, in which you no longer blame anyone, including yourself, for whatever you perceive about yourself is "not good enough" or what it "should be." Instead, you know you own the awesome power over your destiny. This is true freedom, and each time you experience it with something new, you are changed forever!

TO GET THE MOST OUT OF THE *STAGE CLIMBING* PROCESS

❖ **In the pages ahead, you will read about each of the stages.** The first time you read about the seven stages, please read them in order. **Once again—because this bears repeating— please remember that certain things you will read about in Stages One through Four may sometimes be difficult to read about as it pertains to you or someone close to you**. But you will soon learn how to make optimal use of the **hooks** there that you choose to retain. The lower stages act as "shoulders" to stand on when growing. Stage Five may give you a perspective on some of the things in your life that don't provide you with as much fulfillment as you may want them to or expect. **The target Stages Six and Seven will clearly show you where the fulfillment is that may be eluding you and how to get there very quickly.**

❖ Remember that each stage pertains to you, to every one of us and to all of the people in your past and/or those in your life right now. As you read about the stages, be mindful of how the characteristics of all seven stages can explain a part or even many parts of yourself as well as those of virtually anyone else. **I strongly suggest that you reread this section after you have read about the first few stages, so that you can get the clearest possible perspective about how to apply the material to yourself and those around you in the most beneficial way.**

❖ Be mindful of how you or someone else in your life that you are close to or concerned about responds to conflict.

❖ Notice any aspects of your life that you want to change. The first step is to identify the parts of yourself that you will read about in the lower stages. We are or were all there! As you do this, **be aware that many of your best choices and goals will become clearer to you as you read ahead to the higher stages**. The seeds for those higher stages in all life areas reside in each of us, just waiting for us to activate them.

YOUR DEFAULT STAGE

As you read about all seven stages, you will probably notice your tendency to identify with one particular stage more than any of the others, for each of the unique parts of your life (e.g., your relationships, parenting skills, career, approach to spirituality, etc.). **I refer to that particular stage as your *default stage*. Consider this to be your current principal operating stage or *the starting point in your Stage Climbing process for that aspect of your life*.** Most importantly, your default stage tells you where you generally are now. Once you recognize this, you can then clearly determine where you want to be and select the right strategies to get there.

The best news is that you can actually have whatever default stage for any area of your life you want. The stage you *choose* for your default stage is what I refer to as a *target stage*. You may find that in certain life areas you are already at your target stage (either through work you have previously done on yourself or through your natural and organic *Stage Climbing* process), while other areas cry out for change in that direction. *Stage Climbing* will help you clarify this and show you how to bring to fruition the changes you wish to make. **A great universal goal for yourself is to make your target and default stages identical.** In most aspects of life, the higher your default stage the better. A Stage Six or Seven default stage means that you have evolved optimally in that life area.

For the sake of simplicity and brevity, I will "personify" a stage, by speaking of *Ones, Twos, Threes, Fours, Fives, Sixes, and Sevens* when referring to someone with a *default stage* characterized by any of the seven stages. However, please keep in mind that it's extremely rare for even a single aspect of someone's life to be accurately defined *solely* by one stage, or for anyone to possess *all* of the traits associated with any one stage.

Your default stage is simply your automatic position or the stage representing the level of maturity that now comes most naturally to you, most of the time in that specific area of life. **It is *never* accurate to infer that your default stage is always how you operate or the only way you can operate.** You will probably notice that when you think about certain people, you tend to brand them by what you perceive as their default stage in the area of their life where you are most connected to them.

YOUR HOOKS

As you Stage Climb, you'll invariably encounter parts of yourself that act as obstacles standing in your way of living or enjoying life at your chosen or target stage. I call these obstacles *hooks*. Multiple hooks in lower stages can be confused with your default stage. However, hooks are different. They are *anomalies* to the way you normally function. Think of them as your connections to stages *other than* your default stage. **Hooks are simply your thoughts, feelings, and/or behaviors that are characteristic of stages other than your default stage in a given life area. Moreover, in order to be considered a hook, it needs to be identified with a specific stage.**

Beginning with those of Sigmund Freud himself, many theories have been proposed to address the question of why and how we develop hooks. No *one* theory has stood the test of time or rigorous research. **I believe hooks develop for so many reasons—genetic/nature and/or environmental/ nurture—that too often an origin is not clear or even accurately traceable.** For this reason, I rarely spend a lot of time exploring the *origin* of a hook. Instead, I help people identify, understand, manage, and remove them. As you will see, this is an extremely important part of the *Stage Climbing* process, as it is a key to resolving your most daunting issues.

The best news is that taking control of your hooks is very doable. Most of the strategies throughout *Stage Climbing* will help you do this. When working with parents, I help them to raise their children in ways that will be most likely to assure that the child completes the tasks of each stage in an age-appropriate way so as not to create problematic hooks to the lower stages that could have a negative impact later. As each chapter evolves, I will have much more to say about the challenges of passing through each stage.

Sometimes a hook to a lower stage is like a "fly in the ointment." explaining why you have difficulty enjoying life or some important aspect of it. Some hooks are blind spots, meaning that you don't realize you have them, but others around you might. Other hooks, you—and perhaps only you—are very aware of having. In this case, they might be some of the parts of yourself that you choose not to change or to share with anyone else.

The question you need to ask yourself regarding a problematic hook is whether or not you are willing to do what it takes to "unhook" it—that is manage it, remove it, or neutralize it. **I use the word "hook" as a metaphor, because these lower-stage hooks do, to some extent, literally hook you to a lower stage.** They are often what you recognize as your "hang-ups." They can also sometimes work *for* you in certain specific situations—and when they do, enjoy and cultivate them—but as you will see as you read about the lower stages, more often they tend to hold you back.

This is important to remember: *Each time you've gained control over a problematic hook*—and *Stage Climbing* will show you many ways to do that—*you have not only solved a problem, but also broken a pattern*. And to break a troubling pattern is to change your life!

Not all hooks are bad! We also have hooks to the *higher* stages, which give us a peek or feel for what life can be like as we climb to our higher stages. These hooks help us to propel ourselves higher, literally as would a hook at the end of the rope you are using to pull yourself up. So think of a hook as merely a part of you that is uncharacteristically in a higher or lower stage— or as a departure—from your present default stage. **Enjoy the hooks that benefit you and make a commitment to remove or at least neutralize the ones that don't.**

Your default stage, together with your hooks are the prime ingredients that determine your attitudes, beliefs, much of your behavior, and how you *internally* view your life. In other words, **at all times and with respect to any part of your life, you are operating from either your default stage or a hook to a stage higher or lower than your default.** The effect that different hooks have on you can vary greatly.

As you recognize and become the master of your hooks, they simply become more choices. However, the range of the effect of your hooks can be anywhere from minimal to all-consuming. You can think of a hook as a drop of dark ink in a clear glass of water—coloring your life greatly. Or it can simply be an occasional thought that if ignored, does not have to affect any aspect of your life at all.

In reading about the stages, reflect carefully on yourself at each stage. Think of a part of you with hooks in a given stage, now *or* when you used to live life that way. Also, make it a point to recognize honestly and introspectively where you now are. As you will see, each stage has its benefits as well as its drawbacks. The applications in Part II will show you how to implement the material from these chapters, by the stages, to virtually any area of life that interests you.

So **never berate yourself regarding your default stage or your lower-stage hooks. They are what they are for many reasons.** Instead, acknowledge, accept, understand, and honor the reality that at any given time we are all doing the best we can. Then you are free to begin to make choices by asking yourself, "Is this where I want to be or is there something better?" You will see what the alternatives are as you begin to learn and identify with each of the seven stages. At a later time, you may choose to re-read about all or some of the stages, keeping in mind only one aspect of your life (or someone else's) that is of particular interest or concern. The more you are able to relate this material to your own life, the more powerful a tool you will find it to be and the better (and more naturally) you will be able to navigate your *Stage Climbing* process.

The choice is yours whether this book will become a life-changing event for you or merely a good read. All of my work has taught me that teaching powerful theory and state-of-the-art techniques is not quite enough. The action steps and your execution of them are the ingredients this process needs most to work its magic for you.

Start with the crucial assumption that *with the right strategies and the will, there is very little you cannot overcome or achieve.* This will help you to begin to maximize the material and its impact on your life instantly, successfully, and powerfully. I will provide the strategies; what you need to bring is the will and motivation. Then be relentless!

In this dialogue between you and me, I provide many real-life examples, but purposely avoid lengthy case studies. This is my way of helping you to keep the focus on yourself—or whomever else you may be thinking about—as you explore the seven stages. I am excited for you as you begin this journey!

CHAPTER 1

STAGE ONE

Your Dependent Self

"There's a somebody I'm longing to see
I hope that he, turns out to be
someone who'll watch over me..."

— George and Ira Gershwin,
"Someone to Watch over Me"

Picture yourself on a paradise island with people waiting on you hand and foot. You are being taken care of and don't have a care or need in the world that is not being satisfied by someone else. People pay a lot of money for that feeling on a vacation. Kings have conquered countries to provide it for themselves, their families and a privileged few. Having all your needs attended to by others can also be thought of as the definition of ideal infant care.

These are but a few examples of Stage One at its very best. Even though it's a great fantasy and sometimes when life gets overwhelming or stressful we wish for it. But the fact is that few adults can or would consciously choose to remain in that state indefinitely.

Stage One begins at birth and is the stage of development during infancy. Thus, it is optimal to pass through this stage during the first year or two of life. **Stage One is the only *possible* default Stage for infants who are totally dependent on others for just about every need.** So in the Stage One world, oneself and those who play the role of caretaker and wish granter are truly all there is. Early on, infants perceive others as extensions of themselves, who exist merely to satisfy their needs.

Recently, I observed two excellent illustrations of typical Stage One behavior while walking through New York City's Central Park. One was normal and appropriate and the other quite the opposite. The first was an infant sitting on its mother's lap on a park bench, cooing and smiling at passersby who responded warmly. Just a few feet away, a disheveled street person sat on another bench making virtually identical gestures as the baby (he appeared to be unaware of this), to the people who walked past him. Those passersby who had any response at all to this man reacted with disgust. The fact that the same people reacted to the same behavior in completely opposite ways was based only and obviously on one thing — the appropriateness of the ages of the man and the baby with respect to what each was doing. This extreme, yet obvious example illustrates an important aspect of *Stage Climbing:* what works at one stage of life can be quite odd at another! Examples of this phenomenon can be found at every stage.

Stage One is the **Default Stage** in infancy (and sometimes old age and toward the end of life). It is also good to have hooks there when you choose or have no choice but to be taken care of by others, or simply let yourself receive without needing to give back in kind (e.g., when needy, sick, or infirm, or even when letting yourself be pampered or on a vacation).

At each of the first five stages, I will discuss how the maturation process plays out naturally and organically. For the lower stages, proper care, nurturing, guidance, and discipline are some of the major factors that influence how your default stage advances as you age.

At Stage One, parents and caretakers are obviously critical. "Ideal" parents and caretakers (to the extent that such a thing as *ideal* actually exists) provide Stage One infants something akin to unconditional love and nurturing during the first years of life, without expecting much in return. The exception might be the infant's occasional smile or some other endearing form of acknowledgment. However, beyond infancy and most certainly to the extent that adults become stuck emotionally in Stage One, they will characteristically continue to operate as though they and those who enable them were essentially the whole world.

(For the sake of brevity, I will refer to those people having a Stage One default stage or those who are merely operating from Stage One, as *Ones*. I will do so even though this may only characterize a single hook or aspect of their lives.) This is the darkest side of Stage One and is obviously such a distortion of reality for an adult that it could underlie symptoms as severe as those of the most extreme forms of mental disorders.

Your **Ultimate Goal** at Stage One: To have all your needs met with minimal effort or obligation on your part.

As a result of being stuck in this stage, *Ones* can become any of the following: chronically needy and dependent, severely narcissistic and self-centered, highly addicted and/or dependent on harmful substances or even, to an extent, all of those things together. In addition, they will often live life in a state of severe dependency, perhaps even spending an entire lifetime seeking that "mother who was not there" or one who was perceived to have consistently stifled their attempt to do things for themselves. For some *Ones*, the only relationships possible are those in which they are extremely enmeshed or in which they can get away with remaining overly needy and self-involved.

Many *Ones* are experienced by those around them as bottomless pits who are sorely in need of boundaries and most impossible to please in relationships. Also quite often, *Ones* characteristically feel entitled to anything they want. Thus, it's not hard to see how the relationships they form become the basis for those feelings of "entitlement." Moreover, many *Ones* marry their spouses in the first place—at least partially—because they were attracted to them not as the people they are, but to their ability to be a "good provider" or caretaker. For example, it's not uncommon for some men to marry women whom they perceive as extensions of their mother: someone to cook for them, clean up after them, and take care of all of life's annoyances, leaving them free to pursue their careers and hobbies. And of course there are the women who marry "up"—stereotypically younger women who marry older, wealthy men. Such *Ones* sometimes used to be referred to as "gold diggers." These types of relationships (and many variations of them) are far from uncommon.

In the simplest terms possible, happiness at Stage One can be defined as having all of your needs met by others with no effort on your part. Perhaps a notable exception is that smile or some of the many variations of it that develop over time, similar to the way an infant relates to its mother and other caretakers. That first social skill that I sometimes refer to as a "Stage One smile" can be the thing that gets many *Ones* through life. An adult "mother" can have many aliases, such as a pathologically enabling spouse who preempts any attempt at self-sufficiency; a "sugar daddy;" a sheltered work environment or one that inadvertently condones or encourages laziness and non-productivity. Examples include many non-demanding (or even no-show) civil service jobs; and in some cases even a shelter or mental hospital, which could metaphorically be thought of as a giant and reliable "mother."

Happiness and Success at Stage One—When life is easy with no demands or challenges to worry about and having a reliable and dependable provider of all necessities

---

In many cases of course, such as a major or chronic illness, disability or profound mental illness; self-sufficiency truly is impossible. In these cases, our Stage One hooks become healthy mechanisms that help us to cope. However, for others Stage One hooks can foster a dependency on someone in their lives—the government, a charity, or some other body or institution that takes care of them, with no thought about giving anything back or planning to regain self-sufficiency.

The extent to which you may be stuck in Stage One is the degree to which some of these attitudes and beliefs about yourself may govern you:

❖ "I am inadequate"; "I can't do it"; "Life is too hard."

❖ "I am helpless"; (and thus, "I must be taken care of.")

❖ "I must have someone else to satisfy me and care for my every need."

❖ "I have no choices or am incapable of taking the initiative, making my own choices or carrying out any significant change to make my life better."

❖ "I am unable to operate in any capacity other than as a victim."

❖ "I am and always will be unable to overcome my past or upbringing."

❖ "It's no use for me even trying to make things better."

❖ "I must be certain that any decision I make be the right one or I won't able to handle the consequences."

❖ "What's happened to me in the past (e.g., my childhood, etc.) makes living a happy and fulfilling life that I can now take charge of impossible for me."

If we think of a computer as a metaphor for the mind, our beliefs would constitute our operating system. It is our beliefs that create anger in us when someone treats us poorly, anxiety when faced with a difficult challenge or depression when we fail at something. **A major aspect of the *Stage Climbing* process is to change the attitudes and beliefs—ones that underlie any unwanted hooks to the lower stages—to beliefs consistent with your target stage.** The more you do that, the more your "operating system" will be an indicator of the choices you have made as an adult, rather than a collection of self-defeating assumptions that may have been with you since before you can even remember.

Government programs, such as long-term unemployment benefits and welfare, can be godsends to many with a default stage in Stage One with respect to a work ethic. However, as the saying goes, "There's no such thing as a free lunch." A lifestyle grounded in dependency on others can have very high *quality of life* costs. Many people believe that one of the reasons that programs such as the 1960s' "war on poverty" was actually "won" by *poverty* is simple.

By taking away the incentive to use your own powers and skills to rise out of poverty and become truly self-sufficient, discovering whatever you have uniquely to contribute to the world often gets put on the back burner—permanently. Many have told me they've found this same phenomenon to also be true with alimony and other types of "conditional" entitlements. **When the incentive to *underachieve* is taken away, then many will rise to the occasion and connect with their unique purpose and passion to pursue it, as we will discuss in the later stages.** Then, the drive to overcome poverty takes over, becomes second nature, and is often the basis for a major life makeover.

Typical triggers of key **Emotions** at Stage One:

Anger—Being abandoned (even when someone dies), neglected, or deprived by whomever you depend on as your protector, provider, or caretaker. Anger sometimes triggers feelings of helplessness, hopelessness, and victimhood.

Anxiety—Fear of such things as abandonment (such as a relationship—even a bad one ending), physical or mental disability, or extreme poverty; being, living, and/or dying alone. These are situations in which you would be or merely feel unable to survive or change some dreaded fate.

Depression—The self-perception that results from feelings of grief, inadequacy, hopelessness, or self-pity; loss, being abandoned, or having to survive alone.

Grief (over loss) —Self-pity can be quite intense along with anger (at who or what you have lost) about your difficulty separating emotionally. You may also be in denial (i.e., having difficulty believing that someone is gone) or overwhelmed by loss, resulting in conditions such as PTSD (posttraumatic stress disorder) or even major depression requiring intensive treatment.

Similarly to the reality of an infant, *Ones* usually lack the concept of being able to "get up and do something" to help themselves. Some *Ones* are actually at their best emotionally when they are sick and people cheerfully take care of them. Others at Stage One choose to stay in highly dependent and abusive relationships that meet their most basic economic and fear-based emotional needs. **Drug and alcohol addictions are common with Stage One adults who sometimes discover that by taking certain substances, they can easily feel glimpses of how life could be if only they knew how to get there.** In this situation, substance abuse and other forms of self-medication act as anesthesia for the inevitable pain of feeling powerless. When upset, *Ones* will often throw a "tantrum" to mobilize their energy and get attention—or the opposite, which is to retreat into themselves—much like their infant counterparts.

Psychologists have long recognized that there is little, if any, correlation between maturity and intelligence. As you will see, **it's possible to be significantly fixated or stuck in one or more life areas, at this or any stage—for various reasons of nature or nurture—yet still function remarkably well in other areas as an adult.** As we go through all the stages, it will become apparent that most of us retain certain hooks at each stage—including Stage One—even though our default stage may be solidly in the higher and even highest stages.

It's important to note that sometimes we go back to our lower stages during periods of extreme stress or illness, when particular situations occur, or at other times even by choice. Our hooks also serve to help us interact with or even to understand others with that lower default stage. Therefore, when we use our hooks or insights learned through them for those purposes, they serve us well. **It's only when we believe that we are *unable to choose* to function at the higher stages that our hooks become hang-ups that negatively affect our relationships, major life goals, and attitudes.**

Conflict is generally handled at Stage One by doing what is easiest, such as surrendering and/ or allowing some person or force that you consider stronger or more capable than you to take over the situation, thus allowing you to wash your hands of any conflict.

Ones often cannot tolerate conflict and ambivalence. A typical Stage One reaction to conflict is to become absorbed in self-pity and feelings of helplessness. They don't see or even attempt to think about long-term solutions for the underlying issues that may have led to those painful feelings of victimhood in the first place. **When someone disagrees with them, *Ones* typically experience it as abandonment; and *Ones* cannot tolerate feeling abandoned.** They then will become frightened and sometimes combative.

In order to survive, *Ones* can become most proficient at seeking even more pity and/or some type of rescue from others (for example, listening only to "fellow victims" who uncritically support their myopic point of view or by rebounding from one bad marriage to another). Some *Ones* even become proficient at terrorizing others into doing or providing for them by implying or expressing an intention to harm themselves if not cared for in accordance with their demands. Yet paradoxically, this kind of intense dependency usually breeds some degree of resentment in *Ones* toward the rescuer. Thus, relationships with *Ones* often consist of many double binds. **If this situation speaks to you, it fortunately can be turned around; the first step is to recognize what is happening and why, then to commit yourself to change this pattern once and for all.**

Success at Stage One is generally defined as collecting or taking what is thrown your way without being called to task or challenged to pull your own weight. A common staple of Stage One is to ask, "What's in it for me?" without the awareness or even the desire to consider giving anything back to a person or any aspect of the larger world outside of yourself.

> **What Motivates** you at Stage One is whatever feels easiest, safest, and most comfortable.

We who are parents can attest that one of the most difficult things to do is to give our children all we can without enabling them to feel entitled to it. As Warren Buffet wisely said of leaving a fortune to his children, *"I want to give them enough to do everything, but not enough to do nothing."* When parents are unable to perform this often-difficult balancing act, the result in a child can be a sense of entitlement. For example, a parent who repeatedly throws money at an adult child who is having financial problems is providing a Stage One solution that may be, at best, helpful only in the very short term. However, it will not do much to change the pattern (or long-term consequences), as would insisting that he or she resolve the issue without that level of parental help.

> The best **Parenting** for an infant at Stage One provides unconditional love, nurturing, care, and safety during the first year of life. Beyond infancy, the task is to teach them gradually how to fend for themselves.

Sometimes the seeds for becoming those bottomless pits (unable to take responsibility and become adequately self-sufficient) are early on inadvertently planted and reinforced. However, it then somehow becomes the child's challenge to outgrow this. **The best parenting, of course, is about giving guidance that is age appropriate.** This means both accepting and tolerating (while certainly guiding) behavior that is typical of the stage that a child is in. For an infant at Stage One, that is nurturing— providing unconditional love and safety.

Teaching self-sufficiency to a varying and age-appropriate degree becomes optimal thereafter—even to adult children who are relating to their parents through their Stage One hooks! Immature behavior (that is behavior typical of a lower stage), warrants corrective measures. Such measures will help a child of any age to understand how "growing up" with respect to that behavior or attitude is to his or her advantage. Throughout *Stage Climbing*, there will be many illustrations of this. **The best parenting advice I can give is to parent at the stage that is most age appropriate for your child—not higher or lower. Much of the information you will find in *Stage Climbing* can be used as a source of guidelines to help you in this critical and difficult task.**

The archetype of the princess, prince, or even "mama's boy" is one who is raised to have their every need served by others—rarely even eating or dressing by themselves—although quite able-bodied and able-minded. They are examples of normal Stage One behavior for an era of time when a climb out of it would rarely be thought of, let alone attempted. **The problem is that feelings of helplessness, which stem from the underlying belief "I am inadequate," become a predictable by-product of not taking charge of your own life and destiny.** As time goes on, this can become more and more a reinforced part of the character of a *One*, where dependency becomes the natural order of things and eventually can appear to be or feel like the only option.

Spirituality is either non-existent at Stage One or takes the form of the attitude that "God takes care of me and all of my needs; there's nothing I need to do in return." And indeed, whoever does take care of those with a default at Stage One (e.g., parents, spouses, the government, a sheltered work or living environment of some type, etc.) may even be perceived as "God." In addition, it's certainly typical for *Ones* to give a great deal of power to spouses and other caretakers, who can sometimes be extremely abusive without fearing the loss of the relationship. As many former *Ones* can attest, this is a very high price to pay for the illusion of a "safety net"!

Play at Stage One is a very self-involved process. Infants enjoy discovering and exploring their bodies and the sensations self-exploration gives them. In a similar way, **Stage One play for adults is any type of self-pampering: letting yourself be totally taken care of on that vacation at an all-inclusive resort or a luxury cruise, being pampered at a spa, or even lying on a hammock in your backyard with a cold beer on a hot day.** I mention these because they represent healthy and desirable Stage One hooks that you probably would never choose to change. On the other hand, some people who work *too* hard even find difficulty in granting themselves permission to relax or choose to let themselves enjoy these delightful Stage One hooks. (If I ever opened a travel agency that specialized in great pampering vacations, I would consider calling it "Stage One Travels." On page 278 of Part II, I include a tongue-in- cheek breakdown of vacations by all seven stages.)

Pleasurable activities and self-pampering in which pure self-indulgence is the norm can certainly be a good thing on many levels. Spending your free time doing whatever you envision that members of the "leisure class" do is not only okay, but comprises very nice, rewarding diversions. **Many couples find that a custom blend of Stage One-like activities can be an important and positive part of their relationship. For example, one partner pampers and nurtures the other without expecting anything in return, or they take turns doing it, each in their own unique way.**

Some *Ones* are actually envied by others! This is because they are seen to have a blessed and easy life free of conflict and hassle in which someone else provides for them and their every desire. The question as to whether or not that life is a blessed or a very troubled one lies in whether their life and lifestyle is what they want, or one they are stuck in because of chronic feelings of inadequacy. The latter are a constant by-product of the belief that there is no way out, or that no other choice is possible.

Many of the "lived happily ever" stories in folklore have an archetypal "happy ending." moving from "slavery" to freedom in which the protagonist experiences the joy of discovering how different things can be when you take charge of your destiny. However, many stories with romantic themes that appear to end "happily" may—upon follow-up—have the exact opposite conclusion when they result in such things as extreme dependency.

Stage One **attitudes about Sex:** "Putting out" is necessary to keep your partner happy and the relationship intact. On the other hand, Stage One is also the stage that is most identified with sexual addiction, in which a partner is somewhere between difficult and impossible to satisfy sexually (as is the case with most addictions) and therefore might put all aspects of his or her relationship (and/or life) at risk. Sex addicts characteristically believe that sex is exclusively about their own pleasure; and that sex partners are objects who exist solely for that purpose.

Finally, some people, regardless of how evolved they might have been previously, revert to Stage One late in life as part of age-related mental or physical decline, or even by choice in retirement. For example, being your own "caretaker" by providing well for your retirement later on is arguably one of the best things you can do for yourself. The vision and possibility of living a very easy and carefree "Stage One-like" existence in later years is often a great motivator for saving money long before retirement is an issue.

Nursing homes are often strikingly similar to nurseries when it comes to the normal behavior of both the residents and the caretakers. I observed this many times when my mother was in a nursing home. Stage One (in infancy) is the stage where trust begins to develop (Erikson 1963). This is a crucial ingredient for all of our relationships; and no matter how independent we may have been throughout life, it's possible that there will come a time when we once again will have to trust others to take care of us. Hooks in Stage One may be the very thing that helps many to make this sometimes difficult adjustment at the end of their lives. Never let them define you, but honor your Stage One hooks, as you may need them someday, or perhaps even now, should it be necessary to give up your independence due to a medical, psychological, or economic reality.

CLIMBING OUT OF STAGE ONE: WHAT YOU NEED TO KNOW

First and foremost, it bears repeating: **blaming your parents or anyone else for what you perceive as your predicament will only keep you stuck there!** Step one in passing through Stage One (or certain other stages, as you will soon see) is to acknowledge and take responsibility for your Stage One hooks without berating yourself any further for having them. In return for refusing to blame yourself or others, here is the good news: **Any initiative that you decide to take on your own is a step in the right direction to climbing to the higher stages.**

Becoming proactive and self-sufficient in any area of your life in which you may have previously defined yourself as being powerless or stuck is the core of what it takes to dramatically begin the *Stage Climbing* process out of Stage One. You just have to remember to do it. The same applies to helping the *Ones* in your life to grow by supporting them in taking the initiative.

Attitudes that are most helpful for Climbing out of Stage One:

❖ "I can do it/handle it."

❖ "I am tired of being dependent and relying on others. I now want to begin taking charge of my own life."

❖ "Certainty does not exist."

❖ "Too hard implies impossible, which it isn't. Difficult is a challenge I can handle."

❖ "I choose to be free of my past, wherever it limits me"; "I am no longer a victim."

Although this statement could apply more or less to navigating, neutralizing, and gaining mastery over your hooks at any stage, the act of taking the initiative *itself* is generally less of an issue in the higher stages. In Stage One it's the greatest challenge, since that very lack of initiative along with the belief that, "no amount of effort I expend will make things better for me," is what chronically holds you back. This toxic belief (along with the others discussed earlier in this chapter) become the self-fulfilling prophecies that keep your Stage One hooks in place. They can even lock in a Stage One default in one or more areas of life.

For many, dependency can be extremely addicting and hard to give up—especially if someone enables you to stay dependent and/or serves as an ongoing obstacle to change, such as in a controlling or abusive relationship. Therefore, realizing how important it is to commit to and follow through on any step out of your comfort zone is more than half the battle. Freedom and perhaps worlds you would otherwise never know exist, are waiting for your discovery; they lie on the other side of whatever wall keeps you stuck at Stage One.

Listen to those moments of awakening when you realize that whether or not you achieve a desire or goal— and certainly the degree to which you reach your highest potential in life—is up to you and no one else. **Sometimes it helps to visualize your life without the safety net that may be holding you back from taking the reins. Then do something—anything—that brings you even one small step toward your goal. In addition to the obvious benefits, each time you accomplish something you set out to do you prove to yourself that you can.**

I have seen many people in my practice for whom necessity or some form of adversity forced them to climb out of Stage One. The death of, or divorce from, someone on whom they heavily depended may have forced them to take on tasks, missions, and goals they would have characteristically avoided if they could have somehow chosen to remain dependent. **Many people that I have seen in my practice have been shocked at what they could accomplish if only they tried.** For me this has often been an inspiring phenomenon to watch. However, you do not have to wait for crisis or necessity to make this choice. The climb from Stage One is an option available to you any time you want to make it; and it applies to any aspect of your life.

Remember that you *will* retain hooks, however small, to whatever stage from which you climb. Sometimes your hooks to the lower stages are there for no other reason than to help you remember that period of your life, to empathize with others who are still there, or simply to use them whenever it is your choice. **Just be sure that your hooks are there to serve you, never to rule you!** This is always the healthiest reason for us to retain and use our hooks to the lower stages.

WHY DO WE RETAIN OUR STAGE ONE HOOKS?

When your Stage One hooks are not by choice, they can hinder your climb and pull you down. Examples include:

❖ The inability to see how life could be better; (many *Ones* — as well as *Twos* and *Threes* — do not realize that anything better for them exists).

❖ The perceived ease of living some aspects of life at Stage One.

❖ Fear of both success and failure, which would be you telling yourself things such as, "If I take initiative and fail … I wouldn't be able to stand it," or, "If I see myself as inadequate, I won't have to take responsibility for my failures." Also, "If I succeed at something, people will then expect more of me than I could ever deliver."

❖ You have no real motivation, ambition, and/or energy to leave your comfort zone, regardless of how much you tell yourself you "should" want to.

❖ You are hooked on the "rewards" of victimhood and are unwilling to give them up.

❖ Medical issues such as a major or chronic illness or disability; (severe depression and/or anxiety as well as other conditions caused by a chemical imbalance can also thwart your effort to apply the strategies necessary for change. Therefore, please note that these may first need to be treated medically. In many cases, until certain underlying medical conditions are treated and resolved, trying to remove related Stage One hooks might only amount to little more than added frustration).

On the other hand, there are times or circumstances when hooks in Stage One enhance your life. Here are a few examples of Stage One hooks that can serve you in a positive way and when they might come in handy:

❖ When your choice is to be lazy, carefree, or childlike in one or more areas of your life.

❖ The simple experience of the pleasure of sometimes being taken care of without the need to give back on a *quid pro quo* basis. This is often a nice win-win aspect of the best friendships and love relationships.

❖ Coping skills for being dependent or being taken care of when this is necessary. For example, when you are sick or incapacitated and/or have done everything within your power to learn about, make choices regarding, treat, handle, and accept the reality you are facing.

❖ And, of course, when on vacation or enjoying downtime!

If you have one or more Stage One hooks or identify with this stage as your default for an area of your life, read on for specific strategies to better understand or change the impact Stage One may have on you. You may choose to go there now or continue on to Stage Two and consider the action steps later or after you have read about all the stages.

TAKING THE INITIATIVE: CLIMBING OUT OF STAGE ONE

Stage One Action Steps You Can Take Now:

❖ **Identify** areas of your life in which you see Stage One as being your default stage. (For example, it may be the way in which you may relate to aging parents.) Then list any areas in which you may merely have unwanted hooks in Stage One. Title your list: **Things In My Life I Don't Like, But Feel Powerless to Change**.

❖ For each item you have identified, note **which** ones you would like to change and **why.**

❖ Always make sure you know exactly **what's in it for you** to make the changes you have identified. Without solid reasons that are your own (as opposed to someone else's), you simply will not be motivated to leave your comfort zone. This principle applies to all the stages, in varying degrees..

❖ Next, formulate a **simple goal** for each hook or aspect of your life you wish to change. In other words, if you could totally take your life into your own hands with respect to that hook, how would life be different or better?

❖ Now focus on **taking some steps** in the right direction. Make a long list under the heading: **If I were taking the initiative, I'd_____.** (For example, getting information about going to school or an independent financial opinion to help you evaluate the feasibility of leaving your marriage, updating your resume, etc.) Make your list as comprehensive as possible in regard to things you could do to take some initiative with respect to those areas of your life you have identified as wanting to change.

❖ Using the calibrations in Part II as a guide, **challenge** those fears and anxieties that stand in your way of taking prudent action. Never let them hold you back. Settle for nothing less than taking control of your life. **Remember, each time you allow your comfort zone to overshadow your dream or goal, you are strengthening a Stage One hook**. Each time you take action in spite of a fear or anxiety, you are *Stage Climbing*.

❖ Fine-tune and add to your list of **action steps** (ways you can take a desired initiative that you have been avoiding). Add at least one for each hook that you have identified—one that you are willing and committed to do immediately (even today if possible!). Remember, as soon as you begin to take those steps, your *Stage Climb* with respect to that part of your life has triumphantly begun. If you find this difficult, try as an intermediate step simply **acting as if** you could or were taking charge. Visualize pulling it off masterfully! The more you do this, the easier it will become to finally commit to taking those necessary action steps in real time.

❖ Stage One **Resources** include books, audios and Web sites that contain first-person accounts of people overcoming extreme dependency on others and overcoming Stage One realities such as addiction. In addition, books and other resources for information about medication and basic mental health/mental illness issues may be pertinent. Many of these can be found at StageClimbing.*com/resources* (Password: MyStageClimb). I urge you to dig into these resources for both guidance and inspiration for your *Stage Climb* and to help you manage any unwanted Stage One hooks.

CHAPTER 2

STAGE TWO

Your Primitive Self

"I did not have sexual relations with that woman ..."

—Bill Clinton

That quote by Bill Clinton is the one that might perhaps be remembered more than anything else he said during his eight-year presidency. It is merely an illustration of how strongly Stage Two behavior by public figures—by those from whom we tend to expect and look to for much more—can resonate.

Imagine yourself once again the center of the universe—not unlike Stage One. Only this time, you have the impetus and momentum to get up off your chair and take anything you want. Imagine everyone else in your line of vision and beyond, having no feelings or needs—like expendable toys. There are no rules to follow, so no consequences for taking or destroying anything that stands in your way. Have a tantrum and the world satisfies you by delivering whatever it is you are screaming for. Then everything is just fine until you want something else; and when you do, no problem, just find a way to demand or take that too. It's all yours for the asking or taking. That's essentially the world or mind-set of the toddler; and if our species required no other rules or standards for discipline, that would be humankind in a nutshell.

Perhaps in very primitive times it was. Life was good until some stronger or smarter "toddler" preyed upon you. Thus, **a good one-word description of the anarchy of Stage Two is primitive.** We were all there once—personally as a toddler and in prehistoric times as a species—and, most of us on occasion still "revisit" this part of our lives at times, by virtue of our Stage Two hooks.

Now imagine a toddler with the physical and intellectual capabilities of an adult, and you have the somewhat unvarnished profile of a Stage Two default. What a life! For a more amusing rendition of adults celebrating Stage Two anarchy rent any Marx Brothers or Three Stooges film. It's the ongoing spectacle of adults behaving like toddlers that makes them most hilarious.

Stage Two normally begins somewhere between the ages of one and two years old and optimally lasts about two years. We gradually pass through Stage Two throughout the fourth year of life. This is the stage of development in which as toddlers, motivated by a combination of curiosity and our sudden ability to be mobile, we first began to discover our environment and to shift our focus toward what is going on *outside* of ourselves.

At Stage Two, we are naturally uninhibited, playful, and joyous; and these traits become the Stage Two hooks we will most want to preserve throughout our lives. Toddlers, if given the opportunity and are ready to take it, can now become aware of other people in addition to those who act as caretakers. Since for the first time they are mobile, they also have the ability and a natural tendency to begin to "test the limits."

Stage Two is the normal **Default Stage** for toddlers. Your hooks in that stage come in handy mostly if or when in prison; when you are cornered and forced to respond in flight/fight mode; or need to take unusually courageous, defensive, offensive or manipulative action in the moment without regard to long-term implications, in order to get through a crisis or immediate danger; when struggling to survive (for example, when stealing is the only option in order to feed your child). When, however, engaging in delightfully uninhibited joy, fun, and play, you are using the Stage Two hooks you probably want to cherish.

Parents who are unprepared for this sudden change, sometimes become extremely frustrated—even unglued—in their attempts to deal with their child's budding autonomy.

One of the most important and challenging tasks for parents of a child at Stage Two is to begin to teach the very basic rules of living in a civilized society. Ideally, this is done in such a way that when children predictably begin to rebel against those rules, they also learn about the impact and consequences of their behavior as well as the realities and demands of living in the world with other people. A parent needs to be watchful while letting go just enough to allow the toddler to explore. Being mindful of safety while setting limits and encouraging exploration can be a daunting task for parents.

This is the beginning of the development of will. It is also the first sense of power that a child feels. It is certainly called the "terrible twos" for a reason. In addition, it is at this stage where the very first, basic roots of conscience normally start developing, which will bring along with it the first installment of a child's learning respect for authority. To the extent that parents can successfully teach toddlers to learn and accept reasonable limits without losing their zest for life, a healthy sense of autonomy can begin to surface. This is one of the most important aspects of every youngster's development.

At Stage Two, children need to become aware that other people have feelings too; and learn that others are not extensions of—or are there merely to serve—them. This is also the time to learn how to have fun, and to accept the reality that *nobody gets everything they want all of the time.* Twos don't yet buy into this often-inconvenient and sometimes paradoxical fact.

The best **Parenting** for a toddler at Stage Two: To let the toddler explore while teaching/setting limits and minding his or her safety. Most importantly (and at times most difficult), is not to act out *your* frustrations and emotions—especially anger—on your child. Remember, it is your job to teach that toddler civility. If that task is not accomplished now, later on it will become much more difficult.

There are two possible consequences of insufficiently passing through this stage as a very young child. One is the danger of developing a deep sense of shame and self-doubt, which results when a toddler is deprived of the opportunity or simply fails to develop will. Then the child may even grow up to be an adult who is chronically afraid to exercise almost any kind of initiative at all. This is in reality an emotional detour back to a Stage One default or the development of multiple, strong Stage One hooks and any or all of the consequences related to them.

Your **Ultimate Goal** at Stage Two is to have fun, experience joy, and get exactly what you want, while staying under the radar and avoiding any scrutiny, punishment, or other consequences.

More commonly, being stuck at Stage Two can result in a (varying) degree of disregard for rules and limits altogether. For toddlers, play normally involves learning about the world *their* way, and that means whatever is fun suits them. Toddlers love to explore, and they are not yet concerned with the consequences of their behavior. In addition, they are easily bored and tend to do and take whatever appeals to them in whatever way they can and/or feels best at that moment. With this in mind, **it's easy to see how strong hooks at this stage can manifest in extreme risk taking and rebellious behavior as an adult, without any regard to consequences.**

Remember, **it can be quite healthy, and a lot of fun at any age, to hedonistically play hard and be completely uninhibited. That's a great example of how we can call up our Stage Two hooks to serve us.** For example, many couples describe their best uninhibited sex as a wildly enjoyable (and certainly healthy and desirable) Stage Two hook. Thus, **in the higher stages, when you are having fun, experiencing pure joy and even making your work fun, you are choosing to do so under the guidance of your Stage Two hooks.**

However, adults with a Stage two default may become sociopathic or extremely self-centered and narcissistic with some similarities to those at Stage One. The difference is that narcissism grounded in Stage Two does not usually come with helplessness and inaction. Instead, there is an exaggerated sense of entitlement and power—believing they can and "must" have or do anything they want. They are entitled to act out in whatever way suits them, regardless of the effect their desires and actions have on other people or even what others think about them.

Unlike those with a default stage or hooks in Stage One, older *Twos* will typically do whatever it takes—lie, steal, bully, distort, or even commit violent acts to get what they want, believe they are "entitled to," or what their immediate and short-term desires crave. ***Twos* will often do things simply because they can.** If you have ever raised or carefully observed a toddler, you will very likely see this connection.

Sometimes Stage Two hooks can also be profoundly self-defeating. This is especially true for someone with a higher default stage. For example, excessive gambling can wreak havoc on every area of your life, except for the part of you that gets the temporary adrenalin rush that the action triggers. The same can be said for drug and alcohol abuse as well as any other types of addictions such as sexual acting out—that *ignore the long-term cost of short-term gratification*.

***Twos* who use harmful substances do it for recreational purposes** (as opposed to *Ones* who do it merely to self-medicate or provide themselves some relief from life or a painful aspect of it). **Whenever you do things you later regret as part of an addiction, look for the Stage Two hook if you want to understand that behavior logically.** Like toddlers, *Twos* believe they must constantly have their boredom relieved as boredom is a type of discomfort they characteristically can't stand, or have much difficulty tolerating.

The easiest way to satisfy your **short-term** needs is **what you typically seek at** Stage Two.

Indeed, Stage Two can be a very dark default stage to have. With little or no regard for the feelings or rights of others, criminal behavior is common to the degree there are strong hooks in Stage Two. Embezzlers, con artists, other types of thieves and predators, as well as premeditated murderers (if there is also a tendency toward violence), have the most extreme hooks in Stage Two, motivating them to pursue that type of behavior. The ultimate Two could be a serial killer who could take a human life, for example, in order merely to get a minute of his own sexual pleasure. This is arguably humankind at its worst and would be considered the result of a rock solid default at Stage Two.

Opportunities to lure people in and/or reap rewards without paying the necessary dues or playing on a level field are some of the things that **motivate** you at Stage Two.

When adults with a default at Stage Two focus much of their entire existence on self-survival and adopt one of the lifestyles just discussed, one obvious intervention is the criminal justice system. Prison is an institution that at its best—and not necessarily on purpose—is designed to promote an adult version of the kind of remedial discipline offenders may not have had during their early toddler developmental stage. At Stage One, the archetype of "mother" as caretaker is the most influential person; at Stage Two it is the "father" archetype, or the disciplinarian. Prison and the justice system take on the remedial role of one big and harsh "father."

O. J. Simpson has often been cited as a person who while extremely functional in many aspects of his life, is quite dysfunctional and sociopathic in others. What we know of O. J. is an excellent example of someone who had the superb skills of a winner in his chosen field (football), yet was emotionally and behaviorally driven by huge Stage Two hooks (or perhaps a Stage Two default). The complexity and contradictions he has displayed is the very reason so many people became absorbed in his legal case. If our most popular movies and TV shows or the crime novels we read are any indication, our society has always been endlessly fascinated by Stage Two characters and their impact on others. Perhaps this is because they seem to blend in so easily and appear to be so much like the rest of us, until their extremely dark sides become apparent.

Mental health professionals most familiar with this population have described *Twos* as the "ultimate or true free souls." They are free of the need for self-discipline and instant gratification and avoiding any pain of the moment is all there is. To accomplish this, *Twos* can skillfully be whatever they *have to be* at a given moment to get the result they need or want. **Like *Ones*, *Twos* are very focused on and preoccupied with their basic**

survival needs. This is one reason why in prison *Twos* function better than those at any other stage and feel most at home.

A Stage Two reaction to conflict is generally one of fight or flight, or a combination of them. That is, to lash out and/or run away—if at all possible. Thinking that the other person could have a valid point of view, particularly if it conflicts with theirs, is not within their realm. **Their intelligence and ability to charm, mimic sincerity and adapt can help a *Two* learn the system, but in reality, they believe only in fulfilling their own needs.**

Conflict is generally handled at Stage Two by using some form of deception, strong-arm tactic, or doing whatever you have to do, sometimes even without limits, to assure that you get your way. Thus, when acting on Stage Two hooks, you might be extremely charming to manipulate someone, extremely brutal to bully or force them, or any unique combination—that is, whatever it takes to control, overpower and succeed in getting what you want.

Since conscience is largely undeveloped, happiness at Stage Two is simply getting what you want regardless of the effect your actions have on others or any segment of the world. Thus, many live by the motto "The world is my oyster" and the only way to go is being able to manipulate, control, bully, get around, and/or overpower people without any concept of a win-win situation. Most of us have a killer instinct that we use very rarely. Perhaps we reserve it just for such times as when a mosquito is buzzing around our ears on a hot summer night while we are trying to sleep. However, some *Twos* do not particularly care to differentiate between an annoying mosquito and a human adversary. Vivid examples are with the behavior of long-time Stage Two icons such as Charles Manson, Ted Bundy, Al Capone, John Dillinger, Bonnie Parker and Clyde Barrow. They and their fictional counterparts that so many of us find fascinating, such as the Correlones (of *Godfather* fame) and Tony Soprano, are only a few notable representatives of the way *Twos* can be capable of interacting with the world when they are on top of their "game."

Success at Stage Two can be defined simply as getting away with something, whether it's a scam of some type or merely putting something over on someone. Because there is so little sense of positive purpose, hard work is something that *Twos* avoid at all costs. In fact, just about all "for profit" *criminal* behavior generally has one thing in common—that there is very little time spent actually doing any work. As long as their immediate short-term, needs are met, and regardless of whether or not it is at someone else's expense; a strong hook in Stage Two can become a pass to feel perfectly free to act out. Lying, cheating, and conning to deceive increasingly become second nature. **With a Stage Two default, in some cases deception becomes the most comfortable way of life.**

Attitudes or Beliefs behind your problematic Stage Two hooks:

❖ "I *must* always enjoy myself, have and do whatever I want, regardless of the effect I (or my actions) may have on anyone else (or even regardless of the *long-term* consequences I cause to myself)."

❖ "I don't want to change."

❖ "I will be/ do / say whatever I have to in order to get what I want at any given moment."

❖ "Life, and especially any aspect of it that I am concerned with should/must be easy."

❖ "I must always be treated well; and anyone who doesn't is just asking for revenge."

Even when success is obtained, *Twos* ultimately and characteristically are almost certain to find a way to sabotage themselves, often unwittingly. This is because *Twos* have so much difficulty learning from their mistakes. When they are caught, they typically consider the punishment or other adverse consequences they may perceive to be the problem, as opposed to a result of their behavior that prompted it. This lack of insight makes it probable that their behavior will continue to repeat itself. Usually—even if they are able to succeed temporarily by virtue of their intelligence—they will eventually fail. Therefore, in addition to being a very dark stage, Stage Two is also quite a self-destructive one.

Happiness and Success at Stage Two is simply getting away with something or achieving dominance over people. On the positive side, it's sheer joy and the lack of unwanted inhibition.

Stage Two characters you may meet in the workplace include all of those who grab credit for successes they have little or nothing to do with, while dodging the blame for other things for which they may have been completely responsible. They typically have little regard for the impact their behavior has on colleagues, no matter how loyal or undeserving of trouble those colleagues may have been. Sometimes *Twos* even morph into unsavory executives whose practices are characterized by bullying subordinates, illegal financial schemes, and other types of white-collar predatory behavior that can affect anyone in their orbit. Cases such as that of Bernard Madoff are high profile only because of the astoundingly large amounts of money he swindled. However, these types of practices are far from uncommon.

Showman P.T. Barnum famously said, "There's a sucker born every minute." By all accounts, his own default stage was much higher than Stage Two. Yet Barnum's philosophy of why masses will come to seek entertainment through illusion, remains part of the "mission statement" of many *Twos* who are business people, politicians, and others whose success depends on the ability to exploit and deceive others.

A Stage Two politician, for example, is out for whatever he or she can take or steal in the way of money and/or power, with little or no consideration for their constituencies or the needs of anyone else. Like most *Twos,* they know just how to exploit individuals, groups or crowds that give them money, power, and acclaim. They do this by imitating the desired emotions or necessary image and by projecting such traits as warmth, possibly without having a warm bone in their body. However, like *Twos* in any occupation, they can be highly abusive in private when the cameras are turned off.

Although most politicians probably rely on Stage Two hooks at times, successful politicians are likely to be much more complex as we will see as we explore the higher stages.

Twos **typically tend to marry or form relationships with those who are weaker, emotionally dependent, and who will tolerate much abuse while getting few positives in return.** *Twos* are generally one-sided and non-empathetic, emotionally. (That is, until the partner of the *Two* somehow "wises up" and leaves the relationship.) **They usually view friends and lovers as resources for money, sex, power, cover, and position, or simply objects from whom to suck energy.**

What triggers these common **Emotions** in you at Stage Two:

Anger—Being caught, punished (or turned in), confined, or called upon to "pay the piper" and take responsibility for your behavior. Revenge is often the first response to adversaries. Low frustration tolerance or distress regarding anything that is not going your way will characteristically trigger an angry response.

Anxiety—The prospect of losing your freedom, money, or cover; being caught, punished or exposed for your deliberate Stage Two activities.

Depression—Having unpleasant (and usually unexpected) consequences for your behavior, from which you cannot escape

Grief—Loss may become yet another excuse for acting out and displacing feelings such as anger on to others

---

No relationship is above being easily discarded when no longer needed, when someone tries to do some "remedial parenting" with them and set limits, or when something or someone better comes along, or when staying would require some type of sacrifice. Under most circumstances, extreme sexual promiscuity is a Stage Two hook. Moreover, *Twos* are often sexually promiscuous and deceptive about it, while requiring monogamy from their partner. **For a** *Two*, **being able to attach to another person as more than simply an object is unusual.**

In my practice, I have heard many who have been involved with *Twos* describe them as empty suits or hollow, with little real interest in anything other than leaching—emotionally, sexually, or materially—off those who tried to be close to them. This is usually not obvious at the beginning, since *Twos* can be so charming when they have to be and even mimic virtually every emotion there is to get what they want. When someone they still want in their lives has had enough and is threatening to leave, *Twos* can often act contrite and quite conciliatory until that "fed-up" person is back in their camp. However, as soon as the threat is over, a *Two* can be expected to return to their old ways until the next crisis. For this reason, it's not hard to see why there are many love relationships between *Ones* (who can often be easily manipulated through their severe dependency) and *Twos* (who are all too happy to use and exploit them and their vulnerability in any way they can).

Spirituality in the internal sense is not yet present at Stage Two. *Twos* do not believe that God or a higher power of any type exists. It's not that they are atheists *per se*; they just have not yet gotten around to thinking and caring about or developing any spiritual principles at all. They believe that there are no consequences beyond the obvious, as long as you are not caught or exposed. In the case of Charles Manson, his cult members have described him as extremely charming and capable of presenting himself as either normal or even profoundly evolved spiritually. This was until his true motives and intentions were exposed. Manson and others of his ilk are capable of projecting outwardly that they *are* God!

Many *Twos* who use religion as their way of manipulation to deceive others and as a means to an end can mimic religiosity and "spirituality," just as they can other things. They will act piously or observe religious traditions for no reason except to make an impressive impact on or create a false sense of security for someone else. It is never to be confused with true spiritual intentions—which do not fully manifest themselves until the higher stages. Those who have managed to break away from some of the most repressive cults have often described "charismatic" cult leaders in that manner.

Your view of **Spirituality** at Stage Two is rather primitive:

❖ "There is no God."

❖ "There are no consequences or rewards (karmic or otherwise) beyond the obvious that exist in this world, such as getting caught and punished versus getting away with something."

❖ "What you see is what you get."

Just as having hooks in Stage One does not make you a "help-less person," having Stage Two hooks does not mean you are a "bad person." Never forget that since most of us have some hooks in all of the stages, it's quite normal for most to occasionally display minor variations of Stage Two. You may occasionally cheat at cards or throw a tantrum (that may even have been "cute" if you were a toddler) for no good reason or when you did not get what you wanted. Perhaps you sometimes lie or exaggerate to achieve an end or to protect yourself from some unwanted consequence.

You may purposely run a red light or evade a tollbooth (and maybe even blame the cop if you are caught). Or you may take some undeserved credit, are deceptively unfaithful to your spouse, or run an aspect of your business in a dubious manner. These are choices you may or may not regret. Only you can decide, based on your own comfort level with your behavior; and only you in your heart of hearts know the reality of your limits when it comes to acting on your Stage Two hooks. **What would make Stage Two your default stage is the tendency to act that way most of the time, along with the *inability to recognize* that you can choose another way to be that will ultimately provide you with a better life.**

To the extent that an adult has not progressed beyond this stage, the bottom line is that he or she is at best emotionally capable of self-survival. The end of Stage Two is first signaled by the beginning of conscience, where long-term consequences, along with an awareness that others have needs as well, start to become a factor when choosing behavior and making other choices.

CLIMBING OUT OF STAGE TWO: WHAT YOU NEED TO KNOW

It is somewhat unusual for people with a Stage Two default to seek help on their own accord or, for that matter, to be reading a book like this. However, you the reader are likely to be thinking about some of your Stage Two hooks as choices. Most of us are in that category to some degree and can manage our hooks once we recognize them, which is *quite* different from having a Stage Two default. However, the principles regarding problematic Stage Two hooks that you wish to change—mild as they may be—can still apply.

Typically, genuine *Twos* have little or no anxiety or remorse; therefore, unfortunately, there often is little motivation to change. They are characteristically so comfortable blaming others for their problems that their lack of insight repeatedly tricks them into giving themselves a pass. At one point in my career, I spent part of the week doing evaluations and supervising treatment for federal offenders. They rarely took the initiative to seek therapy on their own. Instead, treatment was usually mandated either by the court or in some cases by someone with whom they were involved—such as a spouse—who was tiring of their Stage Two behavior.

In my experience, *Twos* **who thrive in therapy do so only when they can be shown how treatment or the changes that result from working on their issues benefit** *them,* **rather than those who stipulated or requested that they get help**. Thus, if they had wreaked a lot of havoc in their lives or been incarcerated, they sometimes valued treatment as part of a way to achieve their desire to never again be in that predicament.

Attitudes that are most helpful for climbing out of Stage Two:

❖ "Being excessively self-absorbed has thus far not gotten me what I thought/hoped it would, what I truly wanted, or satisfaction around what I have gotten."

❖ "Nobody has *everything* they want."

❖ "I can't always control how people treat me, only my reaction to them."

❖ "Life is not always easy and I choose to accept that."

❖ "There are long-term benefits to me in treating others as I would like to be treated."

Many people whose default stage is higher than Stage Two, but with strong Stage Two hooks, are well aware of how those hooks are self-defeating. If you have a history of failing relationships, losing jobs or losing money that you can't afford to lose (gambling, for example), with your commitment to break this pattern, it can be quickly turned around. Therefore, **to dismantle embedded Stage Two hooks that are not benefiting you, begin by first making the decision and commitment to identify those hooks, take responsi-**

bility for them, and make a commitment to choose different ways to live your life.

Sometimes part of the process is actually to learn guilt and shame in order to help install or strengthen conscience. **This is the only stage where emotions such as guilt and shame can be good sources of insight**. At the other stages, we consider those feelings to be quite the opposite and therefore strive to overcome them. **Learning about and recognizing the long-term consequences of thinking and behaving as a *Two* is the most crucial step in motivating your climb out of this stage.** This means learning from your mistakes, rather than inventing excuses for them, and resolving to walk down the path that is consistent with your long-term goals. For example, **consider modeling and showing *genuine* respect for some of the people who follow the very rules you may have fought up until now.**

Get involved with something larger than yourself. Allow people to help you without exploiting them or jumping to the conclusion that they have an ulterior motive to con *you* in some way. These are the attitudes that will help you to begin developing empathy, which is an awareness of how other people feel and how you would feel if you were the object of the same kind of actions you may be inflicting on others. You undoubtedly were taught the "golden rule" sometime in early childhood. Reconsider it as you work on Stage Two hooks—especially the "as you would have others do unto you" part. You will find many rewarding alternatives to everything Stage Two throughout *Stage Climbing* as well as several strategies to consider and put to work for you at the conclusion of this chapter.

WHY DO WE RETAIN OUR STAGE TWO HOOKS?

Stage Two hooks have two things in common with hooks in Stage One: Both are meant to be temporary stages that we pass through early in life; and when we are operating out of them, there is often little motivation, awareness, and/or confidence that better alternatives exist. These are the major reasons that *Twos* are so resistant to change. However, your Stage Two hooks still come in handy when:

❖ It is your choice (and hopefully under legal and safe circumstances) to engage in uninhibited, and highly joyous hedonistic play—consensual sexual variations unbothered by such things as guilt—typical of a tod-dler's best and most fun-filled *mind-set*. This is your Stage Two hook at its best!

❖ Survival and taking care of yourself first, under unique circumstances, is job one. Examples include when living in a neighborhood environ-ment where Stage Two behavior is the norm, a prison, or a POW setting, or any time when you determine and believe that in order to survive it is necessary to be whatever you have to be in order to handle the reality of the moment.

❖ You do not believe or are unwilling to consider that you have other means of economic survival.

❖ You need to fend off guilt or shame at times when you actually have done something wrong or shameful and perhaps are under fire for it. *Twos* can be quite good at mentally "closing a door" when necessary, by simply refusing to look back or at themselves. Aligning yourself with the present moment is generally a good, healthy, and highly desirable thing. However, most of us have an exceptionally difficult time do-ing that when something very glaring, immediate, or painful is on our minds. Compartmentalization of difficult painful feelings such as ex-treme grief, anger, or anxiety can be a healthy endeavor, and certainly a good skill to learn. *Twos* seem to be able to do this quite naturally.

❖ It is your choice to manipulate or con someone. For example, good poker players depend on Stage Two hooks to win as an important part of the game.

❖ You are willing to accept the consequences, should they occur, but are betting they will not.

❖ You believe—as did Robin Hood—that you are acting for the "higher good."

❖ The energy, drive, and cleverness that often comes so naturally in Stage Two can certainly be put to use for noble and decent things in the higher stages, so feel free to honor that possibility. For some, the seeds of their passion that lead to good things can even be traced to

Stage Two. For example, some of the most effective addiction coun-selors are those who were able to conquer their own addictions. They know all of the tricks and excuses. Ex-offenders sometimes succeed in helping other offenders with their Stage Two hooks far better than other mental health professionals who have never "walked the walk."

❖ Your rewards from Stage Two behavior outweigh any consequences. Thus, you do not see your hooks as problematic. **In other words, you just plain do not want to change.** Again, this is probably the most common reason people choose not to dismantle or neutral-ize the Stage Two hooks they recognize in themselves. If this is your choice, I urge you to remain open to reconsidering it often, especially if you are aware of negative consequences that result from that choice.

LEARNING YOUR LIMITS: CLIMBING OUT OF STAGE TWO

Stage Two Action Steps You Can Take Now:

❖ For your own eyes (of course), **identify** and list areas of your life where you recognize Stage Two hooks (e.g., a tendency to lie about certain things, gamble excessively, overindulge in recreational drugs, etc.). Also list any areas in which you recognize yourself as having a Stage Two default (e.g., your tendency to conduct your career or advance at work by taking credit for undeserved things).

❖ Identify and list some potential **role models** who are getting it right in the areas of your life that you want to change. What would you be doing differently if you were following their lead or the model they pres-ent? How would it be of benefit to you?

❖ Identify what you are **willing to change** about yourself—especially where the changes might not instantly feel gratifying, but could have long-term positive effects for you (e.g., having the type of relation-ship or career you want). As with Stage One, at Stage Two becoming aware of your hooks and making a commitment to do whatever it takes to change them is the lion's share of the battle.

❖ Make a list of **everything** you can think of that could be called: ***"What's in it for me, personally, to climb out of Stage Two?"***

❖ **Reflect** and answer for yourself: ***"Why must I always have what I want?"*** Do you know of any actual person firsthand (celebrities or others you know only by legend do not count) who has everything he or she wants? How could your life be better if you just changed this one belief/attitude/demand?

❖ Consider **involving yourself** in some new form of spiritual endeavor that may have been missing for you up until now. This can be through an organized religion or just simply by discovering your own higher self, as will be discussed as you read about the higher stages.

❖ Whether or not this is new to you, **consider the possibility** that there is a God or higher being who provides karmic rewards and punishments, or that there are other consequences beyond the obvious ones. If that were the case, what might you change in your life and how might you operate differently with respect to the Stage Two hooks you have identified?

❖ With an open mind, read about some of the principles of the **spiritual path** that most interest you. Regard these teachings simply as alternative choices (not dictums) to consider, and then possibly to make, whenever you are ready.

❖ **Think** about *Twos* you know or have known or tried to get close to. These individuals could have been friends, lovers, business associates, or co-workers. Perhaps they related to you through an extremely trustworthy facade, only to prove to be thoroughly untrustworthy. What did these people have in common? See if you can recognize how they may have affected you and even if you might still be susceptible to the manipulation of others like these *Twos* you have identified. And, if so, *how? Are you still affecting others in this way?* With these insights in mind, reflect on other changes you now would like to make.

❖ Stage Two **Resources** include books on sociopathy, criminal behavior (white collar and otherwise) overcoming substance (e.g., drugs, sex, gambling, etc.) abuse, gangs, bullying, finding positive role models, developing spirituality and conscience development. First-person accounts of people overcoming Stage Two habits and behavior can be very powerful. These and many other resources can be found at *StageClimbing.com/resources* (Password: MyStageClimb).

At Stage Three (and beyond, of course), your view of the world becomes radically different.

CHAPTER 3

STAGE THREE

Rule Abider

"Always let your conscience be your guide."

— Jiminy Cricket

Now imagine living in a world where everything is exactly as it "should" be. In this world, rules rule. In other words, all rules are effortlessly obeyed, all authority figures are placated, all norms are satisfied and you can easily stand up to the toughest scrutiny in any area of your life. There are no demands whatsoever being put upon you by any of the "powers that be" that you are not fully meeting or obeying. That same standard is also being met with respect to everyone who looks up to you as an authority.

All rules you are in a position to impose on others are being followed as well. To the extent that you can visualize this "perfect" and seemingly "flawless" world, you are seeing not a scene out of George Orwell's frightening novel *Nineteen Eighty-Four* (actually published in 1949), but Stage Three at its very best. To fit in, you simply need to do and perhaps believe whatever is expected of you by the authority (or authorities) you support or fear. **As a *Three*, that ability and willingness to *fit in and obey the rules* means that life is good.**

The rest of childhood and up until early adolescence is when it's most normal for Stage Three to take place and be your default stage. This is the best time to learn, understand, tolerate, integrate, and even fine-tune the many basic, yet complex rules of living in a civilized society that were first introduced and primitively set in motion during Stage Two. At Stage Three, children rarely yet see themselves as unique or one-of-a-kind individuals; but are optimally moving in that direction. They seek and are most comfortable with solid structure, although at times they can still be as self-centered and egocentric as children in Stage Two,

Stage Three is characterized by the ongoing development of conscience and the desire to fit in, be part of a group and connect with, as well as relate to, peers. You are now capable of some empathy toward others—at least with respect to *your* impact on them.

Stage Three is the normal **Default Stage** through late childhood. As an adult, your hooks there come in handy when in military-type organizations or in other situations in which blending in and enforcing, while not questioning, the rules imposed on you is decidedly the best strategy; and whenever a task or mission requires that others obey you.

During Stage Three, people outside of home become important resources for the first time. Giving can now be a pleasurable experience. Peer friendships can now be chosen. A child's imagination also begins to develop richly during Stage Three. If the fruits of that imagination are encouraged and stimulated by parents and teachers, then this is the best possible scenario for creativity to expand and flourish throughout life. In addition, there is no better time for children to begin to discover that it's highly desirable to listen to their inner voices. They will become a lifelong source of, and channel to, the uniqueness, creativity, and the motivation to take responsibility for taking charge of any aspect of life. At Stage Three, most children begin to develop hooks to the higher target stages. For example, talent in such things as music and sports begin to show up as well as an awareness of giving back through charitable activities.

Primarily, Stage Three is about learning and accepting certain rules that protect our world, save lives, and teach about long-term consequences. Some are no-brainers: not to break things, injure ourselves, maim, murder, or rob people. It is our willingness to adhere to these and many similar rules that makes our species unique and puts us above the primitive nature of Stage Two. **Without our Stage Three nature, humankind probably would not have survived this long.**

The other side of our *lifelong* Stage Three challenge, however, is not only to learn and understand the rules that apply to us and our world at various times, but also to question them when they no longer make sense. For example, a hammer is a very useful instrument, but one with which you can also hurt yourself. The mind is a tool as well, and just like a hammer, the mind has its down side. One misuse of the mind is to maintain many rules that simply do not continue to work, and then to manufacture even more rules that come in the form of reasons why we and others must follow them. **At the beginning of Stage Three, the mechanism to distinguish, question, and dispute rules is barely developed, if at all. Ideally, this gradually changes.**

In addition to parents and peers, another group critical at Stage Three are teachers. Teachers are the professionals who are in a position to have the most important impact on children at Stage Three. Those who meet this challenge certainly and obviously make an indelible imprint on the students they teach, and they can make an immeasurable contribution to the world via the extensive ripple effects that their influence generates. Sadly, however, some teachers do not fully rise to this crucial occasion. I refer here mainly to those who can teach such things as reading and math quite well, but are out of their league when it comes to encouraging creativity, critical thinking, and the benefits of being an individual.

Teachers who operate their careers with a Stage Three default often mistake the creativity of their students for defiance, rather than the higher-stage hook that creativity is. At the extreme, overly repressive and punitive elementary school teachers can not only shut down creativity, but also unwittingly instill a hatred of school and even learning, as well as a broad fear of daring to be different. (This happened to me early in elementary school where a few specific teachers tended to treat any *perceived* act of "defiance" harshly and acknowledged it in as degrading and humiliating a manner as they could get away with. I can remember watching a prison movie when I was a child in first grade. I had such a teacher and actually remember, "envying" the prisoners because they didn't have to go to school. It wasn't until much later, that I was able to change my adversarial view of teachers!)

The best **Parenting** for a child at Stage Three: To provide a solid structure and resolve to do whatever it takes to patiently teach those complex, yet basic, rules of life. By providing loving guidance along with appropriate discipline, children have the best possible environment to learn what it takes not only to fit in, but also to thrive and begin to discover their uniqueness.

Threes rarely believe the old adage that "rules are made to be broken." **To a *Three*, a rule is a rule—simple as that. However, circumstances do not always support the black-and-white thinking that underlies this Stage Three notion**. *Threes* usually have much difficulty accepting or tolerating exceptions to rules. To the degree that Stage Three is their default, adult *Threes* will characteristically tend to become something of an excessive conformist, a rigid rule abider and/or authoritarian personality, letting the fear of punishment, authority, and retribution dictate any—or at the extreme, even every—aspect of life.

Challenging rules or authority is generally out of the question. ***Threes* are often in a box. Closed to new ideas that question their deeply embedded rules, they seek people and situations that merely reinforce their conformity to certain beliefs, lifestyle choices, and ways to behave.** When *Threes* find more comfort in the rigidities they have adopted than any pain they experience as a result of being stifled by them, there is usually little reason or motivation to climb out of Stage Three. **Our "comfort zone" is what I have long referred to in previous books as a "*comfortable state of discomfort*"** (Broder, 1988). Think of that state as an internal force to be reckoned with when deciding to climb out of any stage, but especially the first three.

Your **Ultimate Goal** at Stage Three is to be conflict-free.

Extreme right- or left-wingers in politics, who conform to the strict dictums of an unbending ideology instead of thinking through the individual issues before taking a stand, are usually operating out of Stage Three. By contrast, choosing to be politically liberal, conservative, or moderate because you have thoughtfully considered the alternatives and complexities of the issues important to you would be indicative of higher stages. Stage Three politicians typically see themselves as ruling—or at best, herding—rather than serving their constituencies. To succeed, they often rely on toady-like operatives and followers who provide them ongoing cover and validity. (This is still certainly a step up from Stage Two politicians who are merely there to exploit, deceive, or defraud for power or personal gain.)

Threes are usually most comfortable in a highly structured environment such as the military, for example, where few personal decisions need to be made that require more than adherence to one rule or another. Moreover, just as the typical inmate in the criminal justice system is a *Two*, the typical prison guard most suited for that job would be a *Three*.

Conflict is generally handled at Stage Three by following a set of black-and-white rules that clearly dictate who is right and who is wrong.

Like most Stage Three attitudes, beliefs about gender roles, sexual behavior, making a living, and certain stereotypes tend to be quite rigid and are often defended with self-righteous anger. Prejudice, bigotry, and intolerance are also Stage Three hooks. The television character "Archie Bunker," of course, was a Stage Three icon. For *Threes*, living without set rules about almost anything can be downright frightening and therefore unacceptable. Thus, they will typically look for, and then adopt without question, a rule for everything: how to dress, what to eat, who stays home with the children versus who earns a living, whom to associate with and even what is acceptable to enjoy as a leisure-time activity.

Not making waves, by doing whatever is expected of you and staying on the good side of whomever or whatever you consider the authority to be obeyed as well as your power to rule others are what **Motivate** you at Stage Three.

Most marriages and love relationships grounded in Stage Three that work well are governed by dictums that neither partner challenges. When working on difficult issues with many couples over the years, I have observed that there is often an unspoken agreement that the partners, in a sense, be "psychological clones" of each other. This means that they have exactly the same or at best very similar ideas and values with respect to family, finances, religion, sex, the roles of each partner and family member, child rearing, and virtually all of the major issues that are staples of most relationships. Usually these are not rules they have evaluated and chosen, but those they have adopted uncritically—usually passed on from generation to generation. **It is the degree to which Stage Three is your default stage in a given area of life that determines how much disagreement you can tolerate, whether from a spouse or anyone else.**

The relationship usually will not survive when one partner begins to climb out of Stage Three and challenges some of the basic assumptions by which the couple lives while the other partner remains attached to his or her rigidities. Partners at any default stage can and certainly do grow apart, but when they do it for this reason, I look for the definitive Stage Three hook in one or both partners.

Love Relationships/Marriages, and how partners relate to each other at Stage Three: Both the foundation and the climate for the relationship are grounded in dictums (often clichés or stereotypes) that are usually based on long-standing rules and traditions, but in any case were not willfully chosen. Some examples include: how they met, religious or ethnic background of anyone who is being considered for involvement, who works, who stays home, the nature of their sex life, fidelity, rules such as "all marriages should/must last forever," etc. Disagreements often focus on who's most compliant with whatever rules form the basis of their relationship. Control issues are usually settled by the "book of rules" as well.

It is at Stage Three that spiritual development really begins. However, just like most other things at Stage Three, spirituality is usually

another set of rules to follow without question. Most often, they are the rules of an organized religion—the belief that God will take care of you, but only if you obey his commandments and/or the dictums of the religious branch or organization to which you belong. If not, you incur God's wrath. Fundamentalist-type religious beliefs often appeal to *Threes,* as they leave little or nothing to question or chance. Those, as well as cult-type philosophies, which are mainly grounded in guilt and fear on the one hand and fitting in on the other, tend to give not-to-be-questioned solutions to virtually all inner conflicts.

What triggers these common **Emotions** in you at Stage Three:

Anger—Others who do not follow the same rules or have the same values and beliefs that you do. At its most extreme, this could include prejudice, hatred, or bigotry. Anger at this stage often takes on or results from an attitude of "self-righteousness."

Anxiety—Leaving your comfort zone, especially when "the rules" aren't clear …The possibility of being damned, punished, or killed for doing or perhaps even thinking something different than whatever would be acceptable to a feared authority (real or imagined) … "Shades of gray."

Depression—Being unable to find the answers to a crisis or dilemma within the narrow boundaries of your comfort zone, or the inability to get hold of a clear direction and/or feeling of reassurance from the "book of rules" to which you subscribe.

Grief (over loss)—You practice traditional grieving rituals (such as those of your religion or community) … You may find yourself judging as wrong others who grieve differently than you do.

Religion and spirituality are two entirely different things. Although obviously they can be, and probably are, highly connected for most people. **I define spirituality as something *personal and distinctive* that is *internal* and within each of us. It is connected to our higher self** (whatever form that takes), **and our unique calling or life purpose.** What most organized religions emphasize is how humans are the same as opposed to how we are unique.

When religion is a choice that helps ground you at the deepest levels, it can become the mechanism for true spirituality to kick in. This

is indicative of higher stages. On the other hand, religion by itself is an externally organized set of beliefs that define spiritual things as well as how life is to be lived. *Threes* often turn to the church for reliable help when trying to resolve inner conflicts (e.g., anxiety, depression, or guilt) or relationship/marital issues (such as deciding whether to stay together or about sexual issues). It is at Stage Three that references to those predetermined beliefs as explained by the Bible and clergy are probably the most comforting intervention.

The old cliché that says, "Never argue about religion or politics," is clearly grounded in Stage Three. These are two areas where rigid Stage Three hooks will rarely allow enough flexibility to recognize that there could be a valid alternative point of view that warrants any discussion at all.

In authoritarian and totalitarian societies—which speak to the Stage Three hooks of those who live in them—it is the rules and dictums of the government, its dictator, or other rulers that play the same or a similar role as the beliefs of a church or cult. What connects all these things to Stage Three is the absence of choice that one feels *internally* with regard to them. Of course, merely obeying out of the fear of retribution as opposed to your *belief* in the authorities is not necessarily indicative of Stage Three, as those who were forced to live in a highly repressive environment such as Nazi Germany, the Soviet Union, and other extreme totalitarian regimes have taught us.

> To please authority and be pleased or appeased when *you* are the authority is what you are typically **Needing and Seeking** at Stage Three.

In Stage Three-oriented extended families and social circles, age and position (e.g., being a patriarch or matriarch) grants authority automatically; as opposed to authority being earned. Interestingly, across all stages, the best predictor of a person's career choice seems to be the field of his or her most influential parent. Sometimes not joining the family business or entering a certain career is considered as an affront to the elders in the family who might even declare such "rebels" as family "black sheep." However, don't forget that as embedded as they may be, it's never too late to take a fresh look at those attitudes that no longer serve you.

Most common Stage Three attitudes about Sex:

❖ "Sex comes with a set of rules; and should only be done the right way (e.g., between married people, in the bedroom, missionary position, lights out, etc.)."

❖ Strong belief prevails that any form of infidelity is *always*—and perhaps unforgivably—wrong.

Threes will usually choose to resist change to their "status quo" whenever maintaining it is at all possible. They'll typically define happiness as the familiarity and the safety of *fitting in with those most like them*, in addition to the absence of conflict. Typically, a *Three* will remain conflict-free by consistently choosing to be what they *"should be,"* as opposed to what they *could be*; and by not making waves or in any way challenging the rules or the authority figures in their world that make or enforce those rules.

Attitudes or Beliefs behind your Stage Three hooks:

❖ "I should/must, or should not/must not (insert a rule or dictum that doesn't serve you, but you feel compelled to obey, though you are not required to by any binding authority outside of yourself) _____."

❖ "I must fit in by doing only what I should do and by being what I should be—that which is expected of me—or some dire consequence will result."

❖ "Others should or must do (and even believe) things my way."

Many *Threes* either are content with their lives, simply because they believe there is no other alternative, or they become programmed over time to give in to their anxiety automatically. In other words, they refuse to leave that all too familiar comfort zone. **In my practice, I have observed that those who seek treatment for Stage Three-related issues, normally do so when that "book of rules" they have been living by no longer seems to provide them with solace—the answers or the solutions they are seeking to a**

daunting problem. For example, an illness, severe loss, or need to learn how to cope with some other involuntary change of circumstances (e.g., a spouse leaving or the rebellion of an older child) can be quite a wake-up call. Sometimes as a first step in helping them to work through these issues, the therapist guides them to find an exception or contradiction in their own rulebook that they can grasp, to begin the climb out of Stage Three in the necessary area of life.

A definition of success at Stage Three is the ability to remain on the good side of anyone in a position of authority. Authoritarianism is the Stage Three definition of authority. An authority figure needs not have earned the authoritative quality required by those in the higher stages (i.e., someone you choose to follow by virtue of your respect for them in their role). For example, a physician, an attorney, or any other titled professional can be seen as someone not to be questioned, merely by virtue of his or her title.

To **Problem Solve or when stuck or in crisis, here is where you would typically turn for help at Stage Three:**
The Bible, church, a trusted clergyperson, or a charismatic leader who clearly spells out the rules and/or authority that needs to be adhered to in order to resolve your issue … Also, you might seek an exception or "loophole" in a rule you believe you must follow and someone (a trusted friend, family member, or therapist) to help you adapt to a new way of thinking.

For *Threes*, the rank, position, or title—especially where someone or something holds a "hammer over you"—is what counts. Fear is often the main motivator; and *Threes* sometimes confuse fear with respect. An extreme example is Fascist and dictatorial societies (e.g., Mussolini on the far right and the communism espoused by Marx, Lenin and Stalin on the far left). They could not have succeeded as much as they did if the citizens didn't fear the ruler and look at their societal climate through the lens of Stage Three in order to survive (or at least act as if they did). The genuine dictator *demands* respect rather than *commands* it, whether or not it was earned. Mob behavior where *groupthink* supersedes individual morals is also governed by Stage Three thinking.

Happiness and Success at Stage Three:
Living your life "properly" or righteously by staying within the black-and-white parameters of your world … Not drawing any negative attention to yourself, by fitting in and doing what you "should," as well as doing your part to cause others around you, to "toe the line" as well.

Likewise, bosses at the workplace who operate from Stage Three generally use fear and intimidation to manage their subordinates with a "my way or the highway" attitude. Quite often in authoritarian organizations, Stage Three bosses experience their own superiors in the same way, never questioning someone of a higher position or rank. For many organizations (e.g., military, post office, police and fire departments, and large construction or factory-type operations), this form of "by the book" management is deliberately perceived (and often rightly so) as the only way to accomplish the organizational mission.

Threes have the most fun when doing the "*right*" fun activities exactly as they "*should*" be doing them. That is, fitting in by being like those in your peer group and feeling the support of whatever authority you (correctly or incorrectly) perceive as looking over your shoulder. An environment for fun and play is one that is safe, has a clear structure, and unambiguous rules. *Threes* have a definite awareness of other people; and can usually relate well to members of their "tribe" who conform, have lots in common with them, similar beliefs and attitudes; and most importantly, share the same values and follow the same rules. In fact, if there was an easy definition of those who are most content at Stage Three (either as children in their normal stage of development or adults by virtue of their Stage Three hooks or default), it would be *happy conformists* who live their lives transparently and by "the book."

CLIMBING OUT OF STAGE THREE: WHAT YOU NEED TO KNOW

The good news is that the process of moving beyond this stage is a simple, though not always an easy, one. The first step is to make that choice. Then the main challenge is to become aware of your Stage Three hooks; and recognize that there is a better way for you to live your life. Next, **take a risk or two that undermines whatever stifling rules and beliefs you realize you'd be better off without.** Often, just the awareness of an oppressive Stage Three hook is all that's necessary to quickly move beyond it. This is the *simple* part. However, **what may not be *easy* is the realization that you no longer fit in as effortlessly with certain friends, associates, and family members.**

As you climb, look for alternative ways to both see and resolve conflicts. If the way you have always done something is not getting you the result you want, be open to new ideas (regardless of the area of life; e.g., work, marriage, or friendships). **Dare to be different. Go out of your way to accept others who are different from you.** Work very hard at understanding their point of view and accept that other views exist and may be just as valid for someone else as yours are for you, even though you might not agree with them. This principle also applies to those with whom you used to have much more in common than you do now.

Attitudes that are most helpful for Climbing out of Stage Three:

❖ "I am ready to start examining the unquestioned rules I have lived by (and/or that I have demanded others live by), and even to consider being more flexible and open to new ideas that are now a better fit for me and my life."

❖ "Fitting in is only one of many choices that are available to me."

❖ "Other people have the same wide array of choices regarding how to live as I do."

If living a fulfilling life is the product of the choices you make, then the more choices you have, the better. This is the greatest benefit of dismantling your Stage Three hooks. Thus, for the same reason, **do not insist on acceptance of your higher-stage behavior from those who are operating at lower stages. They may not ever understand you. However, you can certainly choose to understand them.** Allow that sometimes you will forget that old friends and family members cannot relate to certain things about you. Preserving valuable relationships often necessitates your giving those people a pass and accepting the stubborn reality that they are doing the best they can.

However, **be mindful of how you react to people who negate your right to have a point of view different from theirs.** What you say and how you relate to them is not nearly as important as how you feel within yourself when they try to make you wrong for having your own opinion or your own way of doing things that disagrees with them. **You have the power to determine the importance to you of anyone in your life and how much influence they might have on your beliefs, attitudes, and behaviors. Climbing out of Stage Three is about honoring your own personal power.**

Make a special effort to look more to what people do rather than to what they say or to the title, position, or rank they hold. Moreover, if you tend to judge people by the groups to which they belong (e.g., ethnic, racial, political parties, economic status, age, religion, sex and sexual orientation, or some other ideology, etc.), make a special effort to look beyond those factors and to the individual, instead. Whenever you do this, you are indeed moving beyond Stage Three.

WHY WE RETAIN STAGE THREE HOOKS AND WHEN THEY MIGHT COME IN HANDY

Here are some situations in which your Stage Three hooks may serve you:

- ❖ You may prefer to operate out of Stage Three in certain areas of your life where that norm prevails. For example, if you were doing a stint in the military or any place where the decisions are made for you, Stage Three could be your *chosen* default stage—even if temporarily.

- ❖ When helping your children develop conscience; teaching them— without question—to learn the basic rules of behavior for living in our society and how to thrive in their school environment;

- ❖ When it is consistent with *your* spiritual beliefs to do so;

❖ Whenever you want to stay within your comfort zone and live by someone else's rules as a way of eliminating any anxiety related to making your own choices and being responsible for them;

❖ In order to relate at times to certain family members, friends, neighbors, co-workers, and others whom you choose to have in your life or who may not necessarily be in your life by choice;

❖ When you *must* follow someone else's rules (e.g., on an airplane when given safety instructions that must be followed or in an airport going through security, in the hospital when subjected to certain procedures, with specific aspects of your job, when doing your income tax return, etc.), regardless of whether or not you like or agree with them. A hook in Stage Three could be the godsend that helps you handle a difficult environment or task, at least until you can go back to living life by your own default stage;

❖ When you believe you must be in control; and others had better follow your rules—regardless of any "control freak" image you may exude.

AWAKENING TO NEW IDEAS: CLIMBING OUT OF STAGE THREE

Stage Three Action Steps You Can Take Now:

❖ **Identify** and list the aspects of your life where you recognize yourself as having hooks in Stage Three (i.e., where you habitually or even blindly follow an obsolete rule that no longer works for you, no longer applies to you or possibly even conflicts with your life). In what life area(s) might Stage Three be your default stage (e.g., your marriage or parenting style or your role as a supervisor at work)?

❖ Be aware of and **challenge** your thinking whenever you tell yourself some variation of these two Stage Three mantras, **"I must fit in,"** and/or, **"I can do/be only what is expected of me."**

❖ What have you always wanted to do with your life but resisted merely because you were **afraid** to **"march to the sound of a different**

drum"? Make a complete list of anything that occurs to you in answer to this question, along with a list of those risks you *wish* you could take now.

❖ Look at each item on the lists you just made and **ask yourself, "What steps can I take now take in order to pursue what I really want to pursue now, even though it necessitates my being different or on an unfamiliar path and possibly out of my comfort zone"?**

❖ Next, make a commitment to **begin taking some of these risks** you have identified—perhaps very small risks at first, working your way up to the more important ones. The task is to do whatever it takes to bring yourself closer to the higher potential that you recognize for yourself.

❖ Make a special effort to be around and to **relate to people who are different** in some way from those to which you normally relate. At the same time, limit if possible, the amount of time you spend with, and energy you give to certain people. They are the ones that insist that everyone around them must think as they do about such things as politics, lifestyle choices, religion, and other areas (even sports or taste in fashion styles) where you may not agree, but still believe you have a valid point of view.

❖ **Pay special attention** to any tendency you have, to employ a typical Stage Three reaction to conflict—where in a given situation, you passively feel compelled to follow an unchallenged rule or dictum that in reality does not fit for you. Make a strong personal commitment to resist the urge to go in any direction that is not compatible with the goals you have set for yourself or consistent with the life you want to live. If you are in an environment (e.g., your job or a relationship) where challenging the rules is just not possible, simply note this. At the appropriate time, look at and evaluate the long-term implications of staying in that environment. There will be much more perspective on this as we explore the target stages.

❖ Stage Three **Resources** include books on fundamentalist religion, cults, mind control, authoritarianism, totalitarianism, taking charge of

your life, challenging your "shoulds" and "musts" and various management styles, etc. These and many other resources can be found at
StageClimbing.com/resources (Password: MyStageClimb).

You (as well as everyone else on this planet) are different from any other
human being ever created since the beginning of time. Moreover, there will
never be another exactly like you. Do something new each day to honor, rather
than fight or ignore this wonderful reality!

At Stage Four, our unique identities unfold.

CHAPTER 4

STAGE FOUR

Approval Seeker

"The only thing we have to fear is fear itself."

—Franklin Delano Roosevelt

FDR's most recognized quote is actually a paraphrase of something that has been said by many notables and in numerous ways throughout history. It's also the most important mantra that you need to remember about virtually all of your Stage Four hooks.

First, let's look at Stage Four at its best: Imagine yourself being as famous as you could ever want to be, and being wildly admired and applauded— perhaps even routinely receiving standing ovations just for showing up! This level of admiration might come from those who are closest or most important to you (family, friends, neighbors, and others in your life), by crowds of adoring strangers (as celebrities experience) or anything in between.

The idea of being universally well liked and attractive to others, being a celebrity or being a highly popular and admired luminary in your field or social circle are just a few examples of the many possible versions of that desired reward for those with a Stage Four default. These feelings and experiences are highly appealing. However, are they as realistic or likely as you imagine them to be? What are you willing to do for them? How much energy do you wish to expend to achieve these things?

And while we're on the subject, how much money do you spend that you may not even have to buy things you don't really need to impress people that in the grand scheme of things hardly matter? Only you can answer these Stage Four questions. While the thrills that *Fours* seek are always possible for you to experience as fantasies---and you certainly don't have to be Walter Mitty to imagine them---what price do you pay in your life to get or strive for all of that admiration and recognition? How much acceptance and approval do you tell yourself you *need*?

> Your **Ultimate Goal** at Stage Four is to be accepted, admired, and respected by all of those who in any way matter to you; and you may not even have to know them personally.

Here is the other major Stage Four challenge: **Never judge yourself negatively about your Stage Four hooks. Instead, be mindful of what you are doing and consciously notice whether the reward is worth the effort that your Stage Four hooks demand. Either way, I encourage you to resolve to accept *yourself* at least as much as you want other people to accept you.**

At Stage Three, you are naturally drawn (and then tightly attach yourself) to rules and "shoulds" by which to live your life in exchange for feelings of security. At Stage Four, many of those rules no longer give you the emotional security they once did. Thus, your natural tendency is to change direction, start questioning things, and exploring new choices. While "breaking out of the pack" is highly desirable and often feels liberating, it also brings some new challenges right to the surface, such as the anxiety about being accepted, which was not a major issue when you unquestionably "blended in" and conformed at Stage Three.

Self-consciousness at this stage triggers fears of such things as rejection, looking foolish, failure, and isolation, along with a variety of our other most common insecurities. These become the core anxieties that both constitute and underlie your Stage Four hooks. The preoccupation with love and approval from others and the drive to be, or at least seem to be, "perfect," are all common examples of our challenges at Stage Four.

What other people think of you is in fact none of your business! Furthermore, somebody else's opinion of you is one of those things you can least control. Some people will like you because they see you as docile or in their eyes inferior to them in some way. Others could hate you because they believe you are more successful or attractive than they are. Still others could like you for the very reason someone else dislikes you! For example, in the workplace, many of the hardest workers experience scorn or rejection from the others who resent having to live up to the higher standards these hard workers set. **How much of your life you wish to invest in what others think of you—by pleasing and impressing others, being recognized, honored and/or accepted—are certainly things most of us ponder at times. However, for *Fours*, these issues can be all-consuming.**

Stage Four is the normal stage of development during adolescence and up until early adulthood—from the ages of approximately 11 or 12 to around 21. **The psychological task of adolescence is to become secure enough within yourself to establish a solid identity as a *unique* individual.** That uniqueness is a major ingredient for your foundation as a mature adult. Under the best of circumstances, you will build upon this trait for the rest of your life. Typically, adolescents can be obsessed with peer approval, fitting in with groups they select, learning how to make themselves attractive to those they wish to attract, and most importantly at Stage Four, gaining acceptance from those around them.

Quite naturally, a ready-made conflict develops between being that unique individual versus conforming and simply being like everyone else. **Much of the Stage Four conflict, like adolescence itself, is about determining whether to go with what is expected of you—which is typical of the Stage Three "surrender"—or to go your own way.** The latter will often work for you and lead you to good things. Other times it may not, and will bring you back to familiar and deeply embedded, Stage Three-type rules. However, as a *Four*, it's your choice whether and when you follow them. This ongoing dance continues throughout adolescence, until you "figure out" the right mix for you, which is a signal that you are ready to leave Stage Four.

Early love relationships are an important part of the adolescent ritual. In fact, it's been said that a perfectly sane human being goes through something akin to insanity under only two circumstances in life: during adolescence and when *falling in love*. Ironically, both of these are Stage Four challenges.

Stage Four is the normal **Default Stage** throughout adolescence. You are using your hooks here when enjoying the "buzz" or bliss of being adored in a new romance, when selling yourself and/or in a situation where the image you put out to others is important, and when it's your desire to fit into a chosen group where peer approval is required.

Parenting your adolescent child through Stage Four still involves setting limits clearly and dutifully enforcing them. However, the Stage Four balancing act that most challenges *parents* is then to step back and watchfully allow your adolescent to make his or her own mistakes, while still being available to them, when needed, as both a safety net and their most reliable resource. Many parents of adolescents find this to be quite a difficult paradox. Kids will ultimately come to you as a resource for support, guidance, and information to the extent that you let go a bit and respect their quest to discover certain things on their own.

At the same time, however, it's important for parents to administer effective discipline that focuses on addressing any behavior that crosses the line. Parenting *Twos* and *Fours* have this in common, even though most of the other challenges are as different as night and day. Those whose default stage as a parent is at *Three*, where they rule in a highly authoritarian, but not authoritative manner (of course, there are degrees of this) have the most trouble with their adolescents who may have outgrown this approach; and thus tend to rebel against and reject that parenting style. In other words, **parents who relate to their adolescents from Stage Three, can often find dealing with their Stage Four kids akin to pure hell!** A typical adolescent response to such parenting is either to withdraw or act out; seeking whomever they can find outside the house to provide that much-desired modeling and validation. Depending on such factors as the degree of alienation from the home as well as the often-random resources available to the adolescent seeker, this can be anything from an extremely "growthful" experience, to a profoundly destructive one.

The best **Parenting** for an adolescent at Stage Four encourages self-exploration while carefully setting limits, letting go, and allowing your adolescent to make his or her own mistakes—all the while remaining a source of love, support, and guidance that he or she can turn to as needed. However, it is also crucial to provide discipline and "tough love" whenever an adolescent child crosses the line. This could be your last opportunity to be the principle source of influence for your child!

To the extent that you act on your Stage Four hooks, or that Stage Four becomes your default stage as an adult, anxiety, self-doubt, and other forms of insecurity could be your biggest and most difficult life challenges. They can even become your principal, although generally negative, motivators. On the other hand, you might become as self-aggrandizing, highly conceited, and a braggart as the most common image of Donald Trump is, for example, about all the things he owns and has accomplished.

For some *Fours*, life is simply about others admiring or at the very least, thinking well of them. **Stage Four hooks can have the power to torment you to crave being loved and approved of by other people—no matter how insignificant or inappropriate they may actually be.**

That expedition for approval usually begins with parents and teachers. It can then move to peers at all levels—friends, co-workers, neighbors, eventually your children and virtually anyone else in your orbit. There is no limit to how much of your life you can devote to gaining the approval of everyone who either knows you or knows of you. For instance, a gay person who fears "coming out" might choose an opposite-sex partner to spend his or her life with in order to blend in, or as an alternative to perceived rejection from family, friends, or colleagues.

Some of the things that **Motivate** you at Stage Four:
Awards, celebrity, prestige, validation, praise, love, recognition, respect, and approval of you (often in a global way as opposed to merely a specific area of your life); impressing friends, acquaintances, colleagues and relatives (or even the general public).

Adolescence is the ideal time to learn how to handle conflict, since making mistakes then is normally far less consequential than it will be later in life. Perhaps **that's why in many ways, conflict *is* the norm at Stage Four.** For example, if public speaking makes you nervous, think of how your anxiety about it might be a metaphor for how you see conflict. Public speaking usually turns up high on the list (often in first place) when surveys are done of "what people fear the most." Public speaking anxiety is really a Stage Four hook. Your fear of and self-consciousness about rejection, ridicule, or negative judgment by those who hear you speak, could at worst convince you to avoid these situations at the expense of a higher goal or reward for doing the speech. So in this case, your anxiety would win. The same is true for other varieties of performance anxiety, as well—whether triggered by taking a job interview or even connected with sexual performance.

Fours also tend to obsess about such things as being ostracized by a group (or even society) and what they can do to be seen by others as success-ful. **At Stage Four, anxieties about failing can cut very deeply into how you see yourself.** For example; an ended marriage, a financial setback, a lost job or inability to reach an important goal can cause you to overreact by label-ing yourself as "a complete failure." **Berating yourself in a global way can then begin a vicious cycle that affects not just your self-image, but also your ability and willingness to get back into the ring and try again.** In the most extreme cases I've seen, harsh setbacks in Stage Four struggles can even trigger a tendency to give up on self-esteem altogether and revert back to a Stage Two default; with extreme risk-taking, profoundly rebellious, or antisocial behavior, along with a tendency not to care what anyone thinks at all.

> **Conflict is typically handled at Stage Four** by taking the road that produces the most validation from others and the least anxiety.

Self-esteem issues are generally little more than Stage Four hooks. In the best of all worlds, you would have established a foundation of self-confidence to build upon by early adolescence. It's during these years that you would both learn and understand (whether or not consciously) that **the "self" is much too vast, complex, and full of strengths, weaknesses,**

contradictions, and hooks to all seven stages to ever be able to evaluate as though it were merely one thing. In addition to anxiety, symptoms such as (non-medical) depression are often Stage Four (as well as Stage One) hooks. Stress is that *"what if"* fear. *What if* whatever I dread (e.g., lose my status, job or relationship, fail at something important, experience rejection or humiliation, etc.) did occur? We popularly call it stress, but anxiety, depression, and self-doubt are really the labels that are more appropriate.

At Stage Four, how you perceive what others think of you has a strong influence on what you think of yourself. Thus, if the assumption is that others will think less of you, then it's likely that you will think less of yourself. In the extreme, your hooks in Stage Four can even cause self-doubt to become a way of life and negatively color *every* aspect of it.

What triggers these common **Emotions** in you at Stage Four:

Anger—Rejection or disappointment from others whose approval, validation, or love is on some level important to you, jealousy in relationships, or a betrayal by someone you thought was in your camp. Sometimes anger is turned inward to create depression or self-esteem issues.

Anxiety—Being rejected, embarrassed, or seen as inadequate, "a failure" or of lesser worth by someone (or many, e.g., your peer group or even a segment of the public).

Depression—A major rejection or scorn by a person or a group whose opinion you believe has importance to you … When your self-esteem takes a major hit or you put yourself down for some failure, real or perceived.

Grief (over loss)—Blaming yourself for somehow causing the loss as well as for any existing unfinished business that may remain.

Peers and peer validation are therefore perceived as overly important at Stage Four. Much like *Threes*, but for different reasons, *Fours* still have difficulty in truly tolerating those who are too different. But **at Stage Four, you will often tend to select friends who are most like you and then do practically anything necessary to please them, sometimes even at the cost of**

your own integrity. For example, you might find yourself using drugs, getting tattoos, or participating in certain sexual activities merely for acceptance as opposed to your own desires.

Membership in the group you choose to be a part of might be what you consider an essential goal. When you reach it, a clique mentality often develops, where you might become quite enmeshed with fellow members in Stage Three-like "groupthink." Maintaining group membership then becomes crucial, even if this means it's necessary to compromise or disregard some of your own values to do so. Additionally, since feeling accepted and approved of by others can become so strongly tied to your own self-acceptance, then shame and embarrassment feel especially devastating and may even trigger stronger feelings of inferiority with regard to others.

What you are typically **Needing and Seeking** at Stage Four:

❖ To "find yourself";

❖ To "*be* somebody";

❖ To "make something respectable of yourself";

❖ To feel liked/loved and accepted by those in your orbit.

One typical Stage Four reaction to someone with whom you are in conflict is to mount a global and personal attack on that person rather than focusing on the problem that is at the center of the conflict. Another is to act rather unassertively and rush to compliance or perhaps avoid the situation altogether. In either case, the real issue would be glossed over and remain unresolved. *Fours* often find that the act of confronting someone *assertively*—or worse yet, the prospect of being rejected or berated by them, can ignite a level of anxiety that transcends most other types of conflicts.

During adolescence, there is often a tendency to act in a cruel manner by bullying or berating others as a means of artificially pumping up your own self-esteem, or sometimes merely to be part of a group. **To have self-acceptance without having to berate anyone else is to say that you have successfully met a major Stage Four challenge.** If you are part of a family or group that operates in Stage Three, be aware of how you may sometimes have (or had) to *put yourself down* to Stage Three from the higher stages in order to blend in. This same phenomenon can apply to old friendships, sibling relationships, people you work with, or a peer group that you have outgrown emotionally.

Happiness at Stage Four is belonging and feeling liked, loved, honored, or at least recognized and accepted by those whom you value the most. For many celebrities who take themselves too seriously, the general public is part of that "Stage Four network." Since your unique identity is still a work in progress at Stage Four, anything that triggers insecure feelings in you can feel quite painful. So in a way similar to *Twos*, *Fours* will often "be whatever they have to be" to gain acceptance or respect. **When *Fours* lie or mislead, they characteristically do it to impress others, unlike *Twos* who lie to deceive, avoid deserved punishment, and for personal gain.** Many *Fours* live to go out of their way to seek prestige and fame, and love to feel popular and superior, even if they actually realize deep down that this is merely an illusion or a temporary state of mind.

Wanting to *be* an actor in order to *be* famous (a popular ultimate Stage Four fantasy), **as opposed to wanting to act because it is your talent, art, and passion, is an example of Stage Four thinking.** The same can be said for the Stage Four attitude toward love and work**. *Fours* are much more concerned with *being loved*, than with loving another.** A teacher, for example, at Stage Four would characteristically be less interested in doing the work that teaching requires than in *being* a teacher for the stature and position it provides.

A Stage Four politician is more interested in *being admired* and having high popularity than doing something meaningful for the people who elected him or her to power. Thus, the most gratifying part of the job is the prestige and admiration by constituents and others who are impressed by the office. For example, I have seen many doctors and lawyers in my practice who disliked the work they did, but admitted they were hooked on the prestige factor of their professions or even the degree of acceptance from their parents that they perceived for doing a certain type of work (i.e., *being* something rather than *doing* something). I once coined the lighthearted term "beaholic" to describe this all too common Stage Four trait, in which one is hooked or focused on their title and the image it exudes, while not really liking or living up to the actual underlying duties and responsibilities of their role.

Happiness and Success at Stage Four:
Achieving acceptance, approval, fame, and positive recognition; also, keeping personal relationships conflict-free.

In the workplace, *Fours* tend to pay far more attention to how their contributions affect their own self-esteem than to the impact those contributions might have to the larger world outside of themselves. Gaining praise is often a top priority. Wise bosses who recognize the *Fours* among their subordinates use extra praise and validation as a major motivator. *Fours* work best either for or as a "benevolent dictator" type who motivates by setting up an environment characterized by warmth, affection, and the feeling of "family" as opposed to the climate of fear, which is the prime motivator in Stage Three-type organizations. Likewise, ***Fours* who would follow any type of charismatic leaders are often unrealistically idealistic and do so as a way to belong and feel cared for, rather than out of the Stage Three fear of whatever may be the consequences of leaving "the reservation."**

As it is in Stage Three, religion is sometimes a remedy for conflict and insecurity. However, **unlike Stage Three, the purpose of religion is not to avoid "punishment," but to get something positive.** Many *Fours* find such things as prayer and meditation to be excellent antidotes for their anxiety. Sometimes, this might be merely the result of the relaxation that meditation and prayer provide. On the other hand, there is now the capacity to reach for the deeper purpose achieved by handing your problems over to a loving God or higher power. In addition, religious communities and houses of worship often provide that much needed community where acceptance is a given. *Fours* may also experience a rift between their own developing values and those of an organized religion. **At Stage Four, it feels natural to start what for some is the beginning of a lifelong quest of questioning the values that have been instilled in you that you would not have previously dared to question.**

Stage Four hooks can trigger illusion. For example, you may see that which you are anxious about as being far bigger and more threatening than it really is. Things you are depressed about can feel far more catastrophic. **Whatever challenges your self-confidence can be experienced as far more difficult than it needs to be; and things that put you under stress, as far more consequential than the reality of the situation.**

At Stage Four, you are not yet in command of your life. You are still a passenger, not yet the driver. **You may find yourself having at least as much difficulty tolerating certain quirks in others as you have tolerating things about yourself.** *Fours* often suffer a great deal. Examples of this include worry over appearances, feeling badly about things that are hardly important in the grand scheme of life, and even turning your own anger toward something or someone else inward and toward yourself. In a way similar to the lower stages, **Stage Four hooks can also trigger the tendency to self-medicate with drugs or alcohol.**

Your view of **Spirituality** at Stage Four consists of beliefs such as: "God is benevolent," and, "If I do the right thing, God will love me."

To the extent that a marriage or love relationship is hooked in Stage Four, a good part of its foundation is insecurity. Issues such as jealousy, the constant questioning of how much your partner loves you, and sexual performance anxiety can sadly overpower the positives. Sometimes these relationships amount to little more than an alternative to loneliness or the insecurities of being single, rather than genuine expressions of desire for the other person. In other words, the relationship may not be fulfilling; but there is sometimes too much insecurity to leave or possibly even think of broaching the troublesome issues head-on, which could "upset the apple cart." A typical scenario is for one partner to be a chronic "pleaser" who is filled with resentment at the other partner who doesn't seem to reciprocate.

Paradoxically, many relationships between *Fours* can do very well, when both partners' issues are "complementary," making them

able to thrive together. Most romance novels as well as just about every MGM musical contain at least one Stage Four story line, such as jealousy or unrequited love. Fortunately, when both partners relate to each other at Stage Four and one begins to climb, the other may also be open to trying new attitudes, behaviors, and lifestyle changes that could facilitate growth to the higher stages together—both individually and as a couple. This degree of flexibility is rarely possible at the lower stages.

Some Stage Four Attitudes or Beliefs:
- ❖ "What some other person (or people that in the grand scheme of things don't really matter) thinks of me is crucially important."
- ❖ "Rejection by someone else is unbearable and a reason to reject myself."
- ❖ "I must be loved or approved of by others and/or meet their expectations."
- ❖ "I can only accept myself to the degree that I am accepted by others."
- ❖ "I must do well at everything I do. Any result less than perfection is totally unacceptable."
- ❖ "Failing at something (e.g., a relationship, a job, an exam, a sexual performance, or to meet a goal) makes me a total failure (to myself, in the eyes of others, or both)."
- ❖ "I can't stand it when things don't go my way."

No matter how solidly evolved you may be, Stage Four hooks in all aspects of life are quite common. In fact, an adult without Stage Four hooks could be the rarest human specimen there is.

CLIMBING OUT OF STAGE FOUR: WHAT YOU NEED TO KNOW

The climb out of Stage Four simply challenges you to face down and let go of your fears, anxieties, and insecurities. Few tasks in life can be more rewarding. Make a commitment to dismantle each hook that holds you back, that is diminishing the quality of your life, by causing you to fear things that present no real danger. **The main ingredients for your climb to higher stages are the *self-confidence* to succeed as well as undiminished *self-acceptance*, even when you are not successful.** These are merely attitudes that you can choose to adopt, right now.

Rising above or mastering situations that trigger your anxiety—and you know what they are—not only feels great when you do it, but is also the definition of success in gaining control of your Stage Four hooks. You will discover that taking risks, which at the very most could result in rejection or even failure, is indeed a "no lose" situation. For example, if the idea of asking someone for a date or making a presentation produces anxiety for you, do it anyway. If you succeed, then taking this kind of risk the next time will be a bit easier. That's a no-brainer. However, **each time your risk results in that "dreaded" failure or rejection, you also win! In this case, you win by learning that you really *can* handle rejection when it occurs; and *unpleasant as it may be, you will survive it!*** Soon, you will no longer fear rejection or failure very much, regardless of how unpleasant it may briefly feel at the time.

Taking prudent risks and asserting yourself can very quickly bring about a major transformation for you in important areas of life; but never taking the risk is the only *guarantee* I know of that you will *not* get what you want. As Mark Twain said, "At the end of your life you will be more disappointed by the things you didn't do than by the ones you did." How true!

Often we fear what we simply do not understand. It is therefore important to learn as much as you can about every one of your hooks. For example, how have others successfully handled the challenges you are facing? There is no shortage of reading and audio materials that headline virtually every issue in existence. At *StageClimbing.com/resources* (Password: MyStageClimb), you will find many of these highly effective self-help resources.

Many families and peer groups unwittingly provide a breeding ground for low self-confidence and avoidance by encouraging the "safe haven" of the status quo. When this happens, the consequences of your hooks can continue to feel even more daunting. Getting the help you need outside of your familiar circles of support is often the most important step. **Psychotherapy, personal coaching, and group peer support, along with self-help, are the best interventions to help adults climb out of Stage Four.**

Attitudes that are most helpful for Climbing out of Stage Four:

❖ "People who won't accept me for who I am are no longer worth my time and attention."

❖ "There is much more to life than putting boundless energy into fitting in and/or hoping others will admire and/or envy, love and/or approve of me."

❖ "Love and approval from certain people may be nice, but not as essential as I have told myself it is."

❖ "I give myself unconditional acceptance regardless of who else does or does not."

❖ "I can only do my best, and I hereby let go of all versions of that impossible standard called perfection."

❖ "Failing at something does not make me a failure."

❖ "I can handle things even when I don't like them."

Anxiety can sometimes *feel* too intense to permit the kind of risk-taking and self-assertion that the Stage Four climb often requires. Therefore, **strategies designed to zero in on the anxiety directly (as well as depression resulting from such feelings as chronic frustration, for example), are most effective; they can have wide ripple effects that influence positively every aspect of your life.**

In the case of anxiety, hooks to Stage Four are removed by confronting each and every situation that makes you anxious, as well as the beliefs and attitudes you harbor that keep your anxieties in place. Even conditions such as agoraphobia (the literal definition of which is "fear of the marketplace") is actuality the fear of leaving a safe environment, due to the irrational belief that some vague—but dreaded—misfortune will occur that you will be unable to handle.

Discomfort anxiety is the tendency to become angry, anxious, depressed, or otherwise stressed out when things are difficult or frustrating. This includes the tendency to berate and undermine yourself. These, like all Stage Four struggles, can be effectively overcome with the right strategies—many of which are included at the end of this chapter—and a commitment to start using them now, or as soon as you want to see immediate results.

If the world is a "classroom," psychotherapy is tutoring. There are many excellent and well-proven types of therapeutic interventions for feelings of anxiety, anger, depression, phobias, and all of the possible conditions related to them. **Never hesitate to get professional help to learn skills that you have not been able to master in that classroom of life.** This includes some basic skills in conflict resolution, coping with stress and anxiety, and assertiveness training. Life is full of conflicts. However, there is always an alternative to letting conflicts defeat you.

It should be noted that if you are still unable to see progress despite getting the help you need and committing yourself to using the self-help strategies that speak to you in order to make the climb (such as those in this book), there could be a medical reason. It could be a chemical depression or anxiety, or even a thought disorder that needs to be treated *medically*. Psychotropic drugs, such as anti-anxiety and anti-depressant medications, can be invaluable for endogenous or chemically related symptoms.

Depression that is rooted in a chemical imbalance can feel quite similar to depression that is not. The same can be said for anxiety. These disorders need to be diagnosed by a professional. However, medication alone will not resolve your Stage Four hooks and the underlying conflicts, beliefs, or attitudes themselves! Once the medical issues are evaluated and treated, you can once again expect the strategies for working on your hooks to deliver results.

Remember, Stage Four fantasies can be quite compelling and desirable. If you crave adoration from others, your challenge is to determine consciously just how much of your life you are willing to devote to manifesting this and at what cost. And that approval you seek may or may not even be possible for you to get, no matter what you do. Few people would argue that it's nice to be loved or adored, approved of, and accepted by others. However, it's rarely *essential*. So, if this has been an issue for you, **merely changing your expectations in the area of seeking approval can profoundly change your life. The best part is that from now on you can give *yourself* at least as much acceptance and approval as you seek from others.** Then, what somebody else thinks of you will never again take on more importance than you want it to or it deserves.

WHY WE RETAIN STAGE FOUR HOOKS AND WHEN THEY MIGHT COME IN HANDY

❖ **A small degree of anxiety may be a good thing for you in that it could help keep you on your toes in certain situations where optimal performance is important.** For example, many professional performers will say that *some* anxiety gives their performance a positive edge. You may have noticed that same phenomenon when on a job interview or making a presentation, for instance.

❖ **Do not confuse anxiety with fear, even though they might feel the same way.** Fear can navigate you through a truly dangerous situation. It can be a life-saving emotion when it is used to help ensure your physical survival. When there is an actual danger, fear can both alert us and arm our bodies to fight or flee most efficiently. No matter how far beyond Stage Four you have climbed, you will still have access to that channel if you ever need it. Anxiety is more about worry. Most anxiety stifles us. However, even anxiety—a Stage Four hook—can sometimes be a benefit when it alerts you to a situation that cries out for more attention than you may be giving it.

❖ When "in love," your Stage Four hooks can sometimes add to the romantic feelings of being unconditionally loved with the maximum degree of security you often experience. When this is at a fever pitch, life rarely *feels* better. (Just watch your expectations, as this phase of a relationship rarely lasts as long as you wish it would.) **So remember that if your Stage Four hooks are enhancing your life, enjoy them! Moreover, this is true of your hooks at all of the other stages as well.**

❖ When you need to use salesmanship skills strictly and deliberately to impress others or to make an appearance as part of a larger goal, this is also Stage Four at its best.

❖ **In any situation, you can always choose to listen to your Stage Four hooks and then determine that it's in your best interest to take the safe road.** When this is your choice, honor it until there is a better alternative.

ACCEPTING YOURSELF: CLIMBING OUT OF STAGE FOUR

Stage Four Action Steps You Can Take Now:

❖ Note the area(s) of your life in which Stage Four might be your default. **Identify** and list all of the Stage Four hooks you can recognize—especially those you would like to eliminate.

❖ **Imagine getting all of the love and admiration** you could ever want from anyone and everyone on your radar screen (people close to you in your life and/or even those who look at you from a distance). Imagine being a highly popular and sought out luminary in your field. How does that feel? You can certainly create your ideal Stage Four fantasy in your own mind whenever you choose. Take a minute to imagine just what in the areas of acceptance and approval for you would be ultimate. Here are a few other Stage Four questions to consider and reflect upon: How much energy do you put into being loved, adored, "applauded," admired, revered, idolized, and into creating an image for that admiration? Is it worth it (especially if you can create the feelings it provides without expending the frustrating or desperate energy this requires)? If you had complete control of your Stage Four hooks, what would you do differently? What is preventing you from providing to yourself (in the area of acceptance) what you are seeking from others? Write out your reflections to these questions, refer to and revise them often.

❖ Imagine for a moment that you were **absolutely fearless** and immune to anxiety. (For example, you did not *fear* rejection from others, the prospect of looking foolish, or even publicly failing at something you consider important, etc.) What are some things you would do differently, or life changes you would make that perhaps your fears or anxieties now put beyond your reach? Make a comprehensive list of whatever comes up for you, along with an idea or two for a strategy to take at least one *prudent* risk to counter each fear you listed. (For example, begin researching a job change you want to make, asking your boss for a raise, asking someone out for a date, or bringing up a difficult issue that you have been avoiding with a friend or your spouse.)

❖ **What is the worst possible thing that could happen** if what you feared the most, actually became a reality (e.g., a rejection by someone you asked out for a date)? Ask yourself, "Are the consequences really so dire that I need to continue avoiding it or living my life in deference to that fear?" If the answer is yes, then ask yourself "why"? Do not give up challenging these beliefs you have until you are satisfied that you are acting out of *choice*, rather than unwarranted fear or anxiety.

❖ Be aware of how you may be **confusing insight** (the healthy learning that results from both positive and negative life experiences) and **hindsight** (berating yourself for not "knowing then what you know now"). Which of your hooks are fueled by hindsight? What do you *now* need to believe to replace hindsight with insight in one or more important aspects of your life?

❖ Try spending an hour at first, and work your way up to an entire day **acting as if** you were genuinely fearless. Consciously walk and even breathe as though you were fearless. First, try it on a day or at a time when there is not much going on, for example, during a weekend or day off that you can spend alone. Notice what comes up for you. Gradually extend this new mind-set to the times when it would matter most, such as during the week—perhaps to handle a "dreaded" work confrontation. Notice how much easier acting fearlessly becomes, as you are more familiar and comfortable with this attitude and posture. The great performers, such as Sir Laurence Olivier, often had stage fright but knew how to act as if they were in complete control, in spite of it. Soon the jitters would disappear, meaning that they "fooled" themselves as much as they were able to convince everyone else of their self-confidence!

❖ Next, **apply these tools to your biggest fear or anxiety**. First, identify it; and then allow yourself to visualize how your life could be different if this fear or anxiety were gone permanently. Once you have done this, form a detailed strategy to finally obliterate the power of that hook that underlies your anxiety. (Be sure to repeat this step for every major Stage Four hook you have identified, that you want to eliminate.) Then revisit the last exercise and spend time in the situation, specifically *acting as if* you were not afraid of the feared items that haunt you the most.

❖ **Put the spotlight on any and all of the remaining areas** that you are depressed about, anxious about, angry about, stressed about, and that prompt you to question your self-confidence. Sometimes it especially helps to look at each of your issues separately and as though it were your only challenge. How would someone you truly *looked up to* handle the problem you are working on? What would have to change within yourself for you to be able to deal with it as masterfully as the person you most admire could? Whether or not he or she is aware of your struggle (or even aware that you exist), use that person as a model as you proceed to face anything that triggers your anxiety or other types of upset. Working on these aspects of your life can be a major challenge; but conquering them will be extremely rewarding and well worth any effort it takes.

❖ Reserve your highest level of **respect** for people according to what they *do*, not merely what they say, how nice they are to you, or the position they hold.

❖ **Forgive** those toward whom you hold anger. This can be a very liberating experience *for you*. Forgiving does not mean that you excuse their behavior. It simply means that you are *letting go of the pain you feel within yourself* with respect to them. This will free your energy for bigger and better things.

❖ Consider getting psychotherapy, coaching, or other forms of **professional help** with any of the Stage Four hooks in your way that you cannot seem to handle by using the specific strategies in this book (including those in Chapter 14 that zero in on managing hooks across all seven stages).

❖ Stage Four **Resources** include cognitive behavioral therapy or self-help for anxiety, depression, anger, self-confidence, and applications such as dating, beginning new love relationships, changing a job or career, or making major life changes. For many more Stage Four resources please visit *StageClimbing.com/resources* (Password: MyStageClimb).

At Stage Five, the balance of our life roles takes center stage.

CHAPTER 5

STAGE FIVE

Role Juggler

"Be open to everything but attached to nothing."
—The Buddha

I n our modern Western society, **Stage Five is the most likely default stage for most aspects of the life we consider to be that of a "normal adult." Stage Five is also the stage at which we keep our lives working, sane, and together.** As late adolescence morphs into early adulthood, we gradually begin to operate more and more areas of our lives in Stage Five.

Sigmund Freud's description of the "normal adult" is one who is able "to love, work and play" (Erickson, 1963). This is actually where Freud's developmental theory stopped; it is the stage that Freud would have seen—in *Stage Climbing* terms—as a target stage. That definition as paraphrased by many others over the years has come to mean keeping our lives balanced and our roles clear. It should be noted that Freud will always be known for many great things, but being a particularly happy man is not one of them. At Stage Five, keeping your roles in balance and problem-free is typically the definition of winning; but for reasons we will explore in this chapter, **Stage Five often falls short on delivering the degree of happiness you want, expect, or one that is of a *lasting* nature.**

Stage Five is also the most emotionally neutral or *dispassionate* of all the stages. Neutral, in that when making a life change (i.e., bringing something new into your life or taking something out of it), *Fives* are the most likely to evaluate objectively how it fits in with everything else and thus affects the big picture or life's balance. For example, when deciding whether or not to buy a new house, it is your Stage Five self that runs the numbers to determine whether the purchase is financially practical, the house is in the right neighborhood, and has access to quality schools. How you feel about the house itself is incidental at Stage Five. **Other stages tend to be governed more by desire or emotions, be they positive (such as love or joy) or negative (like fear or grief).**

Normalcy, "peace and quiet," and abundance are what you are typically **Needing and Seeking** at Stage Five.

It is also the stage at which we take care of logistics. Chores that you do not particularly enjoy, but that still need to be done, are excellent examples of functions that are performed best from a Stage Five frame of mind. For instance, when commuting to work, you are probably operating out of Stage Five—in the role of traveler—as a means to an end. Managing your portfolio, doing your income tax, cleaning your house, taking out the trash, backing up your computer—for most people who lack an intrinsic interest in such things—or the best attitude for walking your dog on a cold, rainy night when you'd rather be inside sleeping are a few examples of this.

Stage Five is the "normal" **Default Stage** for adults in our society; normal meaning starting in, and then going beyond, early adulthood. You are using your Stage Five hooks when it's important to attend to and create a structure for necessary aspects of your life from which you may or may not get heartfelt enjoyment. Examples include managing finances, doing chores, taking care of health rituals, being around people you would rather not be with, etc. At Stage Five, you provide for yourself and/or family; maintain balance in your life and lifestyle, and often do what is necessary to support your highest (target) stage endeavors. (You will begin to read about them in the next chapter.)

At Stage Five, you are not doing these chores so much out of a Stage Three fear or adherence to rules, but more as part of a larger choice you have made, such as maintaining your assets, having a clean house, or enjoying a dog you love. **You might say we need a Stage Five frame of mind as our built-in "adult supervision" component in order get us through the day.**

At Stage Five, you can now have mature relationships. Since you are finally capable of deep connection without being preoccupied by the love and approval that comes in your direction (as in Stage Four), you are able to choose to reveal much more of your true nature to those close to you without constantly fearing their judgment or rejection. This includes your spouse (or significant other), family and close friends, colleagues, or anyone else who may be important to you. **You can now have deep bonds without becoming too enmeshed, submerged, or obsessed with them. True intimacy can now develop and thrive. No longer do you expect your partner, friends, children, or others around you to be or become clones of yourself.**

The best **Parenting** you can give an adult child at Stage Five is when you recognize that you had a certain number of years to influence your children by example. Chances are that whatever they have not learned from you—regardless of whether or not that was by choice—by the time *they* reach Stage Five, they will most likely choose to learn elsewhere. Therefore, let go of any need to control their lives. Allow and honor the right of your adult children to be independent and different from you. By doing this you will command respect.

However, the *role* in your life that a relationship plays—including the void or slot it fills—can be inordinately important. At Stage Five, those roles can sometimes be even more significant than the people who fill them. For example, if you are seeking a new and permanent love relationship, you might make it a mission to go out and meet suitable candidates in order to fill that slot or void. Then, perhaps you move toward becoming involved with the one that you liked the best. This is in contrast to the higher stages in which you would consider involvement only after meeting the person with whom you believe you would like to spend your life.

Your **Ultimate Goal** at Stage Five: To be content and have comfort and affluence (and/or whatever you believe is necessary for living a good and worthwhile life), as well as all of your roles optimally and satisfactorily covered.

At Stage Five, you are comfortable in your own skin. You are also in a position to feel secure in a richer and deeper sense. With that comes much-awaited feelings of contentment, satisfaction, self-acceptance, and a better recognition of your strengths and weaknesses. You no longer think of or judge yourself in global terms. The idea of taking risks is much less intimidating than it ever could have been in Stage Four or below. You have taken certain risks. Some have not turned out so well, but you realize that you have survived and have been able to use your failures as sources of insight, as opposed to hindsight-based excuses for berating yourself. Therefore, **you now see wisdom and value in leaving your comfort zone at times in order to flourish in almost any desired aspect of your life**. Nevertheless, **to the degree that your default is at Stage Five and whether or not you consciously acknowledge it, you are often likely to think of yourself as the *sum total of your roles*.**

Love Relationships/Marriages—and how partners relate to each other at Stage Five: Each partner dutifully fulfills the other's spouse/relationship slot and all that it entails (e.g., sex partner, financial partner, companion, co-parent, someone with whom to share and have intimacy, etc.). However, in many aspects of the relationship, partners are not necessarily governed by passion or strong attachment that transcends their roles.

A Stage Five marriage or love relationship is about filling various roles as well; lover, friend, co-parent, tennis partner, confidant, great roommate or travel companion, etc. In fact, arranged marriages, which are still common in some cultures and with few exceptions were the rule almost everywhere until early in the last century, are a Stage Five solution to the problem of finding a suitable mate in order to start a family and have children (who will grow into the role of helping with certain tasks, etc.). A more modern counterpart to that is a dating service or Internet-matching techniques that look for role compatibility, first; with the hope that attraction, passion, and real connection between the partners—today's most common requirements for a lasting relationship—will then follow. Those virtues are discussed in Stage Six.

Couples in Stage Five marriages may feel a void once they become empty nesters. Sometimes this will put an unexpected strain on a marriage. A Stage Five solution may be to substitute grandchildren and find a way to live vicariously through them as well as through your adult children. However**, to command respect without demanding it and to accept that your adult children will be different from you is finally possible at Stage Five.** There is much more difficulty with and rigidity about things such as this in the lower stages.

Most common Stage Five attitudes about Sex:
- ❖ "In addition to procreation, sex is a healthy, normal, and nice way to have good sensations as well as an important part of any marriage or love relationship."
- ❖ "Sex is not always orgasmic, but it usually feels good, satisfies my sex drive, and is rarely an issue in the relationship."
- ❖ Both partners generally agree on frequency and preferences regarding how to have sex and the way it is initiated.

You can see how a couple that related well when each had a Stage Four love relationship default (e.g., providing each other with security and validation of each other's self-esteem) could be prone to growing apart at Stage Five. Moreover, many relationships and marriages that were never previously at risk may stop working for either partner when one climbs to Stage Five, and the roles become different or less compatible. The same holds true when a partner does not or is unable to fulfill his or her role well, such as breadwinner or parent. Stage Four relationships also encounter difficulty when a partner outgrows the need for constant validation and then realizes that in reality the relationship provides little else. At the same time, **many marriages that started out in the higher stages, but are no longer passionate, choose to stay together for**

the roles they fulfill in each partner. This is far from uncommon. Such couples are often content with Stage Five as the default—and perhaps even the target—stage for their marriage or love relationship.

Your career at Stage Five would operate under a similar philosophy. If the ultimate Stage Four career fantasy makes you famous, the definitive Stage Five dream is to be rich or at least financially comfortable enough to not have to be beholden to anyone unless you choose to be. **Work fulfills the breadwinner role with external rewards such as money, to be able to afford the type of lifestyle you desire, acceptable hours, good working conditions, an easy commute, etc.** Therefore, the compatibility of your work with your other roles is generally your prime focus. To the extent that your career is at a Stage Five default, you would probably choose to be spending your time in other ways if you did not need the money or such other things as the benefits, or the group affiliation and connections that work provides. Thus, **your work is not yet a part of your soul, life purpose, or a calling. Enjoying your work at Stage Five is** *optional***, no matter how good at it you are.** At Stage Five, you also do not yet require a passionate connection to the actual contribution your work makes to the larger world.

Some troublesome Stage Five attitudes or beliefs:
- ❖ "I can't (or I don't want to) handle (fill in the blank_____) in my life right now— am overwhelmed."
- ❖ "I feel trapped with no way out; I have no choice---My life runs me."
- ❖ "I must keep it all together and step up to the plate with respect to all of my roles and obligations (e.g., spouse, parent, breadwinner, etc.), regardless of whether or not those roles are working or provide me feelings of satisfaction or gratification."

Boredom and discontent with your job or career is extremely common. When someone asks why you do your type of work, a typical Stage Five answer is likely to be, "Because that's my job," or to cite the money, pension plan, or other tangible rewards and/or lack of negatives your job provides you.

For example, if you were a writer motivated at Stage Five, your reason for doing a certain project is not so much because you have something to say, as it is for what you are paid or as a means to get recognition for additional work. School-teachers operating at Stage Five will most likely be more motivated by summers off, the benefit package, shorter hours, and job security than the opportunity to influence and shape the lives of the students they teach. Teachers who are *Fives* see students as a means to job benefits, rather than the other way around.

What triggers these common **Emotions** in you at Stage Five:

Anger—Things or people you perceive as overwhelming you or throwing your life out of balance or control. *Fives* still have difficulty with forgiving adversaries as long as any remnants of an anger-producing situation remain.

Anxiety—Becoming unglued as your roles expand; or worry that circumstances will overwhelm or render you unable to fulfill them effectively.

Depression—Having an important role in your life (e.g., a relationship, financial situation, or career) change (usually a loss) in a way that is undesirable to you and out of your control to reverse or correct; also a general or vague sense of boredom or lack of fulfillment.

Grief (over loss)—The void you experience until you are able to put the pieces (and roles) of your life back together again, often by finding a substitute for whatever or whomever you have lost.

The idea of leaving a job you do not particularly like, but which provides more money and benefits than you could get at another job you may enjoy more, might feel unthinkable—or at least be a very difficult conflict—at Stage Five. (An exception might be if there was so much negative residue from the better- paying job, that it taints other areas of your life or your overall sense of well-being.)

You can take on any number of roles at Stage Five at the same time—for example: leader, follower, admirer, student, mentor, hero, or skeptic. Even hobbies take on a role you want filled in your life, such as that of killing excess time or providing a social outlet. Exercise helps you to maintain your role as a fit and healthy person. Sporting events, perhaps the role of providing a family activity for Sunday afternoons, and vacations can fulfill the role of helping you "recharge your batteries." These are all examples of fine motives for these activities. However, the degree of your actual *enjoyment* of them is not necessarily factored in at Stage Five. Thus, a Stage Five vacation might be visiting a country you have never been to, seeing and busily doing as much as time permits; even though a heartfelt interest or curiosity for the place may not be there. Another example is going to a resort you never really cared to visit, but you need somewhere to go for vacation and it's a bargain.

> Money, benefits, privileges, and respect from others, specifically for how you handle your roles and responsibilities or a particular aspect of your life, are what **Motivate** you at Stage Five.

Fives may still at times have a strong need for uniformity and status quo. Voids in your life that are caused by things beyond your control or created by an empty role, can be quite troubling.** Some examples of such voids are: the feelings of loneliness associated with going through a divorce, separation or the death of a loved one; the loss of job or career; a change in financial or social status; retirement or a serious illness; or the loss of membership in a group that is important to you. Any of these things can trigger a panic surrounding the possibility that you and your existence are unraveling to some extent. Thus, despite how content you may *usually* be, at times a major setback can still feel like your entire life is falling apart. When this happens, you might temporarily revert back to Stage Four and experience many of the same symptoms and feelings of anxiety, depression, or anger that are typical of Stage Four conflict and thus familiar to you. However, during your most reflective moments, you know you have been here before and will bounce back as soon as the crisis is over. As a *Four*, you may not have been able to realize this or come back to normal without more difficulty. Therefore, even a full-blown emotional crisis is generally shorter, tends to feel much less devastating, and is easier to resolve. **Resolution happens quickly when the void is filled again or you realize that you can cope with it.**

Conflict is typically handled at Stage Five by evaluating whether and how the source of your conflict is related to your bigger picture, then by taking the action(s) that come as close as possible to rebalancing your life.

The most important role models to you at Stage Five often include heroes and mentors, usually those who are more advanced or successful in your same field, or who have already achieved certain goals for which you are now striving. Success, happiness, and fulfillment at Stage Five normally result when you believe that you are handling all of your roles well, there are no major problems to deal with and you have met your abundance goals, or at the very least are getting all you are entitled to for your efforts. *Fives* **often speak of the good times as "feeling so normal!"**

Spirituality now has the capability of becoming more of an individual matter. There can be a spiritual element to your relationships. In addition, you are now open to a heartfelt awareness of the world that is greater than you are (to be developed much more in the higher stages). **Unlike in the lower stages, the higher being you worship or your higher self is much more than an authority to fear or to please.** You can now truly experience your spirituality as a source of connection, love, and benevolence. There is the capacity to give some thought to what, in spiritual terms, your place on earth might be. However, too often other responsibilities and aspects of life may conflict with your ability to follow that inner voice, which does not become a constant and essential part of you until Stage Six.

At Stage Five, your religious values can be complex. **Your own values and those of your religion can coexist in certain areas, yet conflict in others.** In addition, you now have a tolerance for those whose thinking is radically different from yours, as long as it does not upset the balance of your roles, which is a major vulnerability at Stage Five. However, you might also experience spirituality as merely another role that you see in a more neutral way—as external, with little drive within yourself to match the activities or practices.

Your view of **Spirituality** at Stage Five:

"Spirituality (often in the form of an organized religion that is most familiar), as well as observing religious traditions, is an important part of life"…"It provides a sense of well-being"…. However, the role of spirituality in life is often confusing and unsettled. In reflective moments you might ponder such questions as, "What is the meaning of life?" or, "Is this all there is?" As well, there can be questions about such things as afterlife, dilemmas about God's role in tragedy and injustice, etc.

The principles of most organized religions are generally a source of goodness, guidance, and wisdom. Places of worship often fulfill the role of community and can provide much support when you are grieving over a death, in crisis, or even as a place to celebrate a major milestone in life, e.g., a wedding, baptism, bar mitzvah, or child's confirmation. It's common for *Fives* to move in and out of their spiritual community, as the role that community plays becomes more or less needed. Remember—this is all within the definition of what's normal, meaning what is most *commonly* believed or practiced in our society.

At Stage Five, you can now recognize and appreciate that growth and learning often comes from a difference of opinion or even through mixed messages. This concept is much more difficult or even impossible to tolerate at the lower stages. However, when your roles conflict with each other or certain ones become incompatible, anxiety may still be the result. In my practice, I have had many people at this stage ponder the question: "Which role (or who) is the "real me?" Another question often asked as part of the struggle with Stage Five issues is that one Peggy Lee immortalized in her standard, "Is That All There Is?"

Fives can be very much like plate spinners and master jugglers. Consider all of your roles in life as plates that need to be kept in the air at the same time. As long as they stay up there, life is good. In some of the roles you play, you may be kind. Other roles may necessitate that you be rather cold. Just as you can have many roles, there is no limit as to how many personas you can have in Stage Five. One necessary skill in keeping it altogether is picking the right *persona* or sub-personality to optimize the role you are playing. Even Captain Bligh—the tyrannical captain of the *Bounty* of *Mutiny on the Bounty* fame—is acknowledged by history to have been a very loving husband and father, yet he is still known as one of the cruelest ship captains of all time.

Your political affiliations at Stage Five are most likely to be with the party you believe will nurture the roles you play. For example, you may vote for one party because it offers you tax cuts and more money in your pocket. Or you may vote for the party that provides the best government entitlement programs, depending on how it fits into your life. The principles or ideology that your political party stands for are not nearly as important to you as what the party will deliver directly to you and yours.

If Stage Five is the norm in our society, it's fitting that the ideal Stage Five government model is a representative democracy. Here you can make a choice as to who represents you based on whatever reasons or emotions you choose to follow, without necessarily having to take the time to understand all the issues in-depth or even develop positions on them. A Stage Five politician will tend to blend in and do whatever is necessary to get the job done and keep his or her constituents onboard without making waves. Championing a passionate ideology is optional and secondary to winning an election.

Happiness and Success at Stage Five:
Keeping all roles and relationships in balance and without problems … Being effective and not overwhelmed … Achieving affluence … Finding a hobby and making time for fun activities as another important way to balance life and "recharge batteries" … "Fun activities" are seen as providing a healthy alternative to work and chores.

Life today can become extremely busy for people who have many different roles. They might include an involved career, activities with professional organizations, hobbies and various other avocations, church or synagogue and raising children while keeping up with all other activities. These roles all speak to different needs; but as they grow, *Fives* often experience life as overwhelming to the point at which enjoying all of them becomes difficult, even if each one alone would be quite nourishing and enjoyable. **When "overwhelm" sets in, things you once thrived on can inadvertently become reduced to mere obligations or even stressors; and actually enjoying them as you once did becomes a luxury for which you no longer have the time or energy.**

Too many activities and roles are often the factor that can be a drain to the quality of your life. For example, a marriage with too many extended family obligations and activities to tend to often leaves little or no time for partners to be lovers or enjoy solitary downtime. **The main thing to remember about virtually anything at Stage Five is to enjoy what you can, but not to expect more in the way of fulfillment than is there. Personal fulfillment is much more a function of Stages Six and Seven, the next two stages you will read about.**

When comfort (and even affluence), a nice, decent family life, an adequate community, religious involvement, the demands you put on yourself to "keep it all together," as well as all—or many of—the staples of what we have come to believe constitute a good life just don't seem to add up to fulfillment, you may find yourself yearning for something more. That something is what we will find at Stage Six, and beyond the boundaries of what is merely "normal."

CLIMBING OUT OF STAGE FIVE: WHAT YOU NEED TO KNOW

At Stage Five, you are far less self-absorbed than in any of the lower stages. Thus, you are now freer to pay more attention to your hooks in the *higher* stages that you will read about next. Think of those higher-stage hooks as glimpses of your potential: what life can soon be like.

A bit of history here is in order. When the human potential movement of the 1960s and 1970s took hold, the people it served the most, were *Fives*, who by societal standards "had it all" (e.g., a well-functioning career, family life, relationships, etc.); but through their higher-stage hooks, knew there was a richer, more fulfilling *inner existence* to be had. In reality, what they were looking for was the ladder to climb from Stage Five to the two higher stages. Such things as encounter groups and other types of personal growth opportunities, which were extremely innovative at the time, were created to facilitate and encourage people to take the steps necessary to leave their comfort zones.

Attitude that is most helpful for Climbing out of Stage Five: "I want to be doing what I love and to feel rewarded **internally** as well as externally."

The result was often one or more major life changes as well as a litany of new and unfamiliar, yet empowering attitudes. For example, long-term love relationships as well as career activities would now have to provide deeper levels of satisfaction and fulfillment, heretofore not necessarily a mandatory requirement. For many *Fives*, a radical makeover was in order, while for others just a bit of tweaking was all that was necessary. Most interestingly, all of this was accomplished by simply and non-judgmentally asking each seeker, *"What do you want to do?"* **The next step was to provide support and encouragement to** *go ahead and do it*. **In other words, keep the roles that work and provide satisfaction, then make whatever major or minor changes are necessary to the ones that do not.**

Along the way, it was just as important to change certain attitudes and life philosophies so that you did not find yourself going backwards in that familiar direction of non-fulfillment. The result was a new world that will never allow things to be the way they were: opportunity and equality for women and minorities, and permission for everyone to follow their dreams and passions. Most essentially, **self-permission is what we came to know as the essential ingredient for living an optimal life or** *reaching your highest potential.*

The Buddha said it best in the quote with which I opened this chapter and what is arguably the most powerful statement ever made about how to reach your potential: *"Be open to everything but attached to nothing."* **This is the core attitude that will most empower you for climbing to the highest stages that follow.** Climbing out of Stage Five simply involves letting go of the roles that are not working—that you keep solely because of your attachment to them—and then trading them for new experiences that ignite or are consistent with your unique passions. Many are fortunate enough to find a mentor to help them do this, to the extent that change is what they want and help is needed to achieve it. For others, psychotherapy or coaching may be an answer.

The best therapy for Stage Five issues zeros in on improving *higher* levels of functioning, rather than merely focusing on personal and emotional problems. In other words, whatever helps you to follow the Buddha, in making choices and seeing them through to fruition is key to your climb beyond Stage Five. This process of choice and change, along with whatever support you may need to see it through, enables you to climb to the coveted Stage Six, the first of our two *target* stages.

A few words about psychotherapy: Over the years, I have trained thousands of therapists and have found that virtually all do best with or "specialize" in one stage or another—whether or not they even realize it. Some therapists do very well with Stage Three issues, some with Stage Four issues, and others with Stage Five issues. **Therapists who are best with Stage Five issues are most comfortable in helping you to explore and facilitate major life changes you *choose*, as opposed to those you have to make for reasons beyond your control.** The types of problems you may need to face along the way often present challenges unlike those at the lower stages. So picking the right therapist to work with in this case is crucial. Several Web sites and other resources for therapists and coaches to help you are provided at the Web site *StageClimbing.com/resources*.

Some people leave one marriage or love relationship (whether or not by their own choice), only to immediately enter into a new one on the rebound; or quickly replace one lost job with another, similar, job without even giving a thought to some exploration of whether a bigger life change may be in order. *Fives* **often err by replacing one role with another, and expect this to provide a permanent solution to their problem.** A reevaluation of the bigger picture will more likely help you to arrive at a much better and more comprehensive solution than by merely switching roles or players. This is the principal reason why rebound romances rarely work on the level of *long-term* fulfillment. **Part of the climb to Stage Six is learning to tolerate the emotional pain triggered by letting yourself feel a void in your life, until you can replace the missing piece with what you *really* desire.** That way you will break your pattern of just settling for whatever is available to you right now—be it a new relationship, job, or anything else—in order simply to end the discomfort caused solely by the void in your life itself. Most importantly, you will have given yourself something much more than just another Band-Aid to get you through a transition or difficult situation.

Many have described life at Stage Five as literally one thing occurring after another, with little to tie it together. To get to Stage Five, your task was to reduce depression, anxiety, stress, and anger, to increase self-confidence and your frustration for tolerance. Then you can function in your chosen roles. The climb to Stage Six makes all this hard work even more worthwhile!

WHY WE RETAIN STAGE FIVE HOOKS AND WHEN THEY MIGHT COME IN HANDY

❖ Whenever the reality of your status quo and the roles it requires blend into your life well, or you simply choose the status quo after weighing all the alternatives;

❖ When you must—or choose—to be involved in activities that you find to be emotionally neutral at best (e.g., doing chores, dealing with certain family members or matters, commuting, or paying the bills);

❖ When interacting with people you would never choose to be around under other circumstances;

❖ When handling obligations and unpleasant tasks or assignments, such as those aspects of your job or the rituals that being a student sometimes require (such as doing expense reports, studying for an exam, or writing a dissertation);

❖ When it is your choice to focus on external rewards such as earning money and other benefits to the exclusion of what you might *prefer* to be doing;

❖ When you need to adopt a persona in order to get something done that is not necessarily in harmony with how you prefer to come across;

❖ When comfort, security, and satisfaction are enough for the fulfillment you seek.

RISING ABOVE YOUR ROLES: CLIMBING OUT OF STAGE FIVE

Some Action Steps To Facilitate Your Stage Five Climb:

❖ In what major areas of your life is your default stage in Stage Five? Also, identify what you see as your Stage Five hooks. As you have with previous stages, **note and list** them.

❖ Next, **identify** those hooks and default stage areas of your life that you want to change (as opposed to those where you prefer to stay neutral or in a "Stage Five frame of mind").

❖ For each item you want to change, **ask yourself, "If I were not attached to a role** (such as breadwinner, husband or wife, father or mother, son or daughter, boss, subordinate, fundraising chairman, friend, or neighbor), **what would be the ideal situation for this aspect of my life?"**

❖ **Never forget that Stage Five can also be the target stage for such aspects of life as your marriage or career.** *If that is your choice, honor it.*

❖ **Ponder** how you believe your life could be simpler, more enjoyable, more purposeful and less overwhelming. Start a journal and write thoughts about this, preferably on a daily basis.

❖ Many Stage Five issues such as being overwhelmed can be addressed by learning **time management skills**. Juggling a busy schedule, multiple roles and obligations (e.g., children, work obligations, and numerous other roles) is daunting. However, don't let yourself fall into the trap of believing that there are no options.

❖ Which roles do you want to let go of? Which would you like to change? Which do you cherish? **Take this opportunity to clarify what's really important to you.** Then vow to stay with the important stuff and let go of as much as possible that is not adding to your life.

❖ To the extent that your default is at Stage Five with an aspect of life, you are generally still motivated more by external rewards than internal rewards. **Pretend that** those external rewards, such as money or prestige, were not a factor. Ask yourself, **"What roles do I then choose to keep?" In addition, remember that sometimes trading one role for another is indeed the best solution to a dilemma. Thus, keeping Stage Five solutions in your arsenal can be quite useful.** You will serve yourself well by regularly asking yourself what it is that you wish to keep (regardless of the externals) as you navigate your climb out to the target stages.

❖ In light of the above assessment, most simply put—**what is it that you want to do/change?** What action steps are you *willing* to take to bring about the changes you want? **What are you fearing** or telling yourself that could prevent you from succeeding?

❖ Next, **set specific goals** as to what you would most like to accomplish with respect to everything you have identified. **How would life be different if you could optimally reach your goal?**

❖ **Resolve to do as little as necessary of whatever you have chosen to discontinue.** Expect some discomfort. Whenever you give up a role, the **void** alone can bring about some uneasiness. Don't get discouraged. Assure yourself there is something far better for you ahead, even if you do not see exactly what it is now. **Act as if the void is a temporary one soon to be replaced by whatever it is that you really desire** in its place (or resolve that ultimately you don't need whatever you have chosen to give up, in any form).

❖ What **sources of help** (e.g., a mentor, support group, coach, therapist, etc.) would be most beneficial to you right now in order to explore and/or facilitate the life changes you want to make, but may be having difficultly doing on your own? **Take a step or two in the direction of getting that help and support.** Visit *StageClimbing.com/resources* for additional ideas.

❖ Remember, Stage Five is the most neutral or dispassionate stage. Our Stage Five chores and activities are often the "necessary evils" and/or means for enjoying or maximizing life at the higher stages. **If you don't expect more satisfaction from doing them than is there, you will be less likely to fight them, procrastinate, or waste more time**. **Plan frequent "Stage Five sessions"** to handle as many of these necessary—but not necessarily fulfilling—chores as possible so that you can clear your schedule for whatever really matters to you.

❖ Stage Five **Resources**(visit *StageClimbing.com/resources* [Password: My Stage Climb]) include literature such as self-help books and audio programs on relationships, careers, life changes, financial issues, time management, stress management and places you can find therapists, coaches, and many other sources of help.

At Stage Six, we rise above our roles and enter the zone of our first target stage.

UNDERSTANDING AND MAXIMIZING OUR TARGET STAGES: SIX AND SEVEN

Now that you have read about the first five stages, it's time to reap the rewards! But first, I suggest you read or reread, "Life at the Target Stages; How Good Can It Be?" on page 19 in the Quick-Start Guide. It's a quick read that will serve to remind you about why this process leading to the target stages is so worthwhile to pursue and how life at the target stages can indeed be your ultimate breakthrough in so many ways. In other words, you will serve yourself well by having the perspective and motivation to do whatever it takes to make Stages Six and Seven—where your highest potential resides— your default stages for any and every important area of your life.

The stages below Six and Seven may at times have been difficult to read about. However, they were necessary, in part so that you could become familiar with all of the factors that may be blocking you from full access to your highest target stages. **The task now is to take the next and arguably most important step in your *Stage Climbing* process: Make a commitment to yourself to become your target stages in whatever part of your life you choose, while retaining the chosen lower-stage hooks that serve you.** Remember, when you are operating out of your target stages, you are using the most *unique, evolved,* and *purposeful* as well as arguably the *best parts of yourself* to achieve almost anything! On a spiritual level, **you are attuned to your calling or purpose and the *source of infinite wisdom* that defines it.** On a personal level, **this is where you love others most deeply and—just in case that's not enough—*feel best about yourself.*** In other words, these stages best characterize why you are here. The next two chapters will give you the tools you need to arrive at and live in these target stages Six and Seven, regardless of whatever circumstances in your life you bring to the table.

It's now time to start thinking about what your *highest potential* would mean to you. Or to phrase the question another way (as many people I've worked with have), **"What do you really want to be when you grow up?"** The target stages contain the blueprint to clarify and bring it all to fruition. You need only to commit to making it your reality.

CHAPTER 6

STAGE SIX

Passion Is Your Path

*"I have learned that if one advances confidently in the direction of
his dreams and endeavors to live the life which he has imagined,
he will meet with an unexpected success... ."*

—Henry David Thoreau

In my practice, my clients are usually working on the climb to Stage Six
when one of them tells me some variation of the following: **"I have 'everything going for me,' but I don't feel happy or fulfilled,"** or, **"I *should*
be happy, but I am not."** For most people, Stage Six is the very definition of
genuine connection, happiness, and fulfillment. We all have hooks there, and
life often feels at its absolute best when we are operating out of this stage.
**As you read on, you will discover that a Stage Six default—*the path to
your highest potential*—in any area of your life, resides within you and is
accessible right now or whenever you choose to claim it.**

Think about our evolutionary process as human beings. For much of
our existence, we worked to survive, and married to procreate and share our
chores. When there was free time, we would likely sleep and do other things for
our ultimate survival. Instead of spending time hand-washing clothes, we are
now free to watch a football game while the machine does it for us.

The quest for enjoyment and fulfillment as we know it today is relatively
new in our evolution; but merely to say that this great concept has caught on
is certainly an understatement! Today we ideally marry for love, and strive to
do the type of work that is most personally gratifying. An entire book could be

written (and many have been) simply on things we do and industries that have been conceived with no other goal but to gratify, fulfill, and make or help us to feel happy. This is all possible now—and to the extent it actually is—simply because we have the time, skills, technology, and resources to give attention to those parts of ourselves that seek higher levels of gratification. **For most people who live in developed countries, fulfillment has now become even more of an issue than survival.** And I would argue that this is the result of the organic *Stage Climbing* process of civilization itself!

Where does your own climb optimally lead you? **The fulfillment that comes to you as a result of doing what you were born to do is a great definition of our frame of mind at Stage Six. Our *passions* are what help us find this zone within ourselves.** Stage Six is the first of our two universal targets in *Stage Climbing*. Regardless of whether or not you are already there, you will probably agree that a Stage Six default is worthy of your aspirations in just about any area of life**. Life is a wonderful occasion. Rising to that occasion means becoming far bigger than your roles. That is the breakthrough to Stage Six. I also see this stage as the major part of a new and apt definition of positive mental health.**

> **Stage Six is the first of the two Target Stages. A Default Stage here breaks you out of the pack starting in early adulthood and takes you through the prime of life and beyond.** Hooks at Stage Six appear all throughout life. You are operating out of Stage Six whenever you are doing what you truly enjoy. That includes when you are loving others in your life (or doing "labors of love" for them); being uniquely creative; or when acting in accordance with purpose, calling, and the core that holds all of the diverse areas of your life together as well as whenever you are feeling the best about yourself and motivated by your passions and desires.

Stage Five has your roles defining you. At Stage Six all of that changes. You know you are something different from the sum of your life roles—something much greater. You are no longer ruled by your ego either. Instead, **your *inner* voice now takes command and guides you.** The roles you play now revolve around you instead of becoming, controlling, or defining you. This is the essential distinction between Stages Five and Six. **Your unique calling, talents, and passion, along with the self-permission to pursue them to the fullest are what launch you to Stage Six.** Instead of shifting your personality to meet the demands of each role you play—although you can certainly still do that when you choose to— you are now in touch with a strong, consistent, and solid layer of integrity within you that holds them all together. This is your core, or at least the seed of it. It has been there all along; but at Stage Six, you are finally allowing it to take center stage and permitting yourself to live by it.

A default stage at Stage Six means your passions and the _internal_ rewards they give you are now ultimately more meaningful to you than anything you could receive from _outside_ of yourself. Up until now, in Stages One through Five, your main sources of motivation, such as financial status, recognition, praise, approval, and even survival have been principally _external_—that is, dependent on forces outside of your own skin and often out of your control. Listening to your passions and living your life accordingly has been perhaps a bonus (actually a Stage Six hook), but not yet your highest priority.

> Your **Ultimate Goals** at Stage Six: To do what you love, are best at and enjoy most… To strive to fill your particular niche perhaps as well as it can possibly be done by anyone, but for your own intrinsic pleasure…To love what you do and the people who matter most to you… **To operate at your highest potential!**

When operating from Stage Six, **you can understand and interact with those in the lower stages without feeling threatened, being preoccupied with fitting in, needing to be like anyone else, or needing anyone else to be like you.** With a default at Stage Six, you recognize, understand, and value the virtues of uniqueness. You no longer need to live vicariously through anyone, including your children. You have your own life; and without exception, honor the right of those around you to prudently and ethically live theirs. You are better able to choose your behavior consciously and without inner conflict.

It is also at this stage where you become a peer to your mentors; and it's not uncommon for your mentors to have rather unexpected and sometimes even negative reactions to how you have evolved, by virtue of *their* hooks in lower stages. Chances are you have pushed the envelope, and discovered that it can actually feel exhilarating and no longer so frightening to leave your comfort zone. **Taking *prudent* risks finally becomes a non-issue, rather than a trigger of your anxiety or an excuse for avoidance.**

What you love and what you hate (or dislike intensely) are your passions at their most extreme. Thus, a passion can be a feeling of strong positive gut-level excitement on the one hand, or of intense negativity on the other. Ignoring your passions can rob you of a huge slice of what life at its best has to offer you. The opposite of ignoring your passions is to listen to them so that they become your inner guides that can always be relied upon at the very least, as great sources of information. **Our positive passions—the things we love, the things that put us most in touch with our feelings of joy and our life's purpose—are the engine or life force behind our creativity, our ability to love others deeply, to enjoy and to accomplish great things.**

Passion is the best currency to help you get what you want at its best. The stronger your passion toward something, the more you will want to become committed to it. **Most of the world's truly accomplished people would probably agree that passion and the willingness to pursue it are the most important ingredients that make success likely. So consider passion to be your roadmap at Stage Six to that path that leads to your highest potential.**

There are few things you will ever discover to be as rewarding as finding your way to that zone of positive passion within you, knowing how to call upon it at any time, how to utilize it maximally, and how to give yourself ongoing permission to go inward to this zone at will. This includes choosing to be *childlike,* to play and experience fun, joy, and happiness as you did at earlier times in your life—times that were perhaps characterized by innocence and actually powered by your very best Stage Two hooks. **At Stage Six, your own "adult self" has no problem letting your "child" take over for a while and responsibly enjoy every minute of it to the fullest!**

Negative passions are equally as important since they serve several purposes. They **tell us what we need to avoid or get away from, such as a bad marriage, an unfulfilling career, or toxic people**. Negative passions can also be the driving force behind a huge cause, such as with Nelson Mandela and apartheid. **They can also be a signal to our dark side, which is usually powered by lower-stage hooks.** No matter what they represent and no matter how hard you try, you have undoubtedly noticed that they are somewhere between hard and impossible to ignore. That's why it's crucial to understand the lower stages and then to manage your hooks there by choosing the role they play in your life.

Conflict is typically handled at Stage Six by simply doing what feels consistent with your own core principles and purpose on a heartfelt level.

Fine-tuning your passion is much like selecting the right fuel for an engine. The very definition of what is often referred to as an "existential crisis" is either not being in touch with, or habitually ignoring, your passions. This is akin to having "Epstein-Barr" (chronic fatigue) of the psyche; and it can take its toll—often with a low-grade depression known as dythemia, chronic anger and bitterness, and even a variety of often serious physical conditions. **I believe that the phenomenon that occurs when we ignore our passions, essentially amounts to fighting our natural and innate *Stage Climbing* process.** Yes, there is a better way!

At Stage Six, doing what you love most and doing it to your maximum satisfaction is now an essential component of your happiness and well-being. You may even wish to challenge yourself at times to proceed with the frame of mind that you are the best there is at what you do—or at least to see yourself working toward that standard. **To win at Stage Six is simply to enjoy what you have, who you are close to, and what you are doing.** Life becomes easier and more flowing. To love, create, and *enjoy* is what puts you *in joy;* and that is the state of mind you are after.

A career or job that merely provides even excellent financial or other external rewards (as in Stage Five) may be painfully unfulfilling to you at Stage Six. Your work is now a part of your purpose or calling. **When you are driven by**

your own passions and desires, chances are you would choose to do the type of work you are doing even if you had enough money to never _have to_ work again. The process of being engaged in an activity you are passionate about is at least as meaningful as the outcome and often more so. **This is partially because Stage Six activities bring out the best in you, including the tendency to feel best about yourself.** For example, if playing golf is your passion, at Stage Six the process and enjoyment of playing the game would be at least as important to you as your score (i.e., the outcome). This is because of how you are feeling about yourself when you are having that experience.

At Stage Six, these **Emotions** and the frustration that underlies them often are (merely) alarms, sending a signal that a problem needs to be resolved or it's time to change course:

Anger—Can be triggered by anything that you believe needlessly distracts you from pursuing your passion or calling. However, forgiveness is a means to let go of an unpleasant situation in order to get back to positive emotions, acceptance, and areas of genuine interest.

Anxiety—Triggers include the prospect of being unable to pursue or receive satisfaction from something you passionately enjoy.

Depression—Being unable to pursue or enjoy that which you love or are passionate about and do best. Depression (as well as other emotions) often acts as a wake-up call at Stage Six.

Sixes are much less interested in *being* something important or prestigious than in *doing or accomplishing* something that is truly meaningful or enjoyable to them. Your passions can even lead you to accomplish great things. And whenever you trade what is passion-driven for something such as more recognition or money (as would a *Four* or *Five*), you will probably take a hit in the area of fulfillment. At the very least, you might experience the tradeoff as a dilemma.

At Stage Six, fun and happiness are defined as fulfilling your passions and purpose in any area of life. You can play as hard as you work. Feel free to enjoy it and leave your inhibitions or anything serious behind, just as you might have as a child. Even if you haven't done it for a while, you have not completely forgotten how to access this wonderful, childlike and light frame of mind. Choose to call it up at will to enhance any area of your life in which more enjoyment is possible (e.g., work, sex, a sport you play or hobby you pursue, having fun with your children, etc.).

At Stage Six, you are naturally and perpetually mindful of long-term consequences, so let go and choose to enjoy! Then work and play can be equally joyous. In fact, work can often feel richer and even more like fun than leisure activities. My routine advice about picking a career has always been to do what you love and what is fun for you. To some, this may seem obvious; but in my experience, sadly, far too few do it. In fact, **I have seen creditable surveys over the years that found that as many as a shocking four out of five people are not happy with their careers! You will spend a lot of time at work. In addition to the *obvious* benefits of enjoying your work highly, you may realize a wonderful standard to set for yourself in all aspects of your life!**

Happiness and Success at Stage Six: The satisfaction of reaching a difficult goal or solving a tough problem … The feelings of excitement and being unstoppable that come from peak performance … Feelings of relaxation and inner peace … The bliss associated with the little things encountered in everyday life, such as the glow of a nice spring day, writing poetry, reading a good book or listening to your favorite music … Exploring novelty and whatever makes you curious … Doing what you really want to be doing (i.e., what you are most passionate about, which often provides the most fun and enjoyment) … When the distinction between work and play disappears … Being with those you love and feeling deeply connected to them … When you can call up the "child" in you at will, connect with those feelings of innocence that result and **let yourself enjoy being child_like_ as appropriate.**

I was sitting on a train recently and overheard two men talking about someone who had worked in their organization. They discussed the fact that he gave up a $250,000 a year job for one that paid less than $50,000. They could not understand why, and thought that person had lost his mind. It is indeed hard to understand this phenomenon when the way you are thinking about such things is in the lower stages—in this case, Stage Five. Moreover**, in my practice, I have helped many people in virtually every field and profession, make career changes out of lucrative fields (e.g., medicine, law, successful family businesses, etc.). The reason: they could not** *happily* **continue doing the work they were doing because of their missing sense of purpose and lack of a passion for it.** That was certainly the reason I switched from accounting (Stages Three and Five) to psychology (solidly Stage Six) early in my career. Yet many of my old accounting colleagues still do that kind of work and love it. For them, the accounting field represents a wonderful Stage Six career choice, whereas for me it simply did not.

What Motivates you at Stage Six are such things as the feeling of satisfaction that comes when doing what you love and were meant to do—dictated by your unique talents at the deepest level … Meeting a challenge ... Performing optimally with passion and ease as opposed to effort and difficulty … Anything that triggers feelings of bliss or where you are having fun **... "If you don't enjoy doing it you either are not doing it right or it's not the right thing for you to be doing," ... The way you feel about** *yourself* **at Stage Six.**

A *Six* who did *not* **quit his or her job after inheriting a large sum of money would also perplex many in the lower stages as to why.** Here is a barometer of how strongly your work default stage is at *Six* versus *Five*: If you asked a *Five* who did not need to work for the money why he or she did, you might hear, "I'd go nuts if I didn't." At Stage Six the answer would be something like, "I love what I do," or, "I wouldn't want to be doing anything else." I believe there's a vocation in each of us that can trigger this kind of Stage Six response. Of course, earning a lot of money for doing something you love enough to do free is obviously what most people would rightly consider a grand slam. If you haven't yet found out what that something is for you, regardless of your circumstances—age, obligations, or any other reasons you may be telling yourself stand in your way—don't abandon the search to discover it until you do. This is certainly a major aspect of reaching your potential, careerwise. Many of the strategies at the end of this chapter will help you get there.

Sixes **can also be quite vulnerable to job and career burnout. This is most common in two situations: when workplace frustrations conflict with your passionate and heartfelt attempts to get a job or a creative mission accomplished, or when your passion changes or evolves to another level that your present job or career simply cannot satisfy.** The term "burnout" uses the metaphor of fire. In my experience, those who are most likely to burn out are the very people who indeed are (or were) most "on fire" with respect to their commitment to what they do.

For example, when at one point in my career I oversaw all of the psychological services of the Philadelphia Police Department, I noticed that burnout occurred frequently with the police officers most dedicated to their job—that is, those who were considered the best of the best and who looked upon their work as their purpose, mission or calling. On the other hand, burnout was almost nonexistent among officers who sought easy assignments and who freely admitted that they were there merely for the job security, early retirement benefits, pension, and the other tangible rewards of being a police officer. **As a rule, by listening to the message your passions send you, the correct course of action for you will be apparent.** Using this information as a fundamental resource for making life changes is an option I urge you to exercise on an ongoing basis.

Typical attitudes about your Career and the work you do at Stage Six:

- ❖ **"I love what I do (and feel best about myself when I am doing it)."**
- ❖ "It is what comes easiest to me, feels most flowing and natural."
- ❖ "I wouldn't want to do anything else."
- ❖ "I feel fulfilled irrespective of the financial and other extrinsic rewards I get."
- ❖ "I get off on the challenge of it."
- ❖ **"If I never again *had to* work, I would still choose to be doing this."**

When you are acting according to your purpose, you are inspired or *in spirit*; and it is actually inspiration that blurs the lines between work and fun. With a Stage Six default, you are now likely to choose spending as little time as possible with anything—work, hobbies, or people—that do not inspire you on some level. The more Stage Six becomes your default stage, the more your *inner* motivators become your driving force in every area of life (Deci & Ryan, 2008). That source of fulfillment is available to you twenty-four hours a day, seven days a week. You only have to remember to seek and connect with it. **Some of the most consistently successful people are those who can line up their passions, talents, intentions, obsessions, and ambitions—then let them reinforce each other in order to create their own distinctive brand of magic. Then wealth and abundance are on track to follow as an effortless byproduct.**

In part, the human species is the most evolved because of a characteristic we as humans have that makes us distinctive: **No two of us want the exact same things when we look inwardly at our passions, desires, and talents.** Just about all foxes, elephants, and squirrels have desires similar to others of their species. However, humans have a consciousness that enables us to have a huge diversity of interests and desires. **The many different directions in which we can collectively go are what enable us to think, process, and thus create the world we have.** This is possible only because of the natural drive in each of us to utilize the unique talents that grow out of the infinite variety of directions our collective passions take us.

What you are typically Needing and Seeking at Stage Six: To accomplish something… Enjoyment of what you do as well as of yourself and who you spend time with … "Enlightenment."

Passion is also a crucial factor in your love relationships, parenting, hobbies, community involvement and virtually everything else that's important to you. Your interest in theater, opera, travel, reading, learning, sports, writing poetry and—of course—your sexual desires are simply examples of parts of your life driven to some degree by passion. If you tend to be politically liberal or conservative at Stage Six, you are operating out of an inner commitment to the principles and values that match your core beliefs. As you've probably noticed, this is quite the opposite of such things as guilt, envy, fear, rigidity, what is directly in it for you or the need to fit in with or impress others who have similar beliefs.

Over the years, many have told me that they have never been passionate about anything. However, **I can't think of anyone who could not find that trait of passion in themselves regarding something.** For example, if you are an avid baseball fan or basketball player, movie or theatre buff, dancer or swimmer, gourmet cook or really enjoy sex, a good novel, a concert, or poetry—then you know you have the *capacity* to be passionate. Yet simply having passion is not enough. It's allowing yourself to value and act on it that puts you in the Stage Six fulfillment zone.

Most likely attitude about Sex at Stage Six: "Sex with my partner is an ecstatically pleasurable experience!"

When your passions are the roadmap, the endpoint may not be apparent at times. But by staying on your path, you will rarely be disappointed. Sometimes, you might have a "been there, done that" experience. When this happens, you will know that it's time to move on to another passion. However, being open to wherever it will take you is usually all you will need to ultimately find what you are seeking.

There are two things that I have lightheartedly referred to as "passion disorders." Obviously one is when passion is missing. The other is when passion is so important that there is a tendency to be neglectful of anything you are *not* passionate about. For example, you may have little or no passion for your work, even though it's necessary to show up in order to make a living (Stage Five), but then you allow your passion for playing computer games and surfing the Internet to take priority over your job responsibilities, perhaps causing you career and then financial problems. At Stage Six, you are able to deal with reality, even when you don't like it. This enables you to carry out choices that make the most long-term sense without conflict, such as minding your job responsibilities and temporarily putting aside the things you enjoy more, while developing a long-term strategy for a job or career change that allows you to do exactly what you really want to be doing. **Once you are comfortable with your passionate self, you can even teach yourself how to act as enthusiastically as you need to in order to enjoy something you may not enjoy under normal circumstances.** Then you can eventually feel or even become passionate when doing a lower-stage activity you would never choose, but that needs to be done. This just takes some practice as well as the degree of maturity that is part of a Stage Six default.

Nobody else can tell you what you are, should or should not be passionate about. Moreover, our specific passions themselves are not consciously chosen. **Passions actually choose or call upon you.** (This is why we commonly refer to a passion your "calling.") Once you hear a passion calling, you are empowered with the choice of whether or not to allow yourself to recognize it, act on it, spend time and resources pursuing it; and learn ways to fine-tune it. This principle certainly applies to career preferences, people you are attracted to, and even the foods you enjoy. You can choose your behavior (e.g., whether to eat that piece of cheesecake), and the people you associate with or make love to, but not your desires themselves. At the end of this chapter, I offer strategies to help you unlock and access those passionate parts of you that constitute your Stage Six core. That core is there and it eagerly awaits your conscious attention in any and every area of your life!

Spirituality for *Sixes* is a highly individual matter. **No definition of spirituality at Stage Six is complete without using the terms *unique* and *higher self*.** Your *higher self* is the internal part of you connected to whatever is your *unique* or distinct image of God, a Godlike higher power within you or a cosmic and energetic connection that can be expressed with or without an organized religion. I personally believe in the Hindu notion that there are many possible paths to God and your spiritual truth. It does not matter whether the route you are committed to is Christian, Jewish, Muslim, Buddhist, through meditation/ yoga, or your own unique combination of any or all of these. It's even possible to be an atheist at Stage Six, provided you would have been open to other spiritual alternatives and possibilities; but instead, connected to a deeply held, inner conviction consistent with atheist philosophy and practice.

There is also a spiritual aspect to your own set of distinctive purposes or callings. **Practices such as meditation, yoga, journaling, journeying,**

and visualization are excellent ways to deepen and enhance your connection to the nearly infinite pool of resources *within you*. I refer to what you may think of as your passionate self, core, soul, or reservoir of insight. The more you connect to the deepest levels of this *source of infinite wisdom*, the more you'll discover and firmly believe that your spirituality, along with all of the answers you need to live your life optimally, exist not outside, but within you. Your challenge, of course, is to access and connect to this source. Any route you take to go inside of yourself to do this is a crucial step in the right direction. **Whether or not your values and beliefs are consistent with those of an organized religion and/or which one, is your call; but at Stage Six, there is no longer a blur between that which is religious** (practices you have learned) **and what is spiritual** (or generated internally)**.**

Your view of Spirituality at Stage Six: "Higher self resides inside of each of us, whose function is to connect us with our unique strengths, calling, purpose, principles, and mission; and our commitment to pursue them"… Spiritual self (or lack thereof) is heartfelt and chosen; it may often call on you to connect with and feel love and awe for the beauty of nature and the world. **Religion may be an important part of your life, but it's not a necessary factor for you to connect to your spiritual source.** *At Stage Six, your connection to that source is direct.*

You can potentially love those you love at Stage Six very deeply. The act of loving someone else is central to you at Stage Six. And it's never grounded in fear or neediness. The love that comes *your* way is the prime motivator at Stage Four. But at Stage Six, **you now know that it's more gratifying to love than to be loved. Whom you love and display loving gestures toward is truly a matter of your choice. But remember, you have no real power at all over who loves you** (or in reality, what anyone thinks of or feels about you). A *Six* saying "I love you," does not need the other person to repeat it back in order for that statement of love to stand. I have heard many people point to this incredible shift in their *ability to love* as profoundly life changing.

Feeling especially good about yourself, when in the presence of someone you love is a very reliable indicator that (for you) your relationship is one at Stage Six. When treating couples in couple's therapy, I have learned over the years to pay far less attention to how partners say they feel about *each other* than how they feel about *themselves* when they are with (or thinking about) their partner. **Use this as a "litmus test." It's a wonderful standard to apply to anyone who's important to you, as well as to evaluate any part of your life, to determine if you are operating from Stage Six.** Whether you are thinking about your significant other, an aspect of your career or avocation, friends or groups to which you belong, **the question is, how do you feel about yourself with respect to them or it?** *The better you do, the more that part of your life is solidly in this coveted target stage zone.* **And for many, this alone could be enough to explain the feelings of fulfillment that make Stage Six so worthwhile.**

You can also be quite happy for other people, even though their good fortune does not benefit you and in some cases may have an adverse effect upon you. For example, a Stage Six politician who lost an election could, on a personal level, be genuinely happy for his opponent's good fortune, while still being quite appropriately sad for himself at having been defeated—and not just for the TV cameras— which would be more indicative of Stage Four. An actor who lost an Oscar can be genuinely happy for the winner whom she believes also gave an excellent performance.

In addition, **you are now better able to disagree with someone, even on a major issue, without anger or defensiveness and without ever thinking less of that individual merely because you disagree about something.** At Stage Six, you have also risen above envy. Although you can be extraordinarily competitive, when appropriate, you know your life, mission, and circumstances are distinctly your own and could never be compared accurately to anyone else's. Therefore, **envy is an obsolete emotion that *Sixes* happily leave behind.**

To the extent that your default stage for love relationships is at Stage Six, you will probably never allow yourself to be in one that is dysfunctional or shallow. Once you and your spouse or partner enjoy genuinely feeling good about yourselves as well as each other when you are together, nothing less will do. Stage Six sex is also passionate and satisfying for each partner. **If by chance you find your marriage or relationship going in a bad direction, you will either take great pains to remedy the situation or decisively accept the painful reality and get out of it quickly.** Insecurities about being alone, which may have tempted you to settle for a chronically unhappy or unfulfilling situation in the past, are staples of the lower stages.

Many, if not most, long-term love relationships begin by virtue of our Stage Six hooks. Hopefully, the relationship will morph into one with a Stage Six default. However, as time and life goes on and passions change or wane, the relationship can move backwards towards Stage Five. As I have pointed out in previous books, namely, *The Art of Staying Together* (1993) and *Can Your Relationship Be Saved? How to Know Whether to Stay or Go* (2002), couples or partners who are unaware or unwilling to work together to keep their passion alive often find themselves moving toward emotional indifference. Sometimes this prompts an affair or a breakup, while at other times it simply reduces the marriage to a content and dutiful collaboration of roles with a permanent Stage Five default unless both partners make a commitment to work on whatever issues need to be dealt with in order to climb back to Stage Six together.

However, please note that **most relationships with a Stage Six default stage are also grounded in a sense of comfort and deep caring for each other that transcends even sex.** Even though most people normally associate passion with sex, **at Stage Six it is your partner you are passionate about, not *necessarily* sex or any other activity you share together.** It's important to remember that sexual desire varies greatly from person to person and can be influenced by many factors, both psychological and physiological. On the other hand, I have seen many couples in my practice who report having great and passionate (Stage Six) sex although virtually every other aspect of the relationship may be in shambles at lower and sometimes even the lowest stages!

The trend toward divorce in recent decades was a revolution brought on by a sudden collective change in consciousness about marital roles. As the pendulum swings in the other direction toward a lower divorce rate, expect more of an evolution. For this, I credit and encourage a relatively new practice for couples to custom design their lifestyle together. As a result, you, as a couple are empowered to make your own choices and to understand that each partner has as much right as the other to be passionate about his or her own needs, desires, and sources of fulfillment. **Marriages that operate by dependency, intimidation, rules, insecurity, and simply by following the role each partner expects the other one to play are less likely to survive one partner's spurt of growth into Stage Six.** At the same time, breakups and divorces at Stage Six triggered by partners growing apart can occur as commonly as in the lower stages.

Stage Six hooks can first appear at almost any age. An eight year old who loves her parents, siblings, or a friend in the same mature way an adult would is an example an early Stage Six hook. Child prodigies in various fields such as music, art, math, sciences, and sports are another obvious example. Most of us can recognize that there was a clue to the roots of our unique talents as far back as early in childhood or certainly by adolescence. I will never miss an opportunity to advise parents (or teachers) to reinforce these early passions and first Stage Six hooks as much as possible. **It is indeed *a great moment* at any time in your life when you are able break out of the pack and believe in yourself enough to use your innate gifts to the fullest.** Someone recently described to me her experience of this as "having the courage first to find and then to follow and ultimately stay on her 'trail of joy.' " For many, life rarely gets better than that.

An actual Stage Six default doesn't usually kick into the major aspects of our lives until at least early adulthood. Then your main obstacles to a blessed life at Stage Six are your hooks in the lower stages. These of course, can come in almost infinite varieties and surface at any time. However, when you come back to Stage Six, you are able to deal with reality even when that reality is one you do not like. **As a *Six*, you will find that the more you believe that you must be what you *can be*, the less likely you will be to let anything or anyone *bring you down* to those lower stages.**

Remember that at Stage Six, as at any stage, you may still sometimes feel a need to react to certain life situations or people as you would have in earlier stages. These are merely your hooks manifesting themselves, often by choice. It's always your prerogative to use those hooks as you see fit. In fact, that's arguably one of the very best uses for your lower-stage hooks. However, **as a *Six*, you can more easily compartmentalize tasks and even people when it's appropriate.**

For example, no matter how much passion and enthusiastic joy might govern your work, you may still have to fill out time and expense reports (Stage Five), flatter a difficult boss or customer/client (Stage Four), follow certain rules that seem anachronistic (Stage Three),demagogue on an issue (Stage Two) or even at times act powerless (Stage One). Then once the matter that is pulling you down is addressed, you can certainly return to your Stage Six default. This becomes an automatic process, to the extent that you have hardwired your Stage Six default. Chapter 14, page 282, contains an exercise with a worksheet to help you do this with any part of your life.

Stage Six relationships *value the person over the role they play in your life such as lover, brother, friend, colleague, mother-in-law or next-door neighbor.* In addition, at Stage Six, the difference between liking or loving someone and merely accepting or tolerating that person is clear to you and rarely in conflict. You can keenly distinguish between a person and his or her behavior. You have gone beyond your need for people to be different from what they are, although you may find yourself at times using every means possible to get someone to change certain behavior (e.g., your spouse, children, colleagues, or others around you). **As a *Six*, you will rarely if ever judge a person based *solely* on how they behave around you or act toward you.** You realize that would be quite an overgeneralization, so you remember not to take it personally when someone is relating to you as part of a role that either you or they are playing (such as boss or subordinate). Rather than globally resenting someone who has disappointed you, you feel little if any conflict in "loving the sinner, but hating the sin."

How Families operate at Stage Six: Whole is greater than the sum of its parts ... Family is held together with love and respect ... Family members encourage and support each other's strengths, ambitions, and personal growth.

To the degree that Stage Six is your default stage, you are no longer a passenger—*emotionally* under the control of others you depend on,

your roles, your fears and anxieties, those whose approval you seek, or even your own ego. Your integrity and sense of self is strong enough to overpower all of these things. **You are now the driver**. Your own embedded values are far more important to you than what anyone could ever tell you your values should be. **Rather than merely being the actor acting out your roles, you are now also the director overseeing them and determining their importance to you.**

At Stage Six, when you find yourself troubled, confused or in conflict, you are best served by whatever practice you use to direct yourself inward in order to *discover and choose* the answer that is right for you. You now know in your mind, your heart, and your gut that the only source of true wisdom that will ultimately work for you, exists and/or is accessible from *within.*

Even though you are motivated mainly through your internal or intrinsic rewards, you will certainly—and can still passionately—desire, accept, or demand external rewards when appropriate. However, at Stage Six, at least in the privacy of your own mind, you see them more as gravy, or as a nice bonus, than as your most important source of motivation. More likely, **you will ask yourself whether whatever you are considering is worth the effort, irrespective of the external rewards. If so, you will go for it. If not, you will most likely let it go.** Of course, even making a lot of money itself can be a Stage Six endeavor, if you truly enjoy the *process* of what you are doing.

Consider this observation of two street musicians within a block of each other—both solo violinists: Musician #1 was playing the violin quite competently, yet still managed a smile for those who put money in his box, and a dirty look to each passerby who neglected to give him a contribution. Musician #2 was also playing very well, but with his eyes closed. He was totally into the music. He appeared to be quite oblivious to passersby, to the point at which you wondered if he knew that anything else existed in the moment but the music he was playing. *He,* ironically, seemed to get a much better rate of contribution from passersby. One could hypothesize that this is because Musician #2 was not only delivering the music, but conveying his passion and enjoyment of it. You could somehow sense that he was absorbed in what he was doing and believed in it at least as much as he wanted his audience to—regardless of whether or not they contributed money. What seemed to govern musician

#1 were the expectations that the street should "take care of him" (Stage One); people who hear his music should pay for it (Stage Three); monetary rewards so that he can make at least part of a living doing this (Stage Five); and the approval of those who passed by him (Stage Four). He appeared to put both his internal and external success that day into the hands of the passersby. Musician #2, on the other hand, was presumably operating out of Stage Six (doing what he loved). The recognition of those who passed by in his case was merely incidental. Even if at the end of the day there was a disappointing amount of money, for Musician #2 the day would arguably still have been at least somewhat worthwhile and enjoyable.

> A Stage Six view toward the purpose of **Wealth**: It ensures that you can continue to pursue what you enjoy the most.

A prestigious house, expensive car, and all the toys and trappings of financial success, for instance, have less meaning to you by themselves at Stage Six than they would have in lower stages. For example, unless cars are an actual passion of yours, no matter how luxurious yours may be, you will come to view it more as a means of reliable transportation and comfort than as a status symbol that will make you temporarily feel better about yourself (as it might in Stage Four). You can now *provide to yourself* (and at bargain rates) whatever *emotional boosts or validation* any of these props may have given you in the past.

If you are an artist, *while you are creating it* you are no longer thinking as much about who will buy your work or what will make it more marketable. **Your primary reward while being creative comes from the *process of creating*.** You can certainly focus on marketing—usually a Stage Five activity for artists—later. Ironically, **many people have told me that once they can change their thinking to focus on the process of creating instead of the outcome or payoff, that more successful payoffs resulted with much less effort!** The creative process often works that way.

A means to get the recognition that may be eluding you is to stop focusing on recognition that depends on others and is more characteristic of Stage Four. Instead, concentrate on improving the level of what you are doing. This is the aspect that really is under your control. It's usually difficult or impossible to be optimally creative while obsessing about what others will think of your creation. Once you remove that pressure and instead decide to concentrate on doing what you were truly meant to do, you can expect to experience some amazing changes. **Something that often surprises many *Sixes* is that abundance finds them the minute they stop chasing it!**

Authority at Stage Six means being *authoritative*; that is a characteristic of someone who people *choose* to look up to, admire, and follow. *Sixes* admire *authoritativeness*, but *not authoritarianism* (which is leadership by the sheer power of rank, force, and fear). **The best way to motivate your Stage Six subordinates—if you are in a position to provide them with an environment in which they can thrive—is to give them a challenge that motivates them intrinsically; that activates their passion, creativity, and all of the synergy that results. Then leave them alone to work their magic.** Power can be a Stage Six passion for some CEOs, political leaders, and others in high positions of authority. However, it is how they use that power that gives a clue to their default stage. Part II has many illustrations of this.

Just as I talked about famous criminals as extreme examples of a Stage Two default**, I mention here a few representative Stage Six luminaries with whom we are all familiar.** Some of those greats include Thomas Edison, Isaac Newton, Galileo, Johann Gutenberg, Jonas Salk, Shakespeare, Michelangelo, Plato, Mozart, Beethoven, George and Ira Gershwin, Cole Porter (as a songwriter, he was certainly a *Six*; however, he started out as a lawyer and, as he described that career, it was characterized much more by Stages Three, Four, and Five), Madame Curie, Louis Pasteur, Charles Darwin, Christopher Columbus, the Wright Brothers, Alexander Graham Bell, Walt Disney, Picasso, Louis Armstrong, Frank Sinatra, Babe Ruth, and Mohammad Ali. Most entrepreneurs, professional athletes, entertainers, tireless innovators, and countless others in every field whose passion has led to excellence are members of this club.

These icons made gigantic, indelible contributions to a world that long survived them; but the best news is that **the Stage Six club is open to everyone. You are operating at Stage Six whenever you are taking full charge of your life by accessing, listening to, trusting, and most importantly, acting on your own unique *inner* resources. *This is the formula you can depend on for reaching your highest potential in any area of your life.***

True democracy is a Stage Six concept in which everyone has an equal voice. Some unusually evolved organizations that are run by and function for highly committed people operate that way. However, I do not believe there is a truly democratic government (as opposed to a representative democracy such as we have in the United States) that has ever survived for long; nor is there currently a society in which a Stage Six (or higher) default was the norm, although such communities have sporadically been reported to exist. This would be the closest thing that I know of to a utopian society.

Sixes still feel their own brand of emotional pain. Becoming *too* attached to your passions and purpose can also create suffering at times. For instance, it can be difficult when you are surrounded by those whose default stages are distinctly lower than yours and you feel conflicted between your obligations and loyalties to them, and to serving what you believe to be your own higher purpose. For this reason, in **many marriages in which one partner climbs to Stage Six in key life areas, while the other partner does not or will not make their own climb, the marriage ceases to exist.** An example is when a breadwinner chooses to make a lifestyle change and earn less money in order to pursue his or her passion. Moreover, in a marriage, once you and/or your partner rise above your marital roles, it is far from a sure bet to assume that both of you will continue to find yourselves walking along the same path.

> How you might view taking care of your *aging* **Parents** at Stage Six: "It's an opportunity to strengthen and complete our relationship while there is the chance."

Sixes do sometimes tend to lose balance in their lives due to excessive preoccupation with one area of life, such as their careers, to the exclusion of family relationships or other important aspects of life. For instance, many luminaries of all stripes have regretted neglecting their families or not taking the time to tend to their own important health issues until it was too late.

At Stage Six, the choice and ability to both love what you do and do what you love is there for the taking. Whatever roles you now choose to take on will most likely be passion-driven and in your long-term best interest; or chances are you will discard them as quickly as possible. **If you now had to choose between success and inner peace, most likely you will conclude that inner peace—a staple of the target stages—trumps success every time they conflict.**

Life does not give you happiness; it only gives you time to use in the best way you can. **Think about those times when you were profoundly happy. Chances are you were in some way connected to something or someone you felt passionate about. That's certainly a great barometer to follow.** Take the time to think and strategize about how you can use the time you have to make this standard apply to any chosen part of your life.

James Dean said, "Dream as though you'll live forever. Live as though you'll die today." That is a great summary of Stage Six!

LIVING YOUR PASSIONS: STRENGTHENING EVERYTHING STAGE SIX

Since this is a target stage, your goal is not to climb out of it, but to widen, deepen, and strengthen Stage Six as your default stage as much as you choose. **I do not know of anyone who has *totally* passed through Stage Six.** Of course, going *beyond* Stage Six is another matter that will be addressed in the next chapter. However, **to the extent that you feel comfortable in your own skin, are enthusiastic and passionate about, as well as at peace with, the life you are living—or the major aspects of it that are most important to you—you are in the Stage Six zone.**

With that in mind and no matter where you are in your *Stage Climbing* process, I offer you some strategies and action steps to quickly make Stage Six your default stage in the areas of your life where you want it to be:

❖ Our **passions** are a major part of what determines our purpose and calling. If you made a list of all the things you feel passionately about and are truly committed to—regardless of what anyone else may think of them—you would have a list of the things that constitute an impor- tant aspect of the **meaning of your life** in the simplest possible terms. Make that list, consult it often and add to it each time a new item oc- curs to you. Keep it handy as a private reference.

❖ One of the Buddha's most enduring metaphors is that of the sun always being there as the natural order of things. Thus, when you can't see the sun during daylight hours, it's due to the sun being blocked by clouds and storms. Think of the **sun as a metaphor** for that comprehensive list of your passions. Then imagine your fears and obstacles (as well as other obvious lower-stage hooks) as the "clouds and storms" that are blocking the "sun" from shining through. This **inner turbulence is what blocks the natural process of *Stage Climbing.*** To the extent that you are living in Stage Six, you have managed to eliminate those storms and clouds from a given aspect of your life. Make another list of all those obstacles you can identify that are still blocking you in some way. Include old hurts you have not let go of from childhood as well as people against whom you still carry resentment. Resolve to use every tool at your disposal — in this book as well with other resources available to you — to work toward permanently eliminating these obstacles as much as possible.

❖ What **hooks into the lower stages** do you now recognize that were not apparent to you earlier? If you can identify some, take the time to revise your strategies as appropriate for acting on those lower-stage hooks (perhaps revisit some of the strategies in previous chapters, as appropriate).

❖ Does your career or job bring you **happiness and a sense of fulfillment**? Is there anything else you'd rather be doing? How about your marriage/love relationship or lack thereof? Is this part of your life working? Are other major aspects of your life bringing you the happiness and fulfillment you seek from them? Make a commitment to yourself to take an inventory of what you want your life to be. What can you work on or improve? **What warrants a deeper commitment? What sorely needs to be eliminated? Perhaps most importantly, what areas of your life trigger in you *the best feelings about yourself*** (a principal factor in determining whether you are operating at Stage Six)? *Sixes* generally tend to find their own way of making the exploration of questions such as these an ongoing exercise.

❖ If all things were possible, **what would you do differently with your life right now?** After you have answered this question for today, try to project ahead to next month, next year, five years, twenty years, and finally to the end of your life. Pretend that you can project yourself forward to those future times and "look back." How would you answer this question differently for today from the perspective of each of these different time periods?

❖ Make a list of times (the more the better) when you were at **your absolute best**—at peak performance, *feeling the best about yourself*: successful, unstoppable, "bulletproof," and full of passion. Select one of the times you just listed (perhaps the one you consider most powerful). Close your eyes and relive that moment. Allow yourself to re-experience the glory of those feelings. See the sights, smell the smells, and hear the sounds while you allow yourself to re-experience that feeling of having "arrived," as fully as possible. Then open your eyes. **Observe the body language, breath, thoughts, and facial expressions that go with the experience that you just relived.** This is your mind and body in a peak state—your zone of passion. This state of mind is something that you can trigger at will. This is also part of your natural frame of mind at Stage Six. You can access it anytime you wish to be in a peak state by setting your intention and changing your body language accordingly; and the more you do it, the more natural it will feel. Eventually this state will come to you automatically.

❖ **If you could be in the peak state** you just identified (body language and all) what would you most like to tackle now? Use this peak state as a foot in the door of what you are most passionate about or trying to accomplish. Identify where you now would most like to apply that zone of passion you just created—which, remember, you can recreate again anytime. I strongly suggest you do this often!

❖ **If you were beyond money**—a billionaire who also had all the time in the world to pursue your dream— what would you do differently with your life? Make sure to include what you would do *after* the "big trip(s)" and the proverbial "spending spree" is over. In addition, what would you do differently if you were to believe yourself to be completely and absolutely in control of your destiny? Make a list of whatever comes to mind. There is no doubt that there are items you have listed that are impossible to do without the money or other resources that are not yet available to you. So when your list is complete, cross those off (just for now, but come back to them in the future whenever you're ready). Then, pick out those things that you could actually accomplish with your present resources. Chances are there are some real passions you can fulfill right now. Go for that "low-hanging fruit" first.

❖ What are your strongest talents? Dare to identify what you consider yourself to be the **"best in the world" at**? There is probably something (or some things). Allow yourself to own it/them. Make another list: **"If I were to do only what I believe I were (or could be) the best at that there is, I would _____."** Make that list as long as possible.

❖ Make a list of the things you are most likely to be doing when you are **feeling the best *about yourself***. Make another list of the people you tend to be around when you feel best *about yourself*. This may take some soul-searching, but it's worth it. These are the people and things that bring out the *Six* in you.

❖ **Spend a set amount of time,** such as one full day (and if necessary, adjust the amount of time up or down to what you are truly *willing* to do), only doing that which you associate with your strongest feelings of passion. Take special note as to how it feels.

❖ If you could have **any mentor in the world** (who is ether alive today or has ever lived), who would that person or those persons be? Take a current dilemma or situation you are considering or with which you are now struggling. When you have something in mind, write a short essay—even a paragraph or two—on how that person would handle (or advise you to handle or resolve) your issue or dilemma. What do your "mentors" *believe* about your circumstances that you would be much better off believing? Keep in mind the fact that you can have as many of these kinds of "mentors" as you want—even different ones for different aspects of your life. With this exercise, think of them (your "mentors") as your "strongest self" (or even the voice of your highest potential) which you can access 24 hours a day.

❖ Is there **an actual mentor**, coach, or therapist who is now available to you in person that you could reach out to for help in manifesting your dream(s) or removing one or more obstacles to it? **The best mentors for you are generally people who have and are still accomplishing for themselves what you are now striving to do.** Consider getting the help you need to get moving—now or as soon as possible—as an important step in your *Stage Climbing* process. Remember, time is the one commodity that cannot be replaced, once it's gone.

❖ **To the extent that you believe, as I do, that from now on the most powerful answers and guidance you seek reside inside of yourself just waiting to be accessed, it's crucial to find a regular practice to tap into this precious source of information, passion, and peace.** Examples include regular meditation, yoga, long quiet and reflective walks, visualization and journeying, or a combination of them that uniquely suits you. They all provide excellent tools to deepen your conscious connection with your inner core. Things that get you there are the best interventions at Stages Six and higher. There are numerous sources of information available to help you develop and enhance these practices as staples in your life. Some of the best books as well as places where meditation and other practices are taught can be found at *StageClimbing.com/resources*.

❖ *Mindfulness meditation* **is an extremely easy thing to learn, yet something that few people (if any) actually master *completely*.** Sit comfortably in a chair with both feet on the ground, close your eyes, and gently focus all of your attention on your breathing (without trying to *change* how you breathe in any way). Do this for a set period of time. If you haven't done meditation before, start with a five minute session daily, then increase it by five minutes per week until you are at somewhere between twenty and thirty minutes per session. **Do**

one or two sessions daily as time and your willingness permits. Simply stay in the present moment while being still, centered, grounded and non-judgmental, while following your natural breath as a guide. Whenever you are aware of your mind taking you in another direction, simply let go of the thought and then let yourself gently drift back to concentrating on your breathing. Doing this while being fully receptive—yet, not attached—to whatever comes up for you, takes some practice; but is well worth it both in the short run and over time. This is meditation at its best and one of many techniques beyond the scope of this book to discuss and explore fully. This paragraph, however, certainly gives you what you need to get started and fully experience it. Moreover, using resources such as those you will find at *StageClimbing.com/resources* to learn a meditation practice more thoroughly (and one that you will do regularly) will pay you incredible short- and long-term dividends in health benefits and an increase in well-being, inner peace, and clarity of thought, intuition, wisdom, and connection to your spiritual self!

❖ Here are some **additional questions** to ask yourself and then make lists of the answers: **"What truly inspires me?"... "What comes easiest to me?"... "What special talents do I have that I am most proud of?"... "What rewards do I find to be most gratifying?"** Eliminate those that come from outside of yourself or someone else (e.g., praise or money). Focus instead on your **intrinsic rewards** (those that come from within, e.g., a sense of satisfaction, etc.).

❖ **What are you willing to do** in order to live the life that a Stage Six default stage could deliver you? What trade-offs would you have to make? What is still holding you back? Where do you go from here? No matter what steps you will ultimately choose to take, *you owe it to yourself to know what your choices are*. Most importantly, empower yourself by acknowledging that it is the choices you have made prior to now that have led to your life circumstances today. Take complete responsibility for them. Then simply **refuse to blame yourself, another person, or any other factor** for an aspect of your life you don't like. If you can do this, you have taken a giant step toward removing and gaining control over any remaining toxic hooks to the lower stages. The same can be said for the reality of what your circumstances *will be tomorrow*—which you can think of as your reward for working on a strong Stage Six default today.

❖ Stage Six **Resources** include yoga, meditation, mindfulness, finding and pursuing passion and dreams, goal setting, manifesting excellence, maximizing peak performance zones and many other practices, traits and skills. You owe it to yourself to read about these resources and learn to put them into practice. Several authors who write, teach, and conduct workshops about different aspects of Stage Six include Jack Canfield, Deepak Chopra, Stephen R. Covey, Wayne Dyer, Mark Victor Hanson, Jack Kornfield, Anthony Robbins, Brian Tracey, Jon Kabat-Zinn, and many others. Their work can be found at *Stage-Climbing.com/resources* (Password: MyStageClimb).

Now imagine that you can take the initiatives you want in all the important areas of life, and imagine you have a well-developed conscience along with a penchant for living by your own rules. You know all too well that chasing other people's approval ultimately returns you little. Your ducks are in a row so that your life is managed well, with all necessities provided. As a bonus, you now enjoy what you are doing, so that you are "in joy" with the categories and aspects of life that inspire and matter most to you. Could there be anywhere else to go? Yes, there is! You can still raise the bar to make the best you can be even better!

At Stage Seven, we are beyond self-gratification and ourselves, and are now ready to use our considerable energies and passions toward a mission that benefits the larger world.

CHAPTER 7

STAGE SEVEN

Benevolence Is Your Calling

*"We make a living by what we get,
but we make a life by what we give."*

—Sir Winston Churchill

A s the ancient Chinese proverb reminds us: "One generation plants the trees; another gets the shade."

If it were not for a calling that we hear in some way to make a greater contribution, then living our lives at Stage Six, along with some handpicked hooks to the five lower stages, would be all we could ever want. Our only remaining challenge would be to find and enjoy more ways to use our passions to gratify ourselves and there would be no reason to climb any higher. Fortunately, for our civilization and those around us, however, as our passions expand, they tend to have other ideas. **Stage Seven—our highest target Stage—takes us *beyond ourselves*.**

When the forces of gratitude and passion work together, practically anything is possible. For starters, **we find might ourselves moving beyond self-gratification. Thus, the major distinction between Stages Six and Seven is that at Stage Seven your focus shifts away from yourself and outwardly to the greater world.** This by no means deprives you in any way— quite the contrary. You are simply no longer *as* motivated by *personal* enjoyment or gratification (Stage Six), money (Stage Five), or praise and recognition (Stage Four). These things are still desirable and nice, and because you retain certain lower- stage hooks, you still might find yourself striving for them. However, as you climb to Stage Seven, they lose their ability to inspire and satisfy you as they once did. At Stage Seven, these lower-stage hooks give way to a stronger desire. The result is a calling you hear *to give something back*. Ironically, **your own personal enjoyment at Stage Seven is optional. Sevens keep the world going by their realization—regardless of how consciously it manifests itself—that there is only so much that they can keep for themselves.**

As a *Six*, you may have found that you became a "victim of your own success," when whole categories of things that used to motivate you no longer do. Sometimes it's merely boredom, one of our most underrated stressors, that tells you it's time to redirect your focus. Often**, I have observed that it's accurate to say that *Sixes* burn out on their own gratification.** However, when you become less interested in merely seeking additional gratification for yourself, something more is needed to bring meaning back to your life. Climbing to Stage Seven subsequently becomes the *natural* way to go.

It is, and always has been, your Stage Seven hooks that call upon you whenever you focus on the needs of others *without regard to what's in it for you*. To the degree you are a Seven, *gratitude*—for all the good things you have been able to manifest and enjoy in your life or simply even for life itself—*joins* passion as your principal motivator and source of fulfillment. As you enter Stage Seven territory, your calling and desire to give back gets louder and louder. **Your passions are still guiding you, but now toward truly caring about something *beyond you*—whatever or whoever that may be.**

Your **Ultimate Goals** at Stage Seven: To change the world in some way—large or small … To have the greatest possible impact on those around you and/or a cause with which you involve yourself.

Like Stage Six, Stage Seven is where goodness can morph into greatness and there is no limit to the potential of where it can all lead. However, **what motivates the Seven in you is the *internal* reward provided by your contribution and service towards a cause or purpose bigger than yourself.**

This expands the definition of altruism at its best, as it recognizes that there is in fact something in it for you. That something is a level of satisfaction connected to a bigger purpose that the stages below Seven, simply couldn't deliver.

A Stage Seven default means that *personal* success is no longer an issue for you. You are beyond thinking in terms of your own success and failure. You have broken out of that pack. Your ego is no longer a factor in decisions you make. I would define this as the *ultimate* personal success. *Sevens* **instinctively understand the simple paradox of happiness: by focusing on your own, you rarely achieve it in a lasting way; but by helping someone else—perhaps many others—to find it, happiness and fulfillment comes back to you almost effortlessly.** Those you help can be individuals, groups, organizations, or nations. They can be close family members, neighbors or friends, animals, the environment, those you recognize in your will that may never have the chance to thank you, people whom you never have nor never will meet, the entire world, or any segment of it. **The desire to help is what all *Sevens* have in common. It is only the mission and the recipient(s) that varies.**

As in Stage Six, whatever you do to go inward and self-reflect, whether by simply listening to your intuition, through meditation, journaling, long silent walks, or your association with a spiritual guide, a role model or mentor, **all the direction you need ultimately resides within you.** What makes Stages Six and Seven similar is that at both stages you are internally directed. However, what makes them differ is that at Stage Seven, you then become committed to something beyond yourself. **Whenever you are helping someone who can't reciprocate with no strings attached, you are operating out of this target stage.**

Your Stage Seven purpose is a highly individual matter. For some, helping one person is enough. For others, nothing short of changing the entire world in some major way will do. Your contribution can range from time or money to a charity that you can easily afford, to your life itself or anything in between. **It's not the size of your mission that is important, only the intent that it be driven by your own true desire to give back as opposed to receive.** Any cause you connect with and decide to pursue, or contribution that you determine in your own way you must do in this lifetime, puts you in the Stage Seven zone.

Stage Seven is the highest stage attainable and the second of our two universal **Target Stages.** A **Default Stage** here in most aspects of life is beyond normal; it would suggest an inordinately high degree of consciousness; but hooks here can develop at any age. You are operating at Stage Seven whenever your focus shifts to a problem that does not affect you directly (or is not necessarily your job or role to address) and you feel the need to be *giving back* without direct benefits to you as a result; or you find yourself asking, "How can I contribute or be of benefit to_____?" For example, **this is certainly the best default stage from which to parent.**

As in other stages, it's doubtful that a real person with an across the board or "perfect" Stage Seven default has ever existed. However, **in a crucial sense, our collective hooks to Stage Seven are what keep this planet going.** The Stage Seven club is open to you anytime at all, and in any area of your life. If at the age of ten, you worked hard to sell Girl Scout Cookies for all the right reasons, or you risked your popularity at school by befriending an outcast or someone far less popular without regard to how you would be viewed by your peers, you probably did so as the result of an early Stage Seven hook. Any act of selflessness can be your ticket. In fact, whether or not you realize it, there are probably many ways you are there already. For example, donating blood—unless you're merely doing it to fit in, get praise, or for other tangible rewards—is a Stage Seven hook in action.

Good parenting that is grounded in love, where you genuinely put your child's needs above your own without regard to any apparent rewards that will come your way, is certainly one of the most common and universal Stage Seven endeavors. Most parents routinely make incalculable sacrifices of time, money, and perhaps their own personal ambitions when raising children and not merely because they "should." This also holds true when you take care of siblings, aging parents, or other family members with special needs—whether those needs are temporary or permanent. Of course, Stage Seven assumes that your true motives are not at the lower stages for doing these things; such as out of guilt-motivated, rigid obligation

(Stage Three), or in order that you would be praised and/or *loved* for it (Stage Four).

Another example is becoming an unpaid resource to, or mentor for someone where even a small amount of your time could mean the difference between him or her succeeding on a healthy path and never finding that path. Can you can think of someone (or several people) who have made that kind of difference in your life?

Additionally, **the most evolved parents, teachers, and scoutmasters routinely use their Stage Seven selves to teach children the rewards of acquiring early Stage Seven hooks of their own**, by emphasizing the pleasure and other *intrinsic* rewards that come back as a result of charitable acts. This is in contrast to serving or contributing merely out of obligation, dictums, or any of the other reasons that are staples of the lower stages.

A Stage Seven act that requires little sacrifice could merely involve sending a blessing, a meditation, or a prayer to a person or cause that could use some positive or healing energy. It is also ordinary people anonymously helping ordinary people. For example, going out of your way to pick up a piece of glass on the beach that is not likely to hurt you, yet might protect the next person walking by, who will never know to give you credit. Helping a blind person with a simple task, or reaching out to an isolated and elderly neighbor—one who has no one else and perhaps nothing to give you back—are but a couple of other examples of the infinite range of Stage Seven contributions. In Part II, there will be many examples of how Stage Seven (as well as all of the others stages) manifest themselves in various careers and professions as well numerous other life applications.

What you are typically Needing and Seeking at Stage Seven: To spread your energy, abundance and/or the feelings of fulfillment you have achieved for yourself to others in some general or specific area.

Your default stage and hooks are highly personal matters. As in Stage Six, at Stage Seven, how you feel about yourself regarding your

activities as a Seven is a great "litmus test." Others can easily be fooled as to whether or not you are acting out of Stage Seven, or a lower stage. The awareness of what's in your heart is accessible only by you. Thus, it's most important not to fool yourself. For instance, if you have sacrificed your own comfort to finance your children's college education, have you done so in order for them to "owe you," and out of the fear that otherwise they will not take care of you should you need help someday in your old age (Stage One)? In order to gain access to a trust fund that a grandparent set up for them, where your real agenda is to net a lot more money for yourself than you actually put out, thus deviously costing your child in the long run (Stage Two)? Because you would feel guilty otherwise since the rule has been drilled into you that, "only bad parents don't pay for college" (Stage Three)? So that your children will love you, praise you, and show you gratitude for their subsequent success in life (Stage Four)? Because it is simply a part of the expected role of parents to help their children reap the rewards of a college education (Stage Five)? As a way of demonstrating and feeling, the joy of parental love (Stage Six)? Or in order to reap the pleasure of seeing them benefit, and perhaps enhance their ability to contribute to the world and to do your share in helping to trigger the many ripple effects that *their* subsequent contribution will entail — even long after you are gone (Stage Seven)? Of course, there can be any combination of these reasons in play via the many hooks we typically have.

Simply note that **at Stage Seven, you never need to be thanked, appreciated, or given any quid pro quo. Your contribution is based on your own principles and values regarding the greater good it will do. Perhaps it's even your way of expressing the gratitude you feel toward someone who once helped you, by passing the energy of that gesture along to where it's needed now.**

Contributions of time or money to charity or a cause you support is similar. **Your true motive is what tells the story.** For example, at Stage Seven, your contribution may be a result of *your inspiration* to benefit the world or a certain deserving subset of it for a cause in which you believe. At times, this could even make your own life more complicated or difficult than it would be otherwise. At Stage Six, it could be the opportunity to *do some type of work that you enjoy doing* for a charity, which you don't have the opportunity to perform as a part of your career or regular life. At Stage Five, it could possibly be to fulfill the *expected role* of giving back (and besides, giving tangibles to charity is tax-deductible). At Stage Four, it could be to receive the *praise and recognition* that often comes from others as a result of giving (many charities even publish the names of their donors, partially for that purpose). Another way to put it is that *Fours* (as well as *Twos*) can act like *Sevens* when the "cameras are rolling." At Stage Three, you may be giving merely to stay out of hell; Stage Two, to convince others that you have pure intentions, so that they fall prey to a scam of yours; and/or Stage One in order, somehow, to actually receive that charity's help.

Once again, almost infinite combinations of any or all of these are possible. In Part II there are numerous examples of how this principle applies to different selected aspects of life.

The role of Charity (giving of time, money or other tangibles to others) at Stage Seven: To move the world or a segment of it in the right direction with respect to something you feel strongly about, where nothing *external* for yourself is expected in return. (*Sevens* need no recognition or tangible rewards for their acts of kindness.)

As can a *Six*, at Stage Seven, you have the capacity to understand all of the people you have passed along the way. Just remember not to insist that they understand you, since that will often lead to your disappointment. **Even more importantly, the higher you go, the more you can now understand *yourself* at your lower stages.** Use this as a gift. Take the opportunity often to gain insight as to why you may have done or thought certain things during an earlier or less evolved time in your life. It is this knowledge that helps you to manage your hooks, let go of the past and stay on your chosen path.

For example, **at Stage Seven you are no longer internally guided by "shoulds" or absolute truths of any kind.** At Stages One and Two, you may still need them to survive. At Stage Three, you generally agree with them, while at Stage Four you try to fight them, but often lose. At Stage Five, you finally start winning the battle of the "shoulds," but they are still a force in your life until you climb to Stages Six and Seven.

Unlike those at lower stages, **Sevens never expect, require, demand, or even ask for any more respect or love from someone else than they are willing to give.** This applies to your children and subordinates, as well as anyone else in your world. At Stage Seven, you know that treating others with genuine respect sets an example, and is your best shot at getting it back. However, you also accept the fact that it only comes back to you as strongly as the other person is capable of sending it and even that other person's inability or unwillingness to reciprocate at all is not a problem for you at Stage Seven. **You now fully understand that if you have *self-respect* you don't really *need* the validation, approval, and respect of others in order to feel worthwhile** (although at any stage those things still feel good).

With a Stage Seven default, you have raised the bar; and have indeed arrived. You can certainly grow, expand, and change missions, but there are no *higher* stages to aspire to. **Since your own personal gratification and fulfillment do not require much of your attention at Stage Seven, you become emotionally freer and more able to put your considerable energy outward toward your calling or purpose.** Your intentions and your behavior match. You are no longer needy or self-absorbed. You are finished with the type of self-destructive behavior that caused you innumerable problems in the lower stages.

However, Stage Seven values can sometimes conflict with other aspects of your life (e.g., one or more important relationships or your day job), making it necessary to change your mission, behavior, or lifestyle accordingly. Yet, painful as these conflicts may be, your core at Stage Seven will survive these tweaks. Any remaining self-doubts will rarely stand up to what you have chosen as your mission. **You have developed a reservoir of inner resources and wisdom to live life at the highest levels of consciousness.**

Happiness and Success at Stage Seven: Achieving the desired impact on a person, a group of people or a segment of the world you most care about … Watching others reap the benefits of your efforts and cheering them on … Being fully connected to your principles and able to perform your mission.

> **Conflict is typically handled at Stage Seven** by carefully listening to the points of view of everyone involved, considering each possibility, then making the decision or taking the action(s) that comes closest to best serving each player as well as the issue itself. You then seek consensus and/or staunchly standby your decision or action and the principles that underlie it.

As a *Seven*, your reaction to conflict would normally be to take the needs and points of view of every concerned or affected person and faction into consideration, in addition to your own. Since you seek no absolute realities or rigid rules to guide you, you understand that the other person has a point of view as well as you do. That does not necessarily mean you buy into it but you will characteristically allow it to become part of the larger picture in resolving a conflict. **You now have not only the capacity for empathy—which is merely an understanding of how the other person feels—but also a deep appreciation of the role empathy plays in your mission.** This prompts you to practice it routinely and perhaps even automatically. For example, a profound tragedy such as the death of a child could trigger a wide range of responses. At Stage One, you could become permanently fixated and even emotionally paralyzed by the feelings of grief and victimhood. However, at Stage Seven, you might find yourself devoting considerable time and money to a mission focused on preventing other parents from going through the experience you did by battling the disease, law, or other circumstances that led to the tragedy. As a *Seven*, you can choose to apply this principle to virtually any life challenge.

The more Stage Seven becomes your default stage, the more your cause can potentially become even more important to you than your own physical or emotional well-being. In other words, your purpose can actually overtake your*self*. While it's not by any means a given or even something that applies to most, many *Sevens* would relinquish their own wealth and personal comforts if those in any way conflicted with their mission. An example is someone who by virtue of their Stage Seven calling chooses a life of pure service (e.g., nuns, priests, and monks) and is able to put aside practically every other aspect of life—material and otherwise.

Again, this is certainly not required or even necessarily Stage Seven-motivated by everyone who does it, only an option that a small percentage of people exercise; and one that sometimes causes more conflict to those around them, than it does in themselves. **However, much more typical is your tendency as a *Seven* to do what you know is the right thing as opposed to what's popular or easier when there's a conflict.** This would come naturally to a politician with a Stage Seven default—routinely ignoring polls and other pressures that summon their Stages Three, Four, and Five hooks. Most notably, at Stage Seven, you are secure enough within yourself to commit to taking what Walt Whitman described as that "road less traveled," (Peck 2003), and focus instead on the world you leave behind.

What Motivates you at Stage Seven are such things as: The opportunity to serve one person or many others in a cause or mission you believe in … To solve a problem that has an impact on people or things that are larger or needier than you and perhaps your circle … The satisfaction of touching one life or many lives.

Spirituality at Stage Seven is indistinguishably connected to your purpose. Your dialogue with God or a higher consciousness is as uniquely personal—as you define God or a higher consciousness. As in Stage Six, you access your spiritual guide by whatever means you use to go inside of yourself. At Stage Seven, you often tend to go a step farther by asking how you can bring a higher consciousness to any situation, problem, or conflict you are facing or recognize—even if it has little or no effect on you directly. **An unshakable commitment to following your inner voice, whether you think of it as listening to God, your higher self or your own intuition, is where you will find the important answers or the direction you seek.**

Many ponder the mystery of whether there is life after death. At **Stage Seven, you are comfortable with whatever conclusion you reach to this great mystery and then remain keenly focused on this life.**

However, you also realize that although to contemplate the afterlife is natural, the ultimate reality is not that important, since either way you would probably not live this life any differently.

Your view of Spirituality at Stage Seven:

In reality, *Sevens* usually come to and live by their own custom blend of spiritual principles. Here are some examples of beliefs that are usually included in that blend:

❖ Laws of spirit apply equally to all of us (e.g., "We are all one"; "Our cores all want the same thing"; "We each have a unique purpose"; Karmic rewards and consequences apply to all actions we take, etc.).

❖ "Those who act badly do so because they lost their way."

❖ "We achieve solace with God by helping/serving others, including even our adversaries (on a personal level)."

❖ "The mystery of whether or not there is an afterlife has no bearing on how this life is lived."

As a *Seven*, your close relationships never have to be limited to those who share your mission, values, or beliefs. Not only can you tolerate those with diverse points of view, but you have a keen appreciation of them. You can choose to encourage those you love, to follow their passion, and reach their potential even if it causes you some personal inconvenience or short-term disappointments. In other words, even in these situations, you can still walk the walk.

A Stage Seven attitude about Sex : "Sex is a way to deepen the loving connection, sometimes even in a spiritual way, between me and my partner who love and care greatly for each other."

A Stage Seven couple who grows apart will never find the partners putting each other in the wrong in order to justify a break-up. Instead, they will have no problem seeing the other person as something separate from their role in the relationship and will react with gratitude for the good things they had, rather than anger about what the relationship did or did not provide. Yet, it should also be noted that many of the greats in virtually every field, have been panned by their children or spouses as "being there for the world, but not for them or their family." The son of one extremely famous luminary once told me, "I can *personally* attest to the adage that 'great men are not necessarily good men.'" Thus, **a reminder that a Stage Seven default in one area of life should not raise the expectation of being at that default stage in another area.**

How partners relate to each other in **Love Relationships/Marriages at Stage Seven**: Couple becomes a team that selflessly works together in a common mission outside of themselves (e.g., raising their children, being active in their community, etc.). You can easily put your partner first and may even put your partner's mission above your own without disdain or expecting a *quid pro quo*. You are beyond being attached to or governed by the expectations of each other.

Personal dilemmas at Stage Seven usually relate to your hooks in Stages Six and below when you find yourself at times torn, for example, between your higher purpose and your own self-gratification, wherever they might conflict. Nevertheless, to the extent that you are operating at Stage Seven, confusion dissolves quickly, you know the next step to take and your values do not fluctuate as life's circumstances change.

Another difference between a calling at Stage Six and a Stage Seven calling is that at Stage Six, the rewards usually are obvious. However, at Stage Seven, it's quite possible for you to be the only one to realize (or perhaps not even fully comprehend) the nature or scope of your impact. **For many people, including some of the greats throughout history, a Stage Six passion can lead to a Stage Seven consciousness and result.** For example, after Marconi discovered how to use radio waves, the world was never again the same. It is hard to imagine life today without radio, television, or even satellite technology. Nevertheless, he was not the first person to explore the existence of radio waves. Many others before him had that vision but were famously judged to be insane (i.e., hearing voices) or, at the very least, quite weird.

Indeed, **many *Sevens* have risked or ruined their reputations—and without personal conflict—to pursue their missions.** In Marconi's case; despite the scorn, ridicule, and adversity, he had the courage as well as the genius to bring his vision to full fruition. This is what puts his contribution at Stage Seven as opposed to Stage Six, which would have been enough had he discovered radio waves as a result of merely pursuing the work he loved to do (as Bell did with the telephone and Edison with numerous world-changing inventions). The difference between people like Marconi and all those who keep their "silly" ideas to themselves is part of the definition of Stage Seven. History is full of examples where the "crazy people" of one era are recognized as visionaries in another.

In fact, **history's Stage Seven icons and luminaries at their best, have the same intention you do when you unselfishly donate bone marrow, your time, or money.** For example, perhaps your contribution will save the life of someone who will somehow go on to have a major impact on the world. Like you, those legendary figures could rarely if ever control the *outcome* of their contribution—only their intentions and the behavior they exhibited to carry those out intentions. It was John D. Rockefeller—the Rockefeller who actually made all of the money—who said, "Think of giving not as a duty but as a privilege."

A Stage Seven view toward the purpose of Wealth: "Wealth is to help and share with others who lack the means you do."

At Stage Seven, you are in good company. Think of the greatest luminaries and sources of inspiration ever! At Stage Six, it is what you live for that's most important; but at Stage Seven, sometimes what you would die for is what sets you apart. The *Sevens* throughout history who are household names, are those who have made immeasurable contributions. As we understand the inner workings of some of history's greats, for example;

Jesus, Moses, Mohammad, Abraham Lincoln, Mahatma Gandhi, Martin Luther King, and Joan of Arc; we realize that **they were known for listening to their inner voices and following their deepest and strongest convictions.** As hardcore *Sevens*, they carried on despite being aware of the potential consequences to themselves including rejection, wholesale ridicule, giving up all of the material perks of a blessed life, and even life itself.

True spiritual leaders, saints, mystics, and sages are all examples of those with a Stage Seven default in those areas of life where we know them best. In many cases, their very existence is (or was) experienced as something holy. They are rare specimens of humanity. In a given time and place and with little or no effort on their part, they could often acquire huge followings. On the other hand, their mere presence sometimes represents such a threat to the segment of their contemporaries who are opposed to their often-radical views, that they become martyred. Many of the greatest *Sevens* were never in their lifetime to know the impact their contributions would make; but we assume that to them, the outcome would not actually have mattered as much as their efforts to manifest what they stood for. What probably kept them going was a rock-solid belief that they were much more than their physical bodies and anything else that is of this world. Most importantly, we all have the power to choose, act on and live by those same convictions. Abraham Lincoln—a member of this coveted group—said, "In the end, it's not the years in your life that count, it's the life in your years."

What is really behind the functioning of those greatest giants in history? Although they have all blazed gigantic trails, we scientists, of course, can only speculate about what was in their hearts. No valid evidence based psychological profiles of them exist. For an *icon* to be considered a true *Seven*, however, there needs to be evidence that more than their own gratification or external rewards was what motivated them to do what they did. That the results they achieved changed the world is not enough to put their contribution in the Stage Seven category. **The pivotal factor is their intention.**

For example, Bill Gates's contributions to the world through his work with Microsoft—numerous and giant as they are—would arguably still be motivated by his enormous and brilliant Stage Six passion for computers and business (a few might even say that a Stage Two business practice here and there may have entered into it as well). However, the unprecedented contributions of huge amounts of time and money he makes through the Bill and Melinda Gates Foundation clearly make him a Stage Seven luminary—in addition to being an iconic Six through the work for which he is best known.

The same is true for Albert Einstein, who famously said, "It is every man's obligation to put back into the world at least the equivalent of what he takes out of it." Einstein's work as a physicist (Stage Six) gave him the giant platform to impact our thinking about world peace and to apply his wisdom to many areas outside of physics (Stage Seven). Of course, we can only speculate. There is no doubt that Oprah Winfrey's show got her much praise and prestige (Stage Four), money (Stage Five), and enjoyment of her work (Stage Six), but it's what she gives back via her many causes such as education in Africa that would cause most to people think of her as a *Seven*.

How you might view taking care of your *aging* Parents at Stage Seven: "It's an honor and graciously loving endeavor to give back."

The *Sevens* in indigenous cultures are often the elders. Using the wisdom they have acquired over a lifetime, their purpose is often to be a source of guidance for both the younger generations and future ones that they themselves may never get to see.

How Families operate at Stage Seven: Family shares deep (perhaps spiritual) values and are guided by strong principles of service outside of the family or "tribe." Children are carefully and lovingly guided by example and through experience to become strong, respectful, productive, empathetic, and highly decent individuals.

Most of our Stage Seven contributions seem quite modest compared to those of the aforementioned giants; but they are by no means any less important in the grand scheme, merely because of the size of the league they play in.

Perhaps it's true that even many of the *Sevens* who had the greatest impact on the world, didn't discover Stage Seven until they were bored, unmotivated, or unfulfilled at Stage Six. However, nobody has to wait for that point in time. **What's most important is your intention behind a Stage Seven act.**

Assuming Stage Seven intentions were what motivated you, here are some examples of ways you can or perhaps have used your Stage Seven hooks to impact the world that's bigger than you and leave it a better place:

❖ Whenever you put the more pressing needs of your children, aging parents, or other family members or friends above your own, such as by caring for those in your life who may be sick or need some help financially—out of desire to help, of course, rather than obligation.

❖ Anytime you give your time or money to a charitable endeavor without regard to what comes back to you in the way of praise, recognition, or any other benefits—tangible or intangible.

❖ Putting your reputation on the line or postponing a goal of you own for another person, a mission or a cause greater than yourself—when it is unlikely that you will experience any direct benefits.

❖ Any act of random kindness that is unlikely to result in so much as a "thank you" from whoever benefits.

❖ Serving in the military or joining and working with a group that stands up for underdogs or the underprivileged as a means of making a difference.

❖ Reporting a crime or blogging about an injustice you are aware of.

❖ Being a whistleblower with potential consequences to yourself, in order to prevent a future injustice.

There are two common and popular templates for our heroes. Stage Six heroes are those such as Mohammad Ali, whose courage enable them to break away from a repressive pack in order to pursue their passions and make their statement. *Sixes* generally are pursuing their passions—at least initially—or their own curiosity, pleasure, sense of purpose related to a calling, and for the enjoyment that comes from maximizing their talent. Then there are our Stage Seven heroes. Some iconic examples include Abraham, King David, St. Francis, Florence Nightingale, and Mother Teresa along with those of her ilk who—whether or not officially—have ascended to sainthood. However, there are countless others who have somehow mobilized their best inner resources—such as love, faith, hope, wisdom, courage, charity, and creativity—to solve an insurmountable problem, create peace, save a life, or positively affect a segment of the world. We can't always name them, because they never sought notoriety for their contribution.

We rarely think of *Sevens* as having fun or needing to enjoy what they are doing. They do their mission because it needs to be done; and the inspiration for doing it—perhaps felt or understood only by them at the time—along with a sense of satisfaction or inner peace, is characteristically all the reward or reinforcement they need. And often they don't even take the time to savor that!

Even the Stage Seven cartoon, TV, and movie heroes who have been with us the longest, such as "Superman" and "The Lone Ranger," make it a point to pass on the enjoyment, rewards, recognition, and acclaim for their acts. Often, our heroes—whether authentic or imaginary—make it look easy. In real life, however, mustering the determination to reach that finish line and resist the urge to quit, rarely is easy. Yet, both Stage Six and Seven heroes tend to live by the old truism, "If you don't enter the lion's den you will never capture the lion."

Often it's significant pain of some kind that mobilizes the *Seven* in you to take definitive action. For example, anger can morph into determination, which can then be directed toward righting a wrong. However, **at Stage Seven, you are able to manage your expectations of people and events, so that your anger does not overpower you or block your ability to seek creative solutions**. *Sevens* are least likely to take things personally but they tend to be most frustrated when they are—or feel—powerless to correct an injustice or make their mission effective. In fact, **at Stage Seven, anger is still an internally destructive emotion, which serves no valid purpose other than to act as an alarm clock or initial activator of your energy.** Beyond that, it only hurts *you* to feel it. Thus, as a *Seven* you will be unlikely to allow yourself to stew with anger for long. Instead, you will most likely realize that prolonged anger is pointless. This makes letting go of your anger while taking decisive, rational, and effective action the most effective choice.

Here are some common triggers and other perspectives regarding these Emotions in you at Stage Seven: As with Stage Six, think of negative emotions and the frustration underlying them as wake-up calls that alert you that a problem needs to be solved, a situation needs to be accepted, or it's time to change course:

Anger—The injustice or misfortune of others (it could be one person, an entire society, or any segment of it) who are unable (as opposed to unwilling) to fend for themselves. You also have no problem letting go of (rather than holding on to) your anger at specific individuals or entities through forgiveness. You will not let your emotions interfere with a larger mission.

Anxiety—When worried about or feeling powerless to combat forces that oppose you when trying to make the necessary contribution that the mission or calling to which you are committed requires.

Depression—Failing to help those to whom you are committed via your calling or mission until you are able to mount a new "plan of attack."

Grief (over loss)—It is typically handled by knowing and accepting the non-permanence of life, life events, and situations that sadly or prematurely change. You understand that everyone grieves in their own way; therefore, you can tolerate and support those who grieve in an entirely different manner. When appropriate, you forgive the people or forces responsible for the loss (including yourself).

For *Sevens*, **forgiving those who have deliberately hurt them tends to be a no-brainer. Forgiving and letting go, when you get nothing in return from the other person (aside from your own inner peace, of course) is a Stage Seven event; and the ability to do that has been described to me by many as a major breakthrough.** As Nelson Mandela said, "Being angry is like drinking poison, then hoping your enemy will be the one who suffers as a result." *Sevens* do forgive easily, though they often have to endure harsh treatment from others as well as mete it out when having to stand up against a person or force that needs to be defeated.

Even at Stage Seven, you most certainly have good and bad days; but you are far past any expectations that life can or should be perfect!

A PERSPECTIVE ON THE TARGET STAGES

Is a Stage Seven default what you want? Before you answer "yes," understand that a default stage here is not for everyone. For many, the rewards of Stage Six are all you could possibly want right now. At Stage Six, you are at the pinnacle of healthy pleasure; and aside from where your Stage Seven hooks naturally take you there is no place else you may truly want to go. For others, Stage Six takes on a "been there, done that" quality that begs for something more. That new plateau, of course, is often what challenges you to go beyond yourself and enter Stage Seven territory.

When you climb to Stage Seven, people who have reliably been support-ive of you up until now often may not be able to understand your thinking. It's highly unusual for anyone to not benefit by climbing to Stage Six from the lower stages in an aspect of life. However, Stage Seven is at times another story, since this often involves bypassing and sometimes even dismantling important aspects of a blessed life that you have put together for yourself and others close to you. Still, **Stage Seven may be the ideal default stage for you as a parent, spouse, and friend, and/or in some aspects of your avocations, career, as well as any other aspect of life. These are choices you can make at any time.**

To both reach and stay at Stage Seven, follow your inner voice in whatever way you channel it. It will not mislead you. You need only listen to the message that comes to you in the form of an intuition, calling or desire. Just remember never to mistake a "should" for a calling (e.g., "I feel guilty about all I have, so I *should* give back", etc.). That's still charity and many would say still virtuous, but your motivation is Stage Three, not Seven.

There is a folk Zen saying: "The wise ones said it couldn't be done; the fool then came and did it." Many causes that have one chance in a thousand of reaching fruition would have been seen as too difficult or impossible in any of the lower stages; but at Stage Seven, that one in a thousand, million, or billion chance might be the only odds you need to bring passionate energy to some important mission. So stay in the lab until the experiment is a success. When your next mission is ripe, that same inner voice will let you know.

Regardless of whether a Stage Seven default is what you are striving for, you can still develop more hooks there; and I certainly encourage you to do that. Rarely if ever will you regret having Stage Seven *hooks*. The action steps that follow offer some help in that area.

GOING BEYOND YOURSELF: EXPANDING EVERYTHING STAGE SEVEN

To the extent that Stage Seven is already your default stage, there is no place to climb to—only new missions to consider and hooks from the lower stages to manage.

That which is Stage Seven is grounded in the truth you most deeply believe. This is the one characteristic that all of Stage Seven has common. **Be in tune with what your truth is and faithfully abide by it, wherever it takes you.**

If there is a recipe to reach Stage Seven and make it your default stage, it is to let the combination of your passion (to manifest something new) and your gratitude (for that which you already have), be the forces that guide you. *Just about all of the Stage Six action steps that focus on accessing your inner resources apply to Stage Seven as well.* In addition:

❖ Make a list of the **qualities of Stage Seven people** you know or know of and admire that in your eyes most put them in this stage.

❖ What do the *Sevens* you have noted **believe** about themselves and/ or their mission that you need to believe (or believe more) about yours? What do you have in common with them?

❖ What **purpose(s) outside of yourself** inspire(s) you or prompt(s) you to care deeply? It could be a charitable endeavor, political issue or candidate, some form of injustice, the environment, an ongoing world problem, or any matter affecting others beyond yourself that you believe you can and/or must become involved with. Your mission could be one that benefits a specific person or group (as close as an immediate family member[s] of your own, a complete stranger, or a specific population such as children or animals) who need some kind of help that you could provide.

❖ **Identify anything that comes to mind where you could see yourself expending the degree of energy toward something that you would have** (in the earlier stages) **if you were looking to benefit yourself directly.** What are some steps you are willing to take in order to maximize your impact toward that cause or causes you've identified? If nothing comes up, let it go for now (but make it a point to revisit this question often) and trust that a Stage Seven mission with the necessary level of inspiration will find or call upon you, when the time is right. Remember; the way in which most *Sixes* go toward Stage Seven is first by simply listening to their inner dialog, concerns and passions, and then by allowing themselves to be guided by them.

❖ Continue your **practice of meditation**, yoga and/or other ways of exploring and deepening your reservoir of wisdom and insight, as you did in Stage Six (see Chapter 6, page 152). Maintaining some form of practice as a permanent staple in your life is as least as important at Stage Seven.

❖ **Visualize** the potential impact on others and the world that your involvement could have. Then ask yourself if you are still interested or inspired.

❖ **Commit yourself** in every way possible to your intention to make a contribution to something larger than you are. You may want to do one Stage Seven act per day or per week. Random acts of kindness, charitable contributions of time or money, and any type of community involvement all count.

❖ Remember that by **acknowledging, supporting, and reinforcing** someone else's Stage Seven behavior or mission, you are in effect operating as a *Seven* yourself. You can take this simple step at any time, by contributing whatever time, money, or other resources you can to a cause you believe in that's being well championed by another committed person or organization.

❖ Spend one day **acting in the Stage Seven mode of being selfless**. In other words, try "walking the walk" of a *Seven* in as many ways as you can. Use this "act as if" technique to see how it feels and what fits you. In addition, never forget that as a *Seven,* there is never anyone outside of your own skin to impress.

❖ There are a few **attitudes you can employ** to manifest what you want in your life. For example, if *you believe, you already have what you want* (at the target Stages Six or Seven); the *Law of Attraction* tells us that you have dramatically increased the odds that it will show up for you very soon. Then, simply keep going, once you know you are on the right track. **Most importantly, make that unshakable commitment to be governed by your own choices, expectations, and inner resources. More than anything else, this commitment to yourself will keep you in your target stages.**

❖ Stage Seven **Resources** include biographies of history's greats, books and tapes on finding a calling/mission, or making various types of contributions to people, the planet and anything that helps you to become inspired—perhaps even on a spiritual level. There are many charities and worthy causes that would love to have you onboard to help them in some way. You'll find much of this and much more at *StageClimbing.com/resources* (Password: MyStageClimb).

In the next section, Part II, we will explore what it would mean to target Stage Seven as well as all of the seven stages, in many selected aspects of your life.

PART II

CALIBRATING YOUR
STAGE CLIMB

The Shortest Path
from Where You Are Now
to Where You Want To Be

Calibrating Your
Stage Climb

Acalibration is a type of measurement that's designed to fine-tune or pinpoint something with as much precision as possible. **In *Stage Climbing,* I use the term "calibration" as a *metaphor* for determining precisely *where you are now* in your *Stage Climbing* process so that you can establish exactly where *you want to be in any given area of your life*. Calibrations simply define each stage for any category to which you choose to apply the principles of *Stage Climbing*.**

In Part I, we focused on each of the seven stages separately. Now it's time to look at some of the many applications you can explore in your *Stage Climbing* process *across all seven stages*. This is a powerful way of putting your *Stage Climbing* process in action and actually observing the results!

The purpose of Part II is to help you to put it all together, by seeing what a default stage and/or hook at each of the seven stages looks like. This section contains numerous applications and examples of life at all seven of the stages that you can compare, reflect upon and tweak into tailor-made insights, attitudes, and goals that fit you exactly. This sampling by the stages is organized into categories of personal issues, relationships, organizations, and institutions as well as selected careers and professions. It's also an ongoing guide for you to consult often in order to stay on your chosen track. Each application and calibration could be expanded to become a complete book in and of itself! For that reason, I have included only the basics for each category and sometimes a special strategy or two. **You may choose to read this section completely or go straight to the applications that most apply to or interest you.** For your convenience, at the beginning of each chapter in Part II (as well as the Table of Contents at the very beginning of the book), there is a list of that chapter's applications.

Remember, the seven stages represent a choice of seven lenses that are available to you, through which to view any aspect of your life. Use these calibrations to make your hooks as well as your present and target default stages much clearer to you. They can also provide you with helpful insights for understanding or resolving an issue—past, present, or future. **Begin by identifying your default stage** —the stage you most identify with in that area of life (or the stage that represents the hook you are working on). Stage Five (which is presented in smaller bold type), is a good starting point for whenever your default stage is unclear to you, since it's generally the most neutral or dispassionate stage. **Then identify your target stage. Once you are clear as to where you are** (your present default stage) **and where you would like to be** (your target stage)**, the only task that remains is to clarify what you need to do to be operating out of your chosen target stage for that part of your life.** You can find help with that whenever you need it, by going back to the strategies at the end of each chapter in Part I (to work on the challenges unique to a particular stage) or Chapter 14 (which contains step-by-step strategies that incorporate all seven stages) as well as throughout the book.

Hooks in Stages One to Four may serve you in certain situations. This is a choice only you can make. However, those lower-stage hooks can also explain your limitations in that life area as well as the obvious benefits to climbing to the higher stages. Lower-stage calibrations can also be seen as examples and reminders of how you used to be (such as during a prior marriage or relationship, what made you choose your line of work, or how you were raised as compared to how you parent your own children). They can also provide you with vivid descriptions of others in your life or choices you are *now* making for yourself. In some cases, identifying your lower-stage hooks can be a wake-up call; or it could be the first step toward self-acceptance in that area of life. **Go back to reflect upon these whenever you can use a boost, some guidelines for relating to others on their own turf, or examples of different points of view.**

The higher-stage calibrations can represent a "rough draft" of your potential target stages or personal goals. There are reproducible calibration forms at the end of each chapter to help you fine-tune them (all reproducible forms are also available at *StageClimbing.com/worksheets, Password*: MyStageClimb). In some areas of your life, you may already be at your target, while others cry out to you for change. Stages Six and Seven (in larger bold type) are the highest default stage aspirations to consider for the areas of your life that matter most. As you will notice, **a Stage Seven calibration usually includes many of the best elements of Stage Six as well as unique Stage Seven characteristics. Your default stage also speaks to your ability to understand others operating at stages below it.** Thus a *Seven* can generally relate to and empathize with a *Six*, as a *Six* can with a *Five*, etc., but not necessarily the other way around.

Your default stage with respect to love relationships and other friendships, work and career issues, hobbies and avocations, your religion and spirituality, etc., can all be uniquely observed here as separate entities. **Once you identify your target, you can literally pick a new attitude or view of life. Sometimes by merely recognizing or working on a lower-stage hook, you will find that your default stage changes or is exactly on target.**

After pondering all the stages in a given category, you may find it helpful **to write down your goals** (aka chosen target stages) **and never stop tweaking them until they fit you and your life situation exactly.** In order to help keep yourself on track, refer to your goals often and until they become second nature or a hardwired part of you. **Chapter 14 offers many strategies to help you do just that.**

Think of climbing the stages as rising to those occasions of life you most cherish. Simply choose your goals and pick the target stages that most represent them. Once you know where you are and where you are going, relentlessly commit to doing whatever it takes to live by your choices!

CHAPTER 8

YOUR MASTER SETTINGS

Fine Tuning the Basic Calibrations
of Your Life by the Stages

I n this chapter, each category represents a different fundamental **Stage Climbing** application that applies to all of us. See which stage(s) in each category comes closest to describing you **now**, versus **where you would like to be**.

However, always keep in mind that through your hooks, you may be able to identify parts of yourself in each of the seven stages.

This chapter includes calibrations by the stages for the following:

YOUR ULTIMATE MASTER GOALS

This first calibration looks at your *Ultimate* **Master Goals,** which are different at each stage. Here they are, broken down by the stages. See which of these speak most to the various areas of your life and how you can best implement the ones you choose:

☐ **Stage Seven—To change the world or some part of it in some way—large or small... To have the greatest possible impact on those around you as well as any cause with which you involve yourself.**

☐ **Stage Six—To do what you love, are best at and enjoy most... To strive to fill your particular niche perhaps as well it could possibly be done—in your own unique way—by anyone, *but for your own intrinsic pleasure*... To love what you do and the people who matter most to you... To operate at your highest potential!**

☐ **Stage Five—To have affluence** (and/or whatever you believe is necessary for living a good and worthwhile life) **as well as having all of your roles optimally covered and comfortably balanced.**

☐ Stage Four—To be accepted, admired, respected, and/or loved by all of those who in any way matter to you, perhaps even regardless of whether or not you actually know them (or they know you) personally.

☐ Stage Three—To be conflict-free.

☐ Stage Two—To get exactly what you want, have fun, and stay under the radar screen— while avoiding any scrutiny, punishment or other consequences.

☐ Stage One—To have all your needs met with minimal effort or obligation on your part.

Note: At the end of every chapter in Part II (and at *StageClimbing.com/work-sheets*), there is a reproducible worksheet to help you make your own calibration for any issue or aspect of your life you would like to change, tweak, or better understand.

YOUR DEFAULT STAGE

This provides some guidelines for when your default stage is *age appropriate* (that is considered normal for your chronological age)… And when that *same* default stage (or a hook in that stage) *best* serves you as an adult:

☐ **Stage Seven—An across-the-board default Stage Seven here would be quite unusual** (if any real person could claim this at all) **and would suggest an inordinately high consciousness; but most of us have hooks here that can develop at any age. However, it's not unusual but highly desirable for almost anyone to strive for a default stage here in an area of life such as parent, spouse, partner, boss, etc. Whenever your focus shifts to an issue that does not affect you directly** (or is not necessarily your job or role to address) **and you feel the need to be giving back without direct benefits to you as a result—or find yourself asking, "How can I contribute or be of benefit to____, or do a 'labor of love' for____?" —you are operating at Stage Seven.**

☐ **Stage Six—A default stage here *breaks you out of the pack* starting in early adulthood, through the prime of life, and beyond. Hooks at Stage Six appear all throughout life—whenever you are doing what you truly enjoy, loving someone else, being uniquely creative, or when acting in accordance with purpose, calling, and the core that holds all of the diverse areas of your life together. Whenever you are motivated by your passions and desires, you are operating out of this target stage.**

☐ **Stage Five— Normal, starting in, and going beyond, early adulthood… When it's important to attend to and create a structure for the necessary areas of your life from which you may or may not get intrinsic enjoyment** (e.g. managing finances, doing chores, being around people you would rather not to be with, etc.); **in order to pro-**

vide for yourself and/or family, to maintain balance in your life and lifestyle and sometimes so that you can support your highest (target) stage endeavors.

☐   Stage Four—Normal stage throughout adolescence… When enjoying the "buzz" or bliss of being adored in a new romance, when selling yourself and/or in a situation where the image you put out to others is important; when it is your desire to fit into a chosen group where peer approval is required.

☐   Stage Three—Normal through late childhood… When in military type organizations or other situations where blending in and not questioning (or enforcing) the rules imposed on you is decidedly the best strategy; whenever a task or mission requires that others obey you.

☐   Stage Two—Normal for toddlers… and in prison, or when you are cornered and forced to respond in flight/fight mode. Or if you need to take unusually courageous, defensive, offensive or manipulative action in the moment without regard to long term consequences. Such a moment could arise in order to get through a crisis or immediate danger and/or when struggling to survive (for example, when stealing is the only option in order to feed your child); or when engaging in totally uninhibited sex or play.

☐   Stage One—The normal (and only) stage for infancy (and sometimes old age and toward the end of life)… When you choose or have no choice but to be taken care of by others; or to simply let yourself receive without needing to give back in kind (e.g. when needy, sick or infirm; or when letting yourself be pampered or on a vacation).

THE STAGE AT WHICH YOU ARE OPERATING

To determine the **Stage at Which You Are Operating** in a specific life area or with a specific situation, issue, thought, belief, attitude, or behavior, ask yourself the question(s) next to the stage they typify. If more than one seems to resonate, be aware of which stage you relate to the most—in the situation or aspect of life you are thinking about:

☐ **Stage Seven—Are the individual and/or collective needs of all others involved in this situation or big picture at least as important to me as my own?** (In addition to Stage Six below.)

☐ **Stage Six—Am I doing, or is my focus on, what I feel passionate about? What truly *feels* right, ethical, and best to me on a heartfelt level? What makes *me* feel best about myself?**

☐ **Stage Five—Am I taking into account that which best affects *all* aspects of my life, and the roles in it that I play?**

☐ Stage Four—Am I being influenced or governed by what others (who have no authority over me) approve of or think of me?

☐   Stage Three—Am I insisting that there is only one way or one set of rules (or beliefs) that I and/or everyone else involved should/must follow?

☐   Stage Two—Am I trying to get away with something, reap a reward I know I am not entitled to or would have no trouble seeing as offensive or problematic if someone else were doing the same thing at my expense?

☐   Stage One—Do I believe I am too dependent, helpless and/or weak to take the initiative and do what needs to be done? Am I being just plain resistant to taking measures I know would benefit me?

ATTITUDES OR BELIEFS BEHIND THE HOOKS THAT DISRUPT YOUR STAGE CLIMB

These are examples of the most common **Attitudes or Beliefs behind the Hooks that *Disrupt* Your Stage Climb** at the various stages. Resolve, on an ongoing basis, to challenge and change any of them that continue to get in your way or hold you back.

To challenge a self-defeating belief, **first ask yourself if that belief is "absolutely true."** Once you've established reasonable doubt as to whether the stifling belief is the truth *and* one you want to live by, **look for a higher stage attitude or belief that works for you to replace it**. Numerous examples of these appear throughout *Stage Climbing* (and in calibration format on the next calibration and throughout this chapter). However, the easiest way to get a higher stage alternative is simply to **ask yourself, "What would I prefer to believe, think or feel about this?"** Then make sure you tweak your answer to that question until the new attitude or belief fits you exactly. **This simple exercise puts your attitudes and beliefs under your control, which can be the critical factor for living your life at the target stages.**

In Chapter 14, there are many more examples of these beliefs and attitudes by the stages, along with a complete step-by-step strategy to help you choose the ones that will best work for you.

Here are the most common attitudes and beliefs with which to start this process, by the stages:

☐ **Stage Seven—"There are larger, grander, bolder, and more challenging missions to undertake."** (This is a disruption only to the degree that it undermines a mission you are committed to and not pursuing.)

☐ **Stage Six—"I must not only have passion, but also *must feel personally gratified around everything I do"* ... "Changing the world that is larger than me—or helping someone else—is not my mission, problem, or concern."**

☐   **Stage Five—"I** *must* **keep it all together and step up to the plate with respect to all of my roles (e.g., spouse, breadwinner, etc.), regardless of whether or not they provide me feelings of satisfaction or gratification."**

☐   Stage Four—"I *must* be loved or approved of by others and meet their expectations"… "Failing at something (e.g., a relationship, a job, an exam, or to meet a goal) makes me a failure (to myself, in the eyes of others or both)."

☐   Stage Three—"I *must* fit in by doing only what I should do and by being what I should be—that which is expected of me—or some dire consequence will result."

☐   Stage Two—"I *must* have and do whatever I want, regardless of the effect I (or my actions) have on others (or even the *long term* consequences I cause to myself)"… "I don't want to change"… "I will be whatever I have to be to get whatever I want at any given moment."

☐   Stage One—"I *must* be taken care of"… "I am inadequate"… "I am a victim with no way out"… "I am incapable of change or taking the initiative to better my life."

YOUR IDEAL ATTITUDES FOR REMOVING A LOWER-STAGE HOOK AND CLIMBING TO A HIGHER STAGE

These are your *ideal* **Attitudes for *Removing* a Lower-Stage Hook and Climbing to a Higher Stage** *that you have chosen* in any area of your life, according to the stage you are operating at presently. Tweak them to fit you exactly and then use them as motivators whenever you need to throughout your *Stage Climbing* process:

☐ **Stage Seven—"On to the next** (perhaps even a bigger or more challenging) **mission!"**

☐ **Stage Six—"Life is good; but there is more to life than my own gratification. It's time to focus on the world that's larger than myself."**

☐ **Stage Five—"I want to be doing what I love, what makes me feel best about myself, and to feel rewarded internally** (as well as externally).**"**

☐ Stage Four—"People who won't accept me for who I am are no longer worth my time and attention. There is much more to life than putting boundless energy into fitting in and/or the hope of getting others to admire or envy, love, and/or approve of me."

☐ Stage Three—"I am ready to start examining the unquestioned rules I have lived by (and/or that I have demanded others live by), and even to consider being more flexible and open to new ideas that are a better fit for me and my life."

☐ Stage Two—"Being excessively self-absorbed, has thus far not gotten me what I thought it would, what I truly wanted or satisfaction around what I have achieved."

☐ Stage One—"I am tired of being dependent and relying on others. I now want to begin taking charge of my own life."

In Chapter 14, there are many more examples of these beliefs and attitudes by the stages for removing problematic hooks along with a complete step-by-step strategy for putting them in place.

HOW CONFLICT IS TYPICALLY HANDLED

How **Conflict** is typically handled at each stage:

☐ **Stage Seven—By carefully listening to all points of view, considering each possibility, then making the decision or taking the action(s) that comes closest to best serving everyone involved— then staunchly standing by your decision or action, if necessary** (In addition to Stage Six and possibly Stage Five below).

☐ **Stage Six—By doing what feels consistent with your own core principles and purpose on a heartfelt level.**

☐ **Stage Five—By evaluating whether or not and how the source of your conflict is related to your bigger picture, then by taking the action(s) that come as close as possible to rebalancing your life.**

☐ Stage Four—By taking the road that produces the most validation from others and the least anxiety (no matter how things shake out).

☐ Stage Three—By following a set of black-and-white rules that clearly dictates who or what is right and who or what is wrong.

☐ Stage Two—By using some form of deception or strong-arm tactic (or doing whatever you have to do, (sometimes even without limits) to assure that you get your way. Thus, to get what you want at Stage Two, you might be extremely charming to manipulate someone, and extremely brutal to bully or force them, or any unique combination thereof—that is whatever it takes to control, overpower and win.

☐ Stage One—By doing what is easiest, such as latching on to, surrendering and/ or allowing some person or force that you consider stronger or "more capable" to take over the situation, thus allowing you to disown any conflict by obeying them and supporting their means of resolving the conflict.

A comprehensive menu for conflict resolution might include something from *each* stage. The key is to choose the most effective approach (or combination of those from several stages) for a given situation or issue. Most of us use our hooks in all of the stages at different times to resolve conflict.

HOW YOU WOULD DEFINE
HAPPINESS AND SUCCESS

This is how you would define Happiness and Success at each stage:

☐ **Stage Seven—Achieving the desired impact on a person/ people/or segment of the world you most care about ... Helping others and seeing them reap the benefits of your efforts ... Being fully connected to and engaged in your principles and purpose.**

☐ **Stage Six—The satisfaction of reaching a difficult goal or solving a tough problem... The feelings of excitement and being unstoppable that come from peak performance ... Feelings of relaxation and inner peace ... The bliss associated with the little things encountered in everyday life, such as the glow of a nice spring day, writing poetry, reading a good book or listening to your favorite music ... Exploring novelty and whatever makes you curious ... Doing what you really want to be doing** (e.g., what you are most passionate about, which often provides the most fun and enjoyment) **... When the distinction between work and play disappears ... Being with those you love and feeling deeply connected to them ... Unconditional self-acceptance ... When you can call up your playful and fun lower stage hooks at will, connect with those feelings of innocence that result and let yourself enjoy being child-like.**

☐ **Stage Five—Keeping all roles and relationships in balance and without problems ... Being effective and not overwhelmed ... Achieving affluence ... Finding a hobby and making time for pleasurable activities as another important way to balance your life and "recharge your batteries"** ("pleasurable activities" are those that provide fun and a "healthy alternative" to work and chores)**.**

☐   Stage Four—Achieving acceptance, approval, fame, and positive recognition (e.g., winning an award) ... Keeping personal relationships happy and conflict-free.

☐   Stage Three—Living your life "properly" by staying within the black-and-white parameters of your world ... Not drawing any negative attention to yourself ... Fitting in and doing what you "should" as well as doing your part to cause others around you, to "toe the line" as well ... The belief that your religious or spiritual path, and yours alone, is most in tune with the divine.

☐   Stage Two—Getting away with something ... Achieving dominance over people ... On the positive side, it's sheer joy and the lack of unwanted inhibition.

☐   Stage One—When life is easy with no demands or challenges to worry about ... Having a reliable, kind and dependable caretaker who is also a provider of all necessities.

The thing to remember here is that **the target stages put our happiness and success firmly under our control. This is what makes your stage climb so empowering!**

WHAT MOTIVATES YOU

What **Motivates** you at each stage:

☐ **Stage Seven—The opportunity to serve one person or many others in your larger community and/or the environment in a cause or mission you believe in ... To solve a problem that has an impact on people or things that are larger than you and your inner circle ... The satisfaction of touching one life** (as a parent, for example) **or bettering many lives.**

☐ **Stage Six—The feeling of satisfaction that comes when doing what you love and were meant to do as dictated by your unique talents at the deepest level ... Meeting a challenge ... Performing optimally with passion and ease as opposed to effort and difficulty ... Anything that triggers feelings of bliss ... The opportunity to be genuinely creative ... Feeling the best about yourself ... "If you aren't having fun doing it, either you're not doing it right or it's not the right thing for you to be doing."**

☐ **Stage Five—Money, benefits, privileges, respect from others for specific aspects of your life** (or a specific role you play such as a manager) **and how you handle your roles and responsibilities ... The need to have all chores and obligations under control.**

☐ Stage Four—Awards, celebrity, prestige, validation, praise, love, recognition, and approval of you (most often in a global way as opposed to merely a specific area of life such as with Stage Five) ... The opportunity to impress friends, acquaintances, colleagues, and relatives (or the public, in the case of celebrities).

☐ Stage Three—Not making waves, by doing whatever is expected of you and staying on the good side of whomever or whatever you consider an authority to be obeyed ... Your power to rule others.

☐   Stage Two—Opportunities to lure people in and/or reap rewards without paying the necessary dues or playing on a level field … Being irresponsible without consequences.

☐   Stage One—Whatever feels easiest, safest, least threatening and most comfortable.

Whenever I speak on the topic of motivation or coach managers on how to motivate subordinates, I emphasize that motivation is never a "one size fits all" process. Whether you are simply trying to nail down what motivates you or how to motivate someone else in order to be maximally effective, it's crucial to understand and acknowledge the default stage from which you (or whomever you wish to motivate) are starting.

In most cases, the target stages then appear quite appealing; as long as you and/or those you are motivating remember that it's still also okay to strive for "lower-stage" or *external* motivators such as money and awards. **The target stages will always offer the bonuses of personal satisfaction, enjoying what you do, and making a contribution to something larger than yourself.**

WHAT YOU ARE TYPICALLY
NEEDING AND SEEKING

What you are typically **Needing and Seeking** at each stage:

☐ **Stage Seven—To serve or help someone or something in distress** (or to prevent some adverse event from occurring) **... to spread your abundance and/or the feelings of fulfillment you have achieved for yourself to others in some general or specific area ... "Enlightenment."**

☐ **Stage Six—To accomplish something ... Enjoyment of what you do as well as who you spend time with ... Feelings of bliss or ecstasy.**

☐ **Stage Five- Normalcy ... "peace and quiet"... abundance... all roles functioning well.**

☐ Stage Four—To "find yourself"... To "*be* somebody"... To "make something respectable of yourself"... To feel liked/loved and/or accepted by those in your orbit... Self-acceptance.

☐ Stage Three—To please authority and be pleased or appeased when *you are* the authority.

☐ Stage Two—The easiest way to satisfy your *short-term* or immediate needs and desires.

☐ Stage One—Safety and security.

Be especially aware of whether or not you are putting energy into seeking what you really don't want or no longer need—perhaps merely by habit. If so, where could that energy better serve you now?

TO PROBLEM SOLVE

To **Problem Solve,** when stuck or in crisis, here is where you would typically turn for help at each stage:

☐ **Stage Seven—Spiritual master of some type who helps you to transcend your ego and access your inner resources to search for the answer(s) you are seeking ... Meditation, prayer, yoga, or any method that works for you to turn inward for guidance or direction.**

☐ **Stage Six—Chosen mentor or coach in the specific area you need help, who is personally beyond the problem or challenge you are struggling with ... Whatever practices best connect you with your inner resources** (such as meditation, for example)**... Many of the same practices as Sevens** (see above)**.**

☐ **Stage Five—Self-help books** (such as this one) **and audio/video programs ... Peers** (talking to people you value) **and all types of peer groups that focus on personal growth or a specific challenge you are trying to meet.**

☐ Stage Four—Psychotherapy for treatment of such conditions as anxiety, depression, anger management, self-esteem issues, and relationship conflicts ... Taking the advice of and adopting the accepted approach of those around you.

☐ Stage Three—The Bible, church, a clergyperson, or a charismatic leader who clearly spells out the rules and/or authority that needs to be adhered to in order to resolve the issue ... An exception or "loophole" in a rule you believe you must follow and someone (a creditable friend, family member, or therapist) to help transition you to a new way of thinking.

☐ Stage Two—Legal counsel ... Behavior modification and other concrete forms of counseling to change errant habits that threaten relationships or freedom.

☐ Stage One—Someone you see as more capable than you are to take over problem and allow you to resume a conflict free existence as much as possible ... Medication and/or drug detoxification for chemical issues.

In my practice, I have seen many sometimes-heartbreaking examples of how people have suffered far longer and more severely than they had to, simply because they were not receiving the type of help that could most effectively help them resolve their issue.

Therefore, a main function of this book is to offer some clarity about this along with resources to help you choose the right source of help. The strategies in this book and discussions in each chapter offer resources that can generally be most helpful by the stages. Additional resources can be found at *StageClimbing.com/resources.*

How to **Respond Optimally to Adults** who are operating at each stage:

☐ **Stage Seven—With gratitude and support for what they contribute.**

☐ **Stage Six—Show them genuine interest about what they do best … To the extent possible, interact with their "passionate selves."**

☐ **Stage Five—Show them respect for how they generally keep their roles in balance and manage important aspects of their lives … Encourage them first to be selective about and then to maximize whatever they take on.**

☐ Stage Four—Praise them, yet be mindful of what is often an inability for them to distinguish between their behavior and their *"self"* as a "total person." Thus avoid all but the most specific criticism or feedback. However, also watch out for their tendency to oversell themselves to you in order to be liked/loved and/or to earn your respect.

☐ Stage Three—Get them on board with your mission; and create the mechanism for them to staunchly support and help you accomplish it… Avoid any argument or debate that puts you at odds with any strong belief they may have (e.g., politics or religion)... When it's possible and in your best interest, be assertive regarding your right to see things differently.

☐ Stage Two—Set limits with extremely clear consequences for violating them… Avoid involvement with them to the extent it is possible if they are in a position to hurt you by being manipulative or deceptive.

☐ Stage One—Establish clear and unambiguous boundaries between you and them… Support any efforts they make to help themselves… Help them to feel secure and problem free… Minimize your expectations of them to produce any results.

This calibration reminds us that no matter how much we are able to execute our own stage climb, we still need to be aware of and deal with others at the stages from which *they* operate.

WORKSHEET

Use this reproducible worksheet to Make Your Own *Stage Climbing* **Calibration for Any Area of Life, Problem, or Issue You Are Working On** [Use calibrations in this section as appropriate for guidelines and reference. For additional help or to download this worksheet, visit *www.StageClimbing.com/worksheets* (Password: MyStageClimb)].

☐ **Stage Seven**

☐ **Stage Six**

☐ **Stage Five**

☐ Stage Four

☐ Stage Three

☐ Stage Two

☐ Stage One

CHAPTER 9

YOUR EMOTIONS

What Triggers Anger, Anxiety, Depression, and Grief at Each Stage?

A nger, anxiety, depression, and grief are among our most common emotions. In this chapter, you'll find calibrations for each of them along with the most likely triggers for these emotions, by the stages. To make the best use of this chapter, notice how your hooks in the lower stages trigger emotions that can throw you off balance in just about any part of your life. **The more you can make a conscious commitment to do a better job in managing your expectations of others and events as well as choosing your battles, the more you become the master of these emotions, rather than the other way around.**

Use this chapter to gain insight on:

In Chapter 14, use Breakthrough Strategies #2 and #3 to address the hooks and issues that power these emotions whenever they are problematic to you.

What typically triggers Anger in you at each of the seven stages:

☐ **Stage Seven—The Injustice or misfortune of others** (could be one person, an entire society or any segment of it) **who are unable** (as opposed to unwilling) **to fend for themselves. You also have no problem letting go of (rather than holding on to) your anger at specific individuals or entities through forgiveness. You will not let your emotions interfere with your larger mission.**

☐ **Stage Six—Anything that you believe needlessly distracts you from pursuing your passion. You see forgiveness as a means to let go of an unpleasant situation in order for you to get back to positive emotions and areas of genuine interest.**

☐ **Stage Five—Things or people you perceive as overwhelming you or throwing your life out of balance or control. At Stage Five, you still have difficulty forgiving adversaries as long as any remnants of an anger-producing situation remain.**

☐ Stage Four—Rejection or disappointment from others whose approval or love is on some level important to you, jealousy in relationships, or a betrayal (real or perceived) by someone you thought was in your camp. Sometimes anger is turned inward to create depression or self-esteem issues.

☐ Stage Three—Others who do not follow the same rules or have the same values and beliefs that you do. At its most extreme, this could include prejudice, hatred, or bigotry. Anger at this stage often takes on or results from an attitude of "self-righteousness."

☐ Stage Two—Being caught, punished (or turned in), confined, or called upon to take responsibility for your behavior. Revenge is often the first response to adversaries. Low frustration tolerance or discomfort anxiety regarding anything that is not going your way will characteristically trigger in you an angry and often vicious response.

☐   Stage One—Being abandoned, neglected, or deprived by whomever you depend on as your protector, provider, or caretaker. Anger sometimes triggers feelings of helplessness and hopelessness.

Whenever anger is more than simply a passing wake-up call, it's very much in your interest to bring it under control. Visit StageClimbing.com/ downloads (Password: MyStageClimb), for your complimentary download of *Overcoming Your Anger*, an anger management MP3 audio that I wrote, which has helped many people around the world to gain mastery over this often-difficult emotion.

What typically triggers **Anxiety** in you at each of the seven stages:

☐ **Stage Seven—When worried about or feeling powerless to combat forces that oppose you when trying to make the necessary contribution that the mission or calling to which you are committed requires ... The prospect of not bringing your mission, calling, or contribution to fruition.**

☐ **Stage Six—The prospect of failure** (or being unable) **to pursue or receive satisfaction from something you passionately enjoy.**

☐ **Stage Five—Becoming unglued as your roles expand; or worry that circumstances will overwhelm or render you unable to fulfill your roles ... The awareness of any form of self-sabotage, where you somehow (usually by virtue of your lower-stage hooks) defeat your own purpose or inadvertently get into your own way.**

☐ Stage Four—Being (or the prospect of being) rejected, embarrassed or seen as inadequate, "a failure" or of lesser worth by someone (or many, e.g., your peer group or even a segment of the public) whose validation is important to you ... Worries about losing a love relationship through some form of rejection.

☐ Stage Three—Leaving your comfort zone, especially when "the rules" aren't clear ... The possibility of being damned, punished, or even killed for doing or perhaps even thinking something different than whatever would be acceptable to a feared authority (real or imagined) ... "Shades of gray."

☐ Stage Two—The prospect of being caught, punished, or exposed for your deliberate antisocial activities ... Losing your freedom or cover ... *Twos* often have a built-in immunity to anxiety. Thus, it can take a lot for them to feel any anxiety at all.

Stage One—Fears concerning such things as abandonment, physical, or mental disability and extreme poverty ... Being, living, and/or dying alone where you would be or even merely feel unable to survive or change a dreaded fate.

If you can use some help with anxiety or such expressions of it as excessive worry, visit StageClimbing.com/downloads (Password: MyStageClimb), for your complimentary download of ***Overcoming Your Anxiety***. I wrote this program to help you attack anxiety at its roots, as well as give you numerous techniques for bringing it under your control whenever it arises.

What typically triggers **Depression** in you at each of the seven stages:

☐ **Stage Seven—Failing to successfully carry out a commitment and/or help those to whom you are committed via your calling or mission.**

☐ **Stage Six—Being unable to pursue or enjoy that which you love or are passionate about and do best.**

☐ **Stage Five—Having an important role in your life** (e.g., a relationship, financial situation. or career) **negatively change in a way that is undesirable to you and out of your control to reverse or correct … Boredom with your life that on the surface has "everything going for it"… A serious illness that threatens your ability to fulfill any or all of your most important chosen roles.**

☐ Stage Four—A major rejection or scorn by a person or a group whose opinion, you believe, has significance to you … When your self-esteem takes a major hit or you put yourself down for some failure, real or perceived … Relationship issues, especially those regarding your feelings for each other that you or your partner are unable or unwilling to address.

☐ Stage Three—Being unable to find the answers to a crisis or dilemma within the narrow boundaries of your comfort zone, or the inability to get hold of a clear direction and/or feeling of reassurance from the "book of rules" to which you subscribe.

☐ Stage Two—Having unpleasant (and usually unexpected) consequences for your behavior, from which you cannot escape … Depression for *Twos* is generally short-lived and will usually convert to anger as soon as an enemy (for the purposes of blame) is established.

☐ Stage One—How you perceive yourself as a result of feelings of grief, inadequacy, hopelessness, or self-pity … The overwhelming prospect of being abandoned or having to survive alone.

Depression is a condition that can be medical, psychological, or both.
More importantly, it can negatively affect the quality of your life and every aspect
of it. To gain an understanding about depression, along with strategies and
exercises to manage it as well as information about when more treatment is
necessary, visit StageClimbing.com/downloads (Password: MyStageClimb), to
download your complimentary MP3 audio, ***Overcoming Your Depression***.
I wrote this program to be a first step toward bringing your mood under your
own control.

How **Grief** (over loss) is typically handled by the stages:

☐ **Stage Seven—By knowing and accepting the non-permanence of life, life events, and situations that sadly or prematurely change … You understand that everyone grieves in their own way, therefore you can tolerate and support those who grieve in an entirely different manner … When appropriate, you forgive the people or forces responsible for the loss** (including yourself).

☐ **Stage Six—By understanding and allowing the process of detachment to happen via your healthy, natural, and emotional grieving process** (e.g., purging painful feelings by crying and then letting go of whatever you have lost in due time) **… Consciously learning how to tolerate the "void of loss" before merely filling that void with another version of whatever you have lost** (such as a new job or relationship).

☐ **Stage Five—Putting the pieces** (and roles) **of your life back together again, often by finding a replacement** (or substitute) **for whatever** (e.g., a job) **or whomever** (e.g., a love relationship) **you have lost.**

☐ Stage Four—By blaming yourself for somehow causing the loss as well as for any existing unfinished business that may remain.

☐ Stage Three—You practice traditional grieving rituals (such as those of your religion or community)… You may find yourself judging others who grieve differently than you do as wrong.

☐ Stage Two—Loss may become yet another excuse for acting out and displacing feelings such as anger on to others.

☐   Stage One—Self-pity can be quite intense along with anger (at who or what you have lost) over *your* difficulty about separating emotionally. You may also be in denial about the loss (e.g., difficulty believing that someone is *really* gone), or overwhelmed by a loss resulting in conditions such as PTSD (post-traumatic stress disorder), or even major depression requiring intensive treatment.

We each grieve in our own way. When we allow ourselves to express our feelings of sadness, they tend to clear out of us naturally and usually lead to acceptance of the loss. However, when this process becomes blocked as it often does for a variety of reasons, grief can lead to chronic depression, anger, anxiety, and a variety of other stifling emotions and conditions.

It's important to allow your grieving process to take place organically. To the extent that you are not able to accept your loss within a reasonable time, look for the emotion that your grief may have morphed into. Strategy #3 in Chapter 14, page 297, is a good exercise for addressing this situation when you find yourself unable to accept a loss.

WORKSHEET

Use this reproducible worksheet to Make Your Own *Stage Climbing* Calibration for Any Area of Life, Problem, or Issue You Are Working On [Use calibrations in this section as appropriate for guidelines and reference. For additional help or to download this worksheet, visit *www.Stage-Climbing.com/worksheets* (Password: MyStageClimb)].

☐ **Stage Seven**

☐ **Stage Six**

☐ **Stage Five**

☐ Stage Four

☐ Stage Three

☐ Stage Two

☐ Stage One

CHAPTER 10

YOUR VALUES

Personal Issues and Attitudes along with Other Common States of Mind by the Stages

This chapter describes **how we typically view certain key aspects of life** through the lenses of each of the seven stages. See how you relate to them with respect to your hooks and default stage in that area of life. Be especially aware of any changes you would like to make as you recognize new hooks for the first time.

By the stages, here's how you are most likely to view these selected aspects of your value system:

Typical *Best* attitudes about your Career and the work you do by the stages:

☐ **Stage Seven—"It's an excellent way** (or the best way I can) **to make the contribution I want to make the most."**

☐ **Stage Six—"I love what I do ... It's what comes easiest to me, feels most flowing and natural ... I wouldn't want to be doing anything else ... I feel fulfilled irrespective of the financial and other extrinsic rewards I get ... I get pleasure from the challenge of it ... If I never again had to work, I would still choose to be doing this."**

☐ **Stage Five—"It's lucrative** (or pays the bills) **and/ or gives me something to do and/or nice contacts and perks."**

☐ Stage Four—"It gives me prestige and/or a steady stream of good people contact."

☐ Stage Three—"It is the type of work my family/ 'tribe' does (or always did) or values most."

☐ Stage Two—"It's an easy way to find lots of opportunities to feel powerful by manipulating and bullying others as well as (perhaps) to make easy money."

☐ Stage One—"It's safe and provides me with feelings of security."

If you cannot identify with the target stages Six and Seven careerwise, you may want to consider this a wake-up call. I have met very few people who couldn't find a way to operate at least out of Stage Six with respect to some major aspect their careers if they really wanted to and were willing to do what it takes to get there. And although getting there may certainly take a lot of effort, the rewards are immeasurable! The next page contains a calibration that takes this concept a step further.

Typical reasons for making **Job or Career Changes:**

☐   **Stage Seven—To move on to serve a higher cause.**

☐   **Stage Six—To seek a greater, more fulfilling, or a more enjoyable personal challenge where *I am doing what I love and really want to spend my precious time doing it!***

☐   **Stage Five—For advancement, more money, fewer hours, easier commute, better contacts and/or benefits, etc.**

☐   Stage Four—May seek change because of not "fitting in," not getting along with, not liking or not being liked by the boss or co-workers … For more prestige … To follow an *emotionally* nurturing boss.

☐   Stage Three—Environment was too unstructured … Need more structure.

☐   Stage Two—Was exposed for violating policy, claiming undeserved credit or other forms of dishonesty or unethical behavior.

☐   Stage One—Job became too challenging and/or less secure.

You may be aware that a job or career change is necessary for you, but feel stuck. If you currently are nowhere near a Stage Six default with your work but wish you were, take this opportunity to ponder what you really want to be doing with this part of your life. Make a list of all the excuses that are holding you back and deal with each one separately, or, for the sake of this exercise, pretend that your excuses simply don't exist.

I have helped folks of all ages and life circumstances to get into careers that were thought to be the domain of people much younger, with more money, fewer responsibilities, etc. *In the end, all things are possible unless you persist in believing they aren't.*

What career or job would put you in your target stage careerwise? Identify the one or ones that would, and as a first step, become committed to getting the information you need to begin taking action. Most importantly, leave no stone unturned in pursuing your dream! Revisit the Stage Six strategies, starting on page 148, and review the resources at *StageClimbing.com/resources* (Password: MyStageClimb) for more help in this area.

Your view of **Charity** **(giving/receiving of time, money, or other tan-gibles to/from others) is a very personal matter.** As you can see, it's not a given that charity is always a Stage Seven endeavor. Thus, your values prevail:

☐ **Stage Seven—To move the world or a segment of it in the right direction with respect to something you feel strongly about, where nothing extrinsic for yourself is expected in return ... Sevens need no recognition for their acts of charity and kindness.**

☐ **Stage Six—Doing some form of work you love** (which you may not have the opportunity to do in your day job or otherwise) **for a cause you believe in.**

☐ **Stage Five—To fill a role in your world that recognizes that those who are more fortunate are expected to provide ... To get tax deductions ... To network with people who may be of some benefit to you in another area of your life ... To do your part in resolving a problem that you become aware of** (which may possibly even affect or have affected you or someone you know or care about)**.**

☐ Stage Four—It's a means for getting recognition, awards, praise, and/or to feel good about yourself.

☐ Stage Three—Charitable giving of time or money is seen as "mandated" or a require-ment for members of the group or religion to which you belong ... Or you believe you "should be" more charitable than you truly want to be.

☐ Stage Two—To find a way to defraud a charity or set one up to use as a scam.

☐ Stage One—To be the recipient of needed help from others or an organization whose charitable values identify you as a "person in need."

When you are looking for ways to best utilize your Stage Seven hooks, infinite possibilities exist. *StageClimbing.com/resources* (Password: MyStageClimb) has contact information for numerous charitable organizations that can use whatever help—time, money, etc.—you can give them. You are a *Seven* in this area, whenever your contribution is heartfelt. And remember the old adage that "charity begins at home."

Your attitude choices regarding the **Environment** by the stages:

☐ **Stage Seven—"Sacrifice or conserve now for the benefit of future/unborn generations."**

☐ **Stage Six—"Do work you enjoy toward preserving it"** (often motivated by a love of nature and the outdoors)**.**

☐ **Stage Five—"It is the responsibility of every good citizen to do his/her share."**

☐ Stage Four—"I'll be admired by others who value the environment, if I am (for example) energy efficient."

☐ Stage Three—*"It's the law* to recycle."

☐ Stage Two—"If I have to wreck it in order to benefit me or my business, too bad."

☐ Stage One—"It's not my responsibility to worry about"... "I'll live off of the environment and use it to my advantage as much as I need to" … "The environment exists for me."

As with charity, only you know your real motives here.

We feel differently about ourselves (and in each area of our lives), according to the stage at which we are operating. Here is how you might generally view your **Self** at each stage:

☐ **Stage Seven**—Grateful ... Determined ... Caring ... Selfless.

☐ **Stage Six**—Passionate ... Happy ... Loving ... Self-accepting ... Whenever you are operating out of Stage Six, you are feeling *the best about yourself!*

☐ **Stage Five**—Content ... Overwhelmed or underwhelmed ... Neutral.

☐ Stage Four—Anxious ... Needing to be loved and/or accepted ... Insecure ... (The opinion of others about you is what often determines your own view of yourself.)

☐ Stage Three—Righteous ... Safe ("as long as I remain a 'good person" or in compliance) ... Powerful or powerless, depending on whether you are the one making or obeying the rules.

☐ Stage Two—Omnipotent... "Above it all."

☐ Stage One—Helpless ... Inadequate ... Dependent.

Which view(s) of your*self* is most appealing? When making a choice or decision**, try factoring in how you might feel about *yourself*** with respect to each of your choices.

Your View of **Spirituality** by the stages:

☐ **Stage Seven**—(In reality, Sevens characteristically come to and live by their own custom blend of spiritual principles. However, these are usually included in that blend.)—**Laws of spirit apply to all of us** (e.g., "We are all one"; "Our cores all want the same thing"; "We each have a unique purpose"; "There are karmic rewards and consequences to consider"; etc.) **... "Those who act badly do so because they lost their way"... "We achieve solace with God by helping/serving others, including even our adversaries** (on a personal level)**"... "The mystery of whether or not there is an afterlife has no bearing on how this life is lived."**

☐ **Stage Six**—Just as Sevens do, Sixes march to the beat of their own drum spiritually— **"Higher self resides inside of each of us, whose function is to connect us with our unique strengths, calling, purpose, principles and mission; and our commitment to reach our potential by pursuing these things"** ... **Spiritual self** (or lack thereof) **is heartfelt and chosen. It may often call upon you to connect with and feel love and awe for the beauty of nature and the world.**

☐ **Stage Five**—**"Spirituality** (often in the form of the organized religion that is most familiar) **as well as observing religious traditions, is an important part of life." How-ever, the role of spirituality in life often is confusing and unsettled. In reflective moments, you ponder such questions as "What is the meaning of life?" or, "Is this all there is?" (as well as questions about such things as afterlife, dilemmas about God's role in tragedy and injustice, etc.).**

☐ Stage Four—"God is benevolent" … "If I do the right thing, God will love me."

☐ Stage Three—Whether an Atheist, a Fundamentalist_____ (name the religion) or anything in between—there is a strict and inflexible set of rules to be followed … "God is malevolent and unforgiving"… "If I disobey God, I incur his wrath (burn in hell, etc.)" … Certain religious dictums teach us how followers are a different and presumably better (or chosen) class of person than are non-followers.

☐ Stage Two—"There is no God" … "There are no consequences or rewards (karmic or otherwise) beyond the obvious that exist in this world (such as the justice system, for example)" … "If you are not caught or exposed and punished, you have gotten away with something completely"… "What you see is what you get."

☐ Stage One—" 'God' is whoever (or whatever) takes care of me."

Your spiritual beliefs are a part of you that can provide inner guidance for many aspects of your life. Many people consider their spiritual selves to be their most reliable source of truth. Practices such as prayer and meditation tend to open this channel wider and wider. In addition to the information in Chapters 6 and 7, *StageClimbing.com/resources* (Password: MyStageClimb) will point you to many diverse views and sources of information and guidance to consider.

Your view of the purpose of **Wealth** by the stages:

☐ **Stage Seven—"Wealth is a way to give back, help and share with others who lack the means I do."**

☐ **Stage Six—Its main purpose is to ensure that you can continue to pursue what you enjoy the most, but not necessarily a factor that motivates you.**

☐ **Stage Five—To acquire material possessions ... To provide for yourself and family and keep all necessary areas of your life functioning optimally ... To not have to work ... To invest and reinvest.**

☐ Stage Four—To acquire status, be envied and accepted by those who are impressed by the trappings of wealth.

☐ Stage Three—To acquire authority and followers of your rules.

☐ Stage Two—To acquire raw and absolute power.

☐ Stage One—To acquire security.

You don't need to be wealthy per se to examine your values here. For example, have you ignored important dreams and sources of fulfillment in order to pursue or maximize your financial goals? If so, has that worked out for you or become a source of regret? Many who have consulted me over the years have been able to change their lives dramatically after clarifying some common dilemmas.

For example: doing the work they love versus what is more favorable financially; staying in an unfulfilling marriage versus taking the financial hits of divorcing when achieving a more peaceful or fulfilling life will result; or pursuing a love relationship that is at best lukewarm emotionally but rewarding financially. These are simply common examples.

I strongly suggest that you set some time aside to ponder some of the "big picture" financial questions that are relevant in your life. Do this with the understanding that there are no right or wrong answers, only choices that are more or less consistent with the path to your highest potential in the most important parts of your life.

It's also been my experience that somehow the money does follow, when your passions and purpose are your guiding forces. Nobody can *guarantee* that, but at worst, you might gain a higher degree of inner peace as a "consolation prize"!

WORKSHEET

Use this reproducible worksheet to Make Your Own *Stage Climbing* Calibration for Any Area of Life, Problem, or Issue You Are Working On [Use calibrations in this section as appropriate for guidelines and reference. For additional help or to download this worksheet, visit *www.StageClimbing.com/worksheets* (Password: MyStageClimb)].

☐ **Stage Seven**

☐ **Stage Six**

☐ **Stage Five**

☐ Stage Four

☐ Stage Three

☐ Stage Two

☐ Stage One

CHAPTER 11

YOUR RELATIONSHIPS

Understand Family, Friendships, Love Relationships, Marriage, Parenting and Sex, by the Stages

The principles of *Stage Climbing* can explain much about your relationships and the issues related to them at all levels. This chapter provides calibrations that can help you **see how people—past or present—fit into and shape your life.** In most cases, you can choose to view or operate any relationship from a higher stage. Additionally, **it's always possible to gain a better understanding and acceptance of someone by identifying the stage(s) at which you relate to each other.** Also, use these calibrations to gain insight regarding how you (and/or someone else in your life) may have operated in a past relationship.

Specifically, in this chapter you will find calibrations by the stages for the following:

How **Families** operate at each stage:

☐ **Stage Seven—Family shares deep** (often spiritual) **values and is guided by both love and strong principles of service both inside and outside of the family or "tribe"... Children are carefully and lovingly guided by example and through experience to be strong, respectful, empathetic, and highly decent individuals.**

☐ **Stage Six—The whole is greater than the sum of its parts ... Family is held together with love and respect ... Family members support each other's passions, strengths, ambitions, and personal growth. They encourage each other to stay on the path to their highest potential.**

☐ **Stage Five—When each member is functioning well in his/her family role, the family thrives. Problems occur when a member deviates from the family norm for a reason that is not clear to the other members** (e.g., when siblings of similar ages are in different stages or children function at higher stages than their parents or other elders, etc.)**.**

☐ Stages 4—When functioning well, members who are headed by a benevolent matriarch/patriarch serve to validate each other. When dysfunctional, self-esteem and self-confidence are unwittingly weakened. Children who witness a lot of anxious behavior throughout their formative years are especially vulnerable to a variety of anxious reactions and anxiety disorders that result from this environment ... Approval and validation is often withdrawn or withheld as punishment.

☐ Stage Three—Family is run rigidly and with an "iron hand" by a tough matriarch/patriarch in an authoritarian manner where stereotypical roles are unquestioned. Respect is demanded, but not necessarily earned. Strict and sometimes severe punishment is mandated for failing to meet the often-stern expectations. Children usually go into the line of work and adopt lifestyles that are expected of them more out of guilt, fear, and lack of reflection (i.e., without even considering other alternatives) than by choice ... Family members are sometimes ostracized or labeled "black sheep "as a punishment for not "toeing the line" or for failing to fit in.

☐   Stage Two—Deception, anger, abuse (can be emotional, physical, and/or sexual), or extreme hedonism without regard for consequences are the staples of this highly dysfunctional family environment.

☐   Stage One—Family members often are extremely enmeshed with each other and feel unable to face the outside world with even a minimal degree of competence or independence.

When operating as a family unit from the target stages, it's obvious that every member benefits on a long-term basis. What changes—whether major ones or small tweaks—can bring different aspects of how you relate as a family to those target stages? Often, simply the awareness of certain blind spots and alternatives to them can trigger a major breakthrough where one is needed.

Ingredients of a **Friendship** by stages:

☐ **Stage Seven—There is a deep mutual respect for the other person and his/her respective commitments and impact** (even if your beliefs, values, or missions differ or are in opposition to each other) **... When appropriate, you have no problem choosing to put the needs of a friend above your own.**

☐ **Stage Six—The connection is one of love and to the core of a person, which underlies and transcends all of his/her roles as well as the circumstances that initially brought you together as friends.**

☐ **Stage Five—Friends are those with whom there is a common role** (e.g., same church, neighbors, colleagues, co-workers, tennis, or travel partners, etc.) **... When the role changes, often the relationship does as well ... Friendships are generally supportive where they can be and don't conflict with other priorities.**

☐ Stage Four—Friends tend to validate and praise each other.

☐ Stage Three—Friends are those who have the same beliefs and/or a connection to the same authority.

☐ Stage Two—Friends are "co-conspirators."

☐ Stage One—Friends are often "fellow victims" or victims and "rescuers."

Take an inventory of the stage(s) at which you relate to some of your most important friends. Be aware of which friendships are adding to your life and which are not. If necessary, how can the ones you value be upgraded?

Love Relationships / Marriages

This calibration suggests that no matter where you are in your *Stage Climbing* **process, there is a relationship for you.** From which stage do you now operate? How about your partner? **Use this calibration to discuss ways you can make your relationship work better** by supporting each other. Also, clarify how you can make the climb together to optimize your relationship. This exercise could permanently raise the bar for both of you, as I have seen it do with so many couples I have worked with. If you are not currently in a marriage or love relationship, but are looking for one, be aware of what you are seeking in a prospective partner as well as where a climb in this part of your life would benefit you. **Here is how partners typically relate to each other by the stages:**

☐ **Stage Seven—Couple becomes a team who selflessly work together in a common mission outside of themselves** (e.g., their children, their community, etc.) **... Can easily put partner first and may even put partner's mission above one's own without disdain or expecting a quid pro quo ... Are beyond being attached to and/or governed by expectations.**

☐ **Stage Six—Partners look to each other as a person to love and support as opposed to someone from whom love, sex, support, and validation are merely expected. There is genuine caring, intimacy, and respect that is not predicated on what you get back. When Sixes tell their partner "I love you," they mean just that.**

☐ **Stage Five—Each partner dutifully fulfills the other's spouse/ relationship slot and all that it entails** (e.g., sex partner, financial partner, companion, co-parent, someone with whom to share and be intimate, etc.) **... Partners are not necessarily governed by passion or a strong attachment that transcends their roles, in many areas of the relationship.**

☐ Stage Four—Partners look to their relationship and each other as a source of love, validation, and approval. There is often an inordinate degree of jealousy and insecurity ... Emphasis is on being loved (receiving) and validated as opposed to loving (giving) ... Fours often try to please partner as a way of getting back as much or more affection. For example, when they say, "I love you," it can mean, "I want you to love me." Fours may often ask their partner, "Do you love me?" and sometimes obsess about that.

☐ Stage Three—Both the foundation and the climate for the relationship are grounded in dictums (often clichés or stereotypes) that are usually based on long-standing rules and traditions. In any case, they were not willfully chosen (e.g., how they met, religious or ethnic background of anyone who could be considered for involvement, who works, who stays home, the nature of their sex life, fidelity, beliefs such as "all love relationships and marriages should/must last forever," etc.) ... Disagreements often focus on who's most compliant with whatever rules form the basis of their relationship. Their "book of rules" usually settles control issues and other conflicts as well.

☐ Stage Two—Usually, one partner strongly dominates the other and/or uses the relationship as a vehicle to act out in a variety of ways ... Deception and even abuse is often the substitute for intimacy where what is not felt can be lied about. For example, demanding that a partner be faithful while secretly they are not.

☐ Stage One—The foundation of the relationship (and often the reason it even came to be) is principally security, dependency, and neediness (e.g., emotionally and/or financially, etc.) ... Either or both partners may be preoccupied with "needing to be needed"... A One often is experienced (and seen) by partner as a "bottomless pit."

In this important part of your life, what changes (for you or you and your partner) **seem warranted?**

A key to good **Parenting** is to compliment what is both age and stage appropriate. Consider this as a very basic guideline for ideal parenting *at each stage of the child* (Note: The calibration on the next page addresses the stages of the *parents*):

☐ **Stage Seven—You only need be proud and feel gratified for having been able to model/encourage Stage Seven behaviors as a parent at those times when you put your own needs aside for those of your children without inducing guilt and by teaching the values of service. To the extent that your children operate as Sevens, they have internalized those values ... Respect from your children flows back to you synergistically.**

☐ **Stage Six—By the time they reach this stage, hopefully you and your children are "emotional equals." However, you are obviously still the parent ... You are parenting your children as Sixes whenever you are enjoying the process of helping them grow in their own direction ...** (Sadly, parents in lower stages will often have difficulty understanding and appreciating their children in the highest stages.)

☐ **Stage Five—You have a certain number of years to influence your children by example. Chances are that whatever they have not learned from you—regardless of whether or not that was by choice—by the time they reach Stage Five, they will choose to learn elsewhere. So let go of any need to control their lives. Allow and honor the right of your adult children to be independent and different from you. You will command respect by doing that, without having to demand it.**

☐ Stage Four—To encourage self-exploration while carefully and lovingly setting limits, letting go and allowing your adolescent to make his or her own mistakes—all the while remaining a safety net and a source of love, support and guidance that he or she can turn to as needed. However, it's also crucial to provide discipline and "tough love" whenever an adolescent child crosses the line. This could be your last opportunity to be the principal source of influence for your child.

☐ Stage Three—To provide a solid structure and resolve to do whatever it takes to teach those complex yet basic rules of life patiently. These are your main challenges with Stage Three children. By providing loving guidance along with appropriate discipline, children have the best possible environment to learn all about what it takes not only to fit in, but also to thrive and begin to discover their own uniqueness via early target stage hooks.

☐ Stage Two—To let the toddler explore, while teaching/setting limits and minding his or her physical safety, are the principal tasks here. Most importantly (and at times most difficult), is not to act out your own frustrations and emotions—especially anger—on to your child. This period can be thought of as a trial run for when your child becomes an adolescent, a stage that is a lot less demanding physically, but can be much more demanding emotionally.

☐ Stage One—To provide unconditional love, nurturing, care, and safety during the first year of life.

Where have you noticed that this difficult balancing act called parenting could use a tweak? You may find it helpful to revisit the parenting discussions in Chapters 1 through 5 to fine-tune your approach, by the stage(s) of your child(ren).

Now, here is how **Parenting** looks by the stages of the parents:

☐ **Stage Seven—**Part of parenting your child from Stage Seven is to see that role as a calling, where putting your needs aside and sacrificing when necessary is done as a labor of love and purpose, never out of guilt or obligation ... Many Sevens choose to become foster parents, adopt needy children, or find and serve in some mission involving children when unable to have their own or when their own children are grown.

☐ **Stage Six—**Those who parent from Stage Six will rarely miss an opportunity to learn more ways to be effective. Parenting is often seen as the most joyous, rewarding, and loving part of life. Observing each aspect of a child's growth can be a mesmerizing experience. Sixes both appreciate and encourage their children's uniqueness. They make a genuine effort to be mindfully present when interacting with their child.

☐ **Stage Five—***Fives* consider parenting their children another major role, albeit an extremely important and rewarding one.

☐ Stage Four— Stage Four parents are often obsessed with being loved, respected, and considered a "friend" by their children.

☐ Stage Three—While teaching rules and values are essential elements of parenting, it's not hard to see how Stage Three parents who make it a practice to rule their kids by fear and extremely harsh discipline, usually miss the mark. In this present era, children of all ages (and others in their lives, such as teachers) have access to many resources and much information that they didn't have in past generations. Therefore, any extreme approach that puts the emphases on fear and other types of harsh behavior may now even be considered emotionally or physically abusive. At best, these anachronistic measures don't translate to effective discipline. Moreover, highly authoritarian Stage Three parents generally have much difficulty being successful with adolescents—in particular—who may rebel to a dangerous degree on the one hand, or, on the other hand, become so fearful that they remain *Threes* both throughout and long after adolescence.

☐ Stage Two—Stage Two parents may be very neglectful or abusive emotionally, physically, morally and/or even sexually for no reason, of course, that even pretends to benefit their children. For example, in extreme cases, *Twos* have been known to use their children to beg, steal, in some cases even deal drugs for them or worse.

☐ Stage One—Parents who themselves operate as *Ones*—regardless of the age of their child—may expect and encourage their children to become "parentified" (which means for the child to act in the role as the parent in one or more major ways), and thus take care of them.

This calibration simply asks you to look at your own values and default stage as a parent and then ask yourself whether you are getting the result that you want.

Some attitudes that govern how *Adult Children* at each stage view taking care of their *Aging* **Parents**:

☐ **Stage Seven**—**"It's an honor and a graciously loving endeavor to give back."**

☐ **Stage Six**—**"It's an opportunity to strengthen and complete our relationship while there is the chance."**

☐ **Stage Five**—**"Taking care of them is my duty. In addition, "saving money now by taking care of them myself is a way I can maximize my inheritance"... However, Fives are quite likely at times to find the experience fatiguing, overwhelming, and in conflict with other aspects of life.**

☐ Stage Four—"Maybe now they will finally recognize/love me."

☐ Stage Three—"Now I make the rules" … "Children *should* 'take care' of their parents when they grow old."

☐ Stage Two—"Now it's my turn for revenge."

☐ Stage One—"What did they ever do for me?"… *Ones* are also likely still to feel entitled to be on the receiving end, no matter how incapable their parents are of giving … *Ones* are least able to accept the reality of when parents die or are close to death, regardless of their age, health, or other circumstances. For *Ones*, it's just about always about themselves, and how almost any circumstance that occurs makes them a "victim."

If there were truly a "selfish" reason to climb to those target stages as a parent, it would be to anticipate that time when the tables are turned. This calibration is one I've seen in play many times. It is often a predictable consequence of the example you set that your adult children follow.

Your attitudes about Sex by the stages:

☐ **Stage Seven—**"**Sex is a way to deepen the loving connection, sometimes even in a spiritual way, between me and my partner. We love and care greatly for each other.**"

☐ **Stage Six—**"**Sex with my partner is an ecstatically pleasurable and** (usually) **orgasmic experience!**"

☐ **Stage Five—"In addition to procreation, sex is a healthy, normal, and good way to have pleasurable sensations as well as an important part of any marriage or love relationship."... "Sex is not always orgasmic, but it usually feels good, satisfies my sex drive, and is rarely a relationship issue." Both partners generally see it as a form of "adult play," agree on frequency, preferences regarding how to do it, and the way it is initiated.**

☐ Stage Four—"Sex is one way I feel needed and loved by my partner"... "Having sex is sometimes necessary to avoid rejection"... In addition, Fours sometimes use sex as an anxiety reducer.

☐ Stage Three—"Sex comes with a set of rules (sometimes merely assumed), and should only be done the right way (for example, between married people, in the bedroom, a certain number of times a week/month/year, missionary position, lights out," etc.)... Strong belief usually prevails that infidelity is always—and perhaps unforgivably—wrong.

☐ Stage Two—"Sex is a means by which to manipulate and control or truly humiliate the other person" ... "I am entitled to be as promiscuous as I care to be"... "I will indulge in whatever comes my way." (Sometimes both the intention and way sexual addiction is acted out can make it a Stage Two endeavor as well as Stage One.) On the other hand, wildly uninhibited and/or kinky sex between consenting adults can also be an expression of healthy Stage Two hooks.

☐ Stage One—"Putting out" is necessary to keep your partner happy and the relationship intact… On the other hand, Stage One is also the stage that is most identified with sexual addiction, where a partner is somewhere between difficult and impossible to satisfy sexually (as is the case with most addictions) and therefore might put all aspects of his or her relationship (and/or life) at risk. Sex addicts believe that sex is exclusively about their own pleasure; and that sex partners are objects who exist solely for that purpose.

There are few discussions that you and your partner might enjoy more than how to bring your default stage as sex partners to those target Stages Six and Seven. For most couples this can have positive ripple effects for every aspect of your relationship!

Start by sharing something your partner may not know (or may have forgotten) about you and what you enjoy sexually. Then reciprocate by listening to your partner's preferences. As simple as that sounds, many couples stop enjoying sex together as they once did because each partner thinks that the other one "should know" or "doesn't care." Many more suggestions on how to enhance this part of your life can be found at *StageClimbing.com/resources* (Password: MyStageClimb).

WORKSHEET

Use this reproducible worksheet to Make Your Own *Stage Climbing* Calibration for Any Area of Life, Problem, or Issue You Are Working On [Use calibrations in this section as appropriate for guidelines and reference. For additional help or to download this worksheet, visit *www.StageClimbing.com/worksheets* (Password: MyStageClimb)].

☐   **Stage Seven**

☐   **Stage Six**

☐   **Stage Five**

☐   Stage Four

☐   Stage Three

☐   Stage Two

☐   Stage One

CHAPTER 12

YOUR CAREER

Selected Occupations and Professions through the Lens of Each Stage

This is how those who do these various types of work see themselves (and/or are seen by others), by the stages. Remember, **rarely does anything less than a complex and unique mixture of several or even all the stages accurately describe the totality of how you see your work in the real world. However, these calibrations might identify some hooks and/or clarify your default stage in this area of your life.**

Selected occupations in this chapter include:

Actors, Athletes, Musicians, and other Performers:

☐ **Stage Seven**—Sees performance as a way to make a statement that will benefit the audience, raise consciousness in some important area, and/or help others such as those who enjoy their performances to maximize their leisure time ... A Stage Seven singer, for example, would see his or her performance as an opportunity to deliver mission driven lyrics to the audience ... A Stage Seven athlete will find ways to use platform to impact a chosen cause.

☐ **Stage Six**—Enjoys the challenge and exercise of talent that goes into the performance. Considers applause as merely feedback for that performance and does not become preoccupied by (or addicted to) it ... Enjoys (for example) acting much more than *being* an actor or *being* a celebrity ... Loves their sport/game as a passion ... Enjoys watching excellence in their field almost as much as playing/performing ... Is inspired by achieving greater and greater excellence, which sometimes involves pushing the boundaries ... This is the stage that players, performers, and fans all have in common.

☐ **Stage Five**—Considers it a job for which external rewards such as excellent pay are most important.

☐ Stage Four—Relishes celebrity… Applause is taken as personal validation … All expressions of audience appreciation are sought, regardless of the quality of a given performance ... Performance anxiety about being judged as well as putting one's self down and hindsight-powered second-guessing as a result of a below-average performance is common.

☐ Stage Three—Can perform only under strict direction with and adherence to "the script." In sports, the referees and umpires optimally operate here by definition (though they certainly can and usually do enjoy the work they do as Sixes).

☐   Stage Two—Uses performance skills or celebrity status to open doors in order to con, exploit or defraud others.

☐   Stage One—Uses such things as the high unemployment rate, the extremely competitive environment for whatever opportunities do exist, difficulties finding work, and other harsh realities of their field, as an excuse not to work harder or at all.

Whenever I work with people in these performance fields, there are two major areas we usually concentrate on. One is learning how to get into peak performance mode mentally. A very effective Stage Six strategy for doing this can be found in Chapter 6 on page 150. The other is to **visualize achieving the best possible performance and outcome**.

This exercise can benefit you regardless of your field:
Simply close your eyes and see yourself getting the exact result you want. Notice how your body and breathing conform to this vision as it becomes more and more real to you. Most importantly, remember to use that posture and breathing as a *starting point* for your next performance. More strategies like this can be found in Chapter Six starting on page 148. Additional resources are at *StageClimbing.com/resources.*

Attorneys:

☐ **Stage Seven—Truly seeks justice; and will choose the branch of law, type of advocacy, and legal positions that will maximize impact** (e.g., become a prosecutor who is sensitive to victims' rights, a public defender, go into community law, help poor people or developing nations, etc.) **and always for the highest motives ... Will not hesitate to take a *pro bono* case that he/she believes in.**

☐ **Stage Six—Loves their particular law specialty and is usually very good at it... Sees law as a fascinating work in progress with much ambiguity, lots of room for exceptions, and as an outlet for creativity.**

☐ **Stage Five—Will practice the branch of law that they see as the most lucrative and provides best connections.**

☐ Stage Four—Seeks specialty, professional environment (e.g., the top firm in their specialty) and/or types of cases that are seen as most prestigious.

☐ Stage Three—Sees law as absolute, rigid, unbending and unforgiving ... Likely to believe that punitive measures should be taken toward anyone (with very little or no exception) who deviates from the letter of law for any reason, regardless of the circumstances ... Also, may enter the field or join the practice run by family members, because that's what is expected of them.

☐ Stage Two—Uses skills and contacts to defraud or take unfair advantage of others.

☐ Stage One—Finds the easiest and most undemanding type of work to do.

In the last decade, many attorneys have consulted me to discuss a possible career change they were anticipating. At first, their most common complaint is usually being fed up, burnt out, or disillusioned with the law and the "hassles of practicing it" in this present era. However, at the end of the day, the vast majority of attorneys actually tended to stay in the legal profession, opting instead to change specialties or firms so that their day-to-day activities were more consistent with what they saw as their passion-driven interests, calling, and whatever clearly connected them to their chosen career target stages.

The good news is that like the legal profession, many fields offer the opportunity to do this type of tweaking, making a more drastic career change unnecessary. How might that possibility relate to you, if you are thinking about making a career change?

Business Owners:

☐ **Stage Seven—Sees customers as clients who have entrusted them with a need, and who are to be served with sincerity and care ... Reaches out to charities as a resource for them ... Would rather send customer/client elsewhere than not be of genuine service** (believing that is a good long-term business strategy as well as life principle) **... Is truly committed to the long-term benefits of giving value.**

☐ **Stage Six—Enjoys the game of business as well as the special challenges of the specific type of business they are in ... Is always looking for additional ways to use the opportunity their business provides to be creative ... Is focused on meeting the various challenges business requires ... Also sees profits as means for expansion as well as a method of evaluating business decisions and objectives.**

☐ **Stage Five—See customers as dollar bills and opportunities that they will lawfully** (and within whatever may be their personal "code of ethics") **sell to and profit from as much as possible ... Business direction is profit motivated. The bottom line is what matters and drives practically all decisions.**

☐ Stage Four—May undermine business through lack of assertiveness (by not using hard edge when appropriate or by overreacting when handling a difficult problem), avoiding making unpopular decisions and being over-cautious due to anxiety about making mistakes and failing ... *Fours* seek recognition for themselves, from within and outside of their organization.

☐ Stage Three—May also go into the family business, not out of choice, but because of unquestioned tradition, to avoid family alienation, to stay in comfort zone, or to alleviate the irrational fear of poverty... Will employ very little creativity and/or avoid giving much attention to changing trends ... May seek business with lots of rules and structure (e.g., a franchise).

☐   Stage Two—Consciously operates some type of predatory, fraudulent, or unethical enterprise … Would not hesitate to use or bend bankruptcy laws liberally, for example.

☐   Stage One—Seeks and chooses an easy path (perhaps the family business or some other turnkey operation) in order to make things easiest for themselves … Will often fail in business due to a lack of initiative and commitment to hard work.

I have spoken to, consulted for, and coached many business owners who see their role as an entrepreneur in Stage Five terms. Indeed, maintaining profitability is job one. However, a very common question many business owners face is how to keep their businesses profitable while "cashing in" on the rewards that operating out of the target stages provides.

Usually, this is not only doable, but with a little creativity, can even lend itself to more *opportunities that are profitable*. For example, charitable endeavors provide contacts that may not otherwise be accessible, and enjoying what you do while being creative, sets up a higher level of motivation for accomplishing the mission of your business. (Also, see the Calibration for Executives and Managers on page 256.

Construction and Tradespersons:

☐ **Stage Seven—Appreciates the contribution their projects make to the larger world and to future generations.**

☐ **Stage Six—Enjoys the work of their chosen trade, the creativity of applying specialized skills to difficult tasks and seeing projects come together ... Values the subtleties as well** (e.g., working outdoors, being "in the moment" with a high level of concentration, etc.) **... Supports new technology and more advanced and efficient ways of doing the job ... Strives to learn more and more in order to have maximum impact by enhancing their value to the company and/or industry.**

☐ **Stage Five—Is motivated by such things as good pay and benefits, decent hours, and the freedom of not having to do or think about work after hours.**

☐ Stage Four—Finds the camaraderie and feeling of belonging or being part of a group to be an important aspect of the work they do.

☐ Stage Three—Skips any pretense of creativity in favor of the traditional ... Often believes "they don't make things like they used to" and can feel quite threatened by new advances and technology.

☐ Stage Two—Looks for ways to exploit their system and those they work with for personal gain and profit ... Takes credit for work they haven't done ... Has little or no regard for fellow workers.

☐ Stage One—Depends on such things as unemployment, union protection, and other people (who they work with, and/or for in their field) for job security and support for exerting as little effort as possible ... Seeks easiest possible work with least responsibility for the results they produce (or lack thereof)... If possible, will get others to do their share of the work.

**Many of those who are most successful and have had the largest over-
all impact in their industries came up through the ranks.** Your ability to do
this is usually a function of your attitude about the work you do and your ability
to both succeed and to make a difference.

**Set some short-term (less than three years) and long-term (over three
years) goals for where you would like to see your career go.** Become
committed to them and take whatever steps you can toward those goals. Then
watch them become reality!

Executives/Managers:

☐ **Stage Seven—Keeps the focus on the greater good ... Encourages subordinates to become a vital part of organization's mission ... Cares about members of the team beyond merely their immediate use to the organization.**

☐ **Stage Six—Motivates subordinates to care, be creative and thrive, because it makes good business sense ... Encourages them to help the common cause by reaching their potential ... Reinforces and values a subordinate's right to give dissenting opinions** (would prefer access to the entire mind of a subordinate as opposed to only the part of their mind that agrees with them) **... Wants the brightest, most capable, and creative people around them and provides the environment to maximize their talents ... Are not threatened by the prospect of being compared to subordinates who outshine them in certain areas.**

☐ **Stage Five—Focuses on fairness in the workplace and giving tangible rewards for good performance ... "Makes the trains run on time."**

☐ Stage Four—Gives and seeks ample praise and personal validation ... May feel threatened by a subordinate who is "too competent" or getting too much recognition ... Believes (often erroneously) that the deference or respect they get from subordinates is toward them personally rather than related to their role as boss ... Often covers for subordinates in order to be liked.

☐ Stage Three—Rules by setting up a fearful or highly rigid atmosphere ... Heavy, unforgiving, and unbending on discipline ... Discourages and often punishes dissenting opinions of subordinates, even if they make a great deal of sense and are given with the best of intentions regarding the bigger picture ... However, this management style also has its place in certain industries or types of organizations that need to be run using a military-type approach.

☐ Stage Two—Deceives, manipulates, takes advantage of, harasses, abuses, and/or bullies subordinates in a predatory and often very personal and/or inappropriate manner.

☐ Stage One—Makes job of subordinates (as well as their own) as easy, safe, and sheltered as possible ... Not focused on productivity... Often has his or her own job through nepotism or cronyism ... Might reinforce a subordinate's feelings of inadequacy when it comes to them finding a better job or when a conflict arises ... Overdelegates, allows, and engages in buck passing ... Rarely rises to top management.

For successful executives and managers, motivating subordinates to be the most effective they can be is usually one of their highest priorities. The trick is to help them see your mission as their mission. In the hands-on work I've done in consulting for and coaching managers, I have observed that the best ones have a sometimes natural ability to size up a subordinate in terms of what motivates them presently and what could motivate them to do their absolute best.

This roughly lines up with your employee's default versus target stage. Therefore, consider using this *Stage Climbing* principle to help those you manage *want* to give you the best of themselves day after day. Moreover, train those under you to manage their subordinates to do the same.

An added bonus to the production you will get from those you can properly motivate, is that there will be less turnover due to them not only feeling good about their jobs, but also about *themselves* in that role.

Military/Law Enforcement Personnel:

☐ **Stage Seven—The calling is nothing less than a cherished opportunity to join and contribute to the assigned mission in order to help saves lives and property, "Save the planet" or be involved in an aspect of that … See themselves as warriors against evil for the greater good … Motivated by the opportunity to do heroic acts, regardless of whether they are personally recognized for what they do … They realize and accept the reality that their mission could result in extreme sacrifice and even death.**

☐ **Stage Six—Military or law enforcement offers a unique opportunity to do the specific kind work they love to do.**

☐ **Stage Five—Government benefits take care of family, medical needs, perhaps even housing, and provide a good pension as well as many other perks. In addition, there are often great opportunities for advancement.**

☐ Stage Four—Thrives on the image and potential for admiration and hero worship that "the uniform" provides in certain circles … Often works for and/or is motivated by the recognition, awards, and medals.

☐ Stage Three—Regardless of whether in a high position (providing an opportunity to give orders) or a low position (which often requires the endless taking of orders), thrives on the structure of the authoritarian environment that military or law enforcement organizations must have in order to function most effectively.

☐ Stage Two—Sees their position as a foot in the door that comes with an opportunity to rip off the government, shake people down, and/or act out in a variety of different ways (possibly even including brutally for brutality's sake).

☐ Stage One—Joins military or law enforcement field to be taken care of by a system they perceive as providing the ultimate level of recession-proof job security and benefits, which extend to all basic needs… Seeks easiest and safest assignments … Will retire early or as soon as they can max out their benefits.

Having served as the stress manager and chief psychologist for the Philadelphia Police Department (PPD), as well as having been in the Army Reserves (as a very young man), I came to genuinely respect the management styles of these fields. **It's clear that the management of law enforcement and military organizations is very much grounded in Stage Three, and for good reasons—namely life and death.** However, I have also observed a huge number of *Sixes* and *Sevens* on the job. This is in no way a contradiction. Those who put their lives on the line for little money set a target stage standard that few fields could ever match. However, they are also quite prone to burnout, as well as a variety of extreme job stress issues. There are no easy answers here.

At the PPD, we taught stress management skills at every level and we would generally use special therapeutic interventions to do whatever could be done to restore the passion and zest for the job when treating burnout and other stress-related disorders. Fortunately, we were usually (though not always) successful in turning things around. **The paradoxical fact is that the more *passionate* you are about your work** (in any field)**, the *more susceptible* you may be to burnout.**

Physicians, Nurses, and Other **Health Professionals:**

☐ **Stage Seven—To** make the greatest impact possible on those who put their health and lives into the hands of these helping professionals ... To save some lives and greatly improve the quality of others' lives by applying their skills to cure as well as reduce pain and suffering.

☐ **Stage Six—They** have great passion for the specific work they do, along with an intense interest in the new developments that affect their field and thus increase the ability to be maximally effective.

☐ **Stage Five—The field is lucrative, recession-proof, and will always offer opportunities.**

☐ Stage Four—For the admiration of those they help as well as those impressed with the prestige of the profession to which they belong.

☐ Stage Three—Would choose to adhere to the established and often rigid rules that govern traditional procedures, rather than being sensitive to the unique needs of the actual patients who rely on their services, as well as others who have to deal with them.(such as coworkers, subordinates, or family members of patients).

☐ Stage Two—Uses position of power to exploit vulnerable people under their care (e.g., financially or sexually)... Misses no opportunity to overbill, for example.

☐ Stage One—Uses the security of the field to meet their needs, while doing only the absolute minimum... Shows little or no concern at all for those who depend on them.

In the past decade or so, many physicians, nurses, and health professionals have *passionately* participated in the huge breakthroughs of their fields (hopefully as a function of operating from their target stages), and have also become disillusioned by many of the economic changes that are realities of their profession. For example, malpractice premiums and lawsuits, managed care and other cost-control measures, have driven some of the best from the field. However, their work could not be more important.

In most cases, these professionals start out with a Stage Six (and/or Seven) default with respect to their careers. Nevertheless, as these realities—which are unrelated to the actual work they signed up for—take their toll, many I've spoken to seem to have all but forgotten the sense of purpose and calling that got them into the field in the first place.

This is extremely unfortunate! Regardless of your field, if this phenomena speaks to you (as it undoubtedly applies to many fields that are changing in certain ways and not for the better), go back to the basics. What do you really want to be doing? How has your calling changed? Are you simply burnt out because of some aspect of things (perhaps even minor) that can be changed? Or is a major makeover (aka a career change) in order?

Whatever you come up with as you ponder these questions, make it a priority to get your career back to at least a Stage Six default. *If you have operated there before, it will be quite difficult to accept anything less.*

Politicians:

☐ **Stage Seven—Would not concern himself/herself with being re-elected, being popular, or being anything for that matter ... It's only the cause(s) that they seek or are in office to take on and the problems they hear a calling to resolve, for the good of their constituency** (and beyond) **that's important to them ... Has no hidden agendas ... Says and believes the same things in private as in public ... Is humbled by the sense of duty that comes with their position and the opportunity to serve ... Cares about and is focused on the world he/she leaves behind.**

☐ **Stage Six—Loves public policy and focuses on doing the work exceptionally well that each aspect of it requires ... May even truly enjoy the challenge of an election campaign and the opportunity to inspire others by getting out their message.**

☐ **Stage Five—It's a job that provides power, contacts, and perhaps a social circle that he or she may otherwise have no access to, but is not yet a calling. Thus, it's still about them, not the people they serve.**

☐ Stage Four—The most gratifying part of the job is the prestige that comes with it ... Being liked and admired by constituents and others who are impressed by the office held ... Stage Four politicians are governed by polls and often obsessed with their own popularity or lack thereof ... They will tend to see their role and position as more of an honor (being in office) than a duty (to deliver on promises, for example).

☐ Stage Three—They see themselves as ruling rather than serving their constituencies. In extreme cases, they would have no problem even supporting the principles of an authoritarian or totalitarian dictatorship, were they in that kind of system or society ... In addition, extreme left- and right-wingers, for example, and their often staunch and toady-like—sometimes idol worshipping—followers who never go beyond ideological dictums to carve out positions, are generally operating out of Stage Three. Talking points are considered sacred and never to be challenged.

☐   Stage Two—A politician who is out for whatever he or she can get away with and/or steal in the way of money, power, and favors … Uses charisma to deceive … Will say or do anything necessary to get into office and hold on to power, often through deception and demagoguery.

☐   Stage One—To the extent that an opportunity for a *One* in this field exists, it would be a very low-level situation in which the government is seen as an undemanding and unlimited resource to fulfill personal and security needs (for example, patronage and "no-show" jobs they consider "entitled to").

Politicians present us with one of the best examples of "stage diversity"! Most of us who follow politics could name a national or local politician (past or present) with a clear default in each of the seven stages. Moreover, most politicians have career-related hooks in nearly all of the stages. Love them or hate them, that's what makes politicians such compelling figures.

In your career (or another important area of your life), where you perhaps have a default in one certain stage and recognizable hooks in most of the other stages, how do you keep it all together? Do a calibration of the "politician" in you, who may sometimes operate out of many stages at once (in your job or marriage, for instance). Then, do some tweaking to decide if you really need to operate that way to optimize that part of your life.

Psychotherapists:

☐ **Stage Seven**—Sees their own life's work as being a healer and force to help and improve the lives of patients/clients and all of the people that those who they help might impact ... Does some *pro bono* work ... May see mission as simply helping as many people and as deeply as possible ... Sees (and sets up) **office as "sanctuary" for clients/patients to work on their most daunting issues and life problems** (In addition to Stage Six below).

☐ **Stage Six**—Finds helping people to be challenging and intrinsically rewarding ... There is also a level of affinity and a solid layer of empathy for the populations they treat ... Will religiously stay within their area(s) of expertise and do only what they know and do best. Whatever that is, Sixes tend to do it very well.

☐ **Stage Five—Consider it a fine profession with flexible hours, a customized work environment and a nice income.**

☐ Stage Four—Likes *being* a therapist as a way of gaining deference and admiration from patients/clients.

☐ Stage Three—May apply their favorite dogmatic theory or technique—in a highly authoritarian manner—to every case they treat, regardless of whether that approach is the best in a given situation… Insists that patients/clients conform to *their* personal values and instructions if they ever want to get better.

☐ Stage Two—Will exploit (e.g., financially, sexually, etc.) patients/clients as prey whenever and however it suits them ... May also breed dependency as Stage One therapists do, only *Twos* do it consciously, deliberately, and without regard for the impact on client/patient ... May present themselves as an expert at something, regardless of how untrue that may be. In this regard, they can also be quite dangerous.

☐   Stage One—Without realizing it, they breed dependency by training their patients/ clients to need therapy—and them—far more than any healthy treatment would dictate. This is often in order to have their own emotional and financial needs met. Thus, their therapy often serves the therapist more than it does the patient/client (whom, of course, it is meant to serve).

Having a sense of the default stage of the therapist you choose to work with can be quite important. Many therapists (but certainly not all) are less than effective when trying to help clients who have presenting issues that typify higher stages than the therapist's own default stage in the life area they are treating. So how do you know if your therapist is in over his/her head?

Tell your therapist or prospective therapist exactly what you are looking for from him or her, your therapeutic goals, and the results you expect or wish to achieve. If you can walk away from that initial meeting feeling that you've been heard and that you and your therapist are on the same page, a second session is in order.

As long as you're in therapy, keep your eyes open and challenge your therapist whenever you are unclear as to where you are going or whether **your goals** are being honored and addressed. If your therapist doesn't welcome that, then he or she is probably operating from a lower stage than you might need.

Teachers at all levels including **College Professors:**

☐ **Stage Seven—Will take every possible opportunity to recognize a student's potential and help him or her find a way to maximize it ... Marvels at the impact their work can have on the future of their students** (and all who are touched by them) **and the world, for an infinite period into the future ... Can tolerate, respect, and perhaps even encourage a student's dissenting points of view ... Makes it a practice to distinguish their own editorial view when presenting subject matter** (particularly with topics that are controversial) **... Respects students as unique individuals.**

☐ **Stage Six—Loves their subject and the art of teaching it ... Constantly finds new and more effective ways to get the job done ... Considers the creativity of students to be one of their most important resources ... An affinity for the type of students they teach is an added bonus ... Cares deeply about the impact of their work**

☐ **Stage Five—Are often motivated mainly by the benefits and favorable work conditions** (e.g., hours, the summers-off schedule, etc.) **that teaching provides ... "There's no better job schedule-wise for someone raising school age children to have"... Might consider students merely as a means to the rewards and benefits their job provides ... Sees little reason for innovation when standard curriculum is available.**

☐ Stage Four—Feels superior to students ... Enjoys the deference, but like Stage Four bosses, they often mistake it for genuine respect and affection.

☐ Stage Three—Derives satisfaction from the almost "dictatorial authority" aspect that the job often provides ... Can be extremely harsh with discipline ... Has a "one size fits all" mentality when dealing with students and classes.

☐   Stage Two—Sees students as "prey" to be exploited.

☐   Stage One—Are able to get by doing the absolute minimum … May still be on the job, but only because bureaucracy, unions, and tenure protect them.

I can think of nothing that's more important to the long-term health of our society than the work of good teachers. The ripple effects of a good education can reverberate indefinitely. While many teachers rise to the occasion, many don't. Sadly, the importance of their work seems to have gotten lost for so many of the teachers I have spoken with over the years—in a similar way to what health professionals have experienced. However, regardless of the age or life stages of the students you teach, the option and power is still yours to pick the stage from which you operate.

Try this simple exercise: Picture the type of students who would motivate you to operate from Stages Six and Seven routinely. Then if you are not there already, develop a strategy to be working in the exact setting with the type of students *where you know you can perform optimally*. However, **make sure your focus is on the students.** *They*—**not your superiors, not the school board, not the parents, not your peers**—*are your legacy*.

This simple shift (which may apply to you even if you are in a different field altogether) **can reverse burnout and get you back to the target stages where you belong, and very quickly.**

Writers and Speakers:

☐ **Stage Seven—Are in tune with the ripple effects their work could have on their audience, the many people they and their audience will impact and perhaps even the larger world ... Feels very fortunate to have the opportunity to do this kind of work even though it may be a tough field sometimes ... Work speaks to a higher calling ... Would easily pass on top engagements in favor of less lucrative or prestigious ones that would better provide them the platform to get out their exact message in their own way ... They believe so much in their message that a great presentation of it comes quite naturally and can be inordinately effortless for them** (in addition to Stage Six below)**.**

☐ **Stage Six—Loves to communicate their message and feels passionate about what they have to say or they would be doing/saying something else ... Chooses professional organizations as a way to find mentors and enhance skills.**

☐ **Stage Five—Likes the flexibility of hours, perks, pay, and contacts their field provides them ... Will write and speak about topics and in formats that are most marketable and lucrative ... Are often commissioned to write or speak about topics and say things they might even disagree with, if they like the engagement and compensation ... Sometimes have "publish or perish" mentality ... Joins professional organizations to network and maximize opportunities.**

☐ Stage Four—Likes the prestige of being a writer or speaker ... Cherishes good feedback as a means of self-validation ... Often motivated or troubled by the anxiety over deadlines and their performance feedback (e.g., what others think of their work etc.).

☐ Stage Three—"Preaches to the choir" in a highly conventional and expected way, with an underlying fear-based message (usually some variation of "what would happen" if and/or when some tradition is violated, rule is broken or some drive toward change—which is framed as totally wrongheaded or evil—is not defeated).

☐ Stage Two—May use skills and opportunity to defame, deceive, demagogue, and deliberately spread false information for an undisclosed personal gain.

☐ Stage One—Communicates a variation of the "we are all victims" theme, with emphasis on the "hopelessness" of a problem and little—if any—strategy for solution or to help the audience "rise above" victimhood.

These fields are also very close to my heart. **Having the skills to write and/ or speak well are important. But the more crucial thing is *what you say.*** We all have a unique message. What is yours? Unless writing or being an orator in and of itself is your passion, it's your message and your commitment to it that puts you in the higher stages.

What do you feel passionate about that you'd like to share with others? At Stage Six, it's what *you want* to share. At Stage Seven, it's what *someone else really needs to hear*. In these fields, Stages Six and Seven ideally go together. Working from the target stages and getting your message out is what makes building your platform (usually a Stage Five endeavor) worthwhile in the end. Determining what you have to say that meets this standard is your target stage challenge.

WORKSHEET

Use this reproducible worksheet to **Make Your Own *Stage Climbing* Calibration for Any Area of Life, Problem, or Issue You Are Working On** [Use calibrations in this section as appropriate for guidelines and reference. For additional help or to download this worksheet, visit *www.Stage-Climbing.com/worksheets* (Password: MyStageClimb)].

☐ **Stage Seven**

☐ **Stage Six**

☐ **Stage Five**

☐ Stage Four

☐ Stage Three

☐ Stage Two

☐ Stage One

CHAPTER 13

ORGANIZATIONS AND INSTITUTIONS

They Operate by the Stages Too

J ust as the **Stage Climbing** model can explain the motives and attitudes of individuals, couples, and families, it **fits organizations, institutions, and other groups as well!**

In this chapter, see how a very small sampling that includes the following organizations and institutions operate by the stages:

Here is how **Business Organizations** operate by the stages:

☐ **Stage Seven—Policy is established and management is very conscious of giving everyone—employees, customers/clients, and other associates—the fairest possible treatment as well as the highest regard ... Customer service is a genuine part of the company's mission statement and reinforces its intention to make the optimal impact** (as opposed to merely being a marketing tool) **... Does pro bono work, donates goods or services to community and/or a portion of profits to charity ... Is environmentally and socially conscious ... Encourages that same high-minded behavior in employees.**

☐ **Stage Six—Creativity is valued and reinforced in an environment that listens to the opinions and suggestions of all staff ... Extraordinary efforts are made to formulate maximum use of all talent** (considered a major resource) **for the long-term good of the organization, including its bottom line.**

☐ **Stage Five—Perks, money, and benefits are mainly used to manage employees in a conventional environment in which the management style is tailored to the primary mission of the company, which is maximizing profits ... Other than bottom-line profit making, almost everything else is considered incidental.**

☐ Stage Four—Management sees value in pacifying, being kind to employees, and/or often defers (whether or not by choice) to labor union.

☐ Stage Three—Runs by strict rules, including an unbending chain of command and unquestioned authority (e.g., assembly-line factories, large construction projects, post office, etc.) ... Most valued are "yes men/women"; "company men/women"; toadies; and those who maximally blend in and follow the system and "party line" without making any waves or bringing attention to themselves.

☐ Stage Two—Operates on a foundation of lies, deception and fraudulent practices.

☐ Stage One—Provides a "sheltered environment" for employees ... Deliberately hires people who have a hard time finding work and/or would be most likely to latch on for the sake of job security.

Businesses must obviously make profits to survive and prosper. **The best-run business organizations are the ones that can hit their goals in the crucial profit area while operating from the higher stages whenever possible. I believe that all things being equal, an operation that emphasizes optimal motivation of its employees and other target stage values will have the best *long-term* profit potential.**

Government by the stages and in its simplest terms would operate like this. However, as in the case with all institutions and organizations, unique combinations of these are certainly possible:

☐ **Stage Seven—Utopian society, which may exist only in theory and folklore** (in addition to Stage Six below).

☐ **Stage Six—True democracy in which each person has an equal say** (like Stage Seven, ideal theoretically, but highly impractical).

☐ **Stage Five—Representative democracy** (such as USA and most other Western countries).

☐ Stage Four—Benevolent dictatorship.

☐ Stage Three—Authoritarian and/or charismatic dictatorship (or possibly even a totalitarian one in which oppositional words and thoughts are as punishable as forbidden deeds).

☐ Stage Two—Rogue state in which government exists and rulers are in power through the blood or exploitation of its citizens and/or weaker nations … When anarchy reigns.

☐ Stage One—"Client state" of another nation that supports them and receives aid as a reward for their dependency or because poverty is so profound that there are no other ways to keep it going and feed its people.

These are some examples of Miscellaneous **Organizations** that specialize in serving those at various stages:

☐ **Stage Seven—Communities of the elders and luminaries of their chosen fields.**

☐ **Stage Six—Artistic, creative, professional, and spiritual communities** (that value and encourage uniqueness and freethinking).

☐ **Stage Five—Business organizations.**

☐ Stage Four—Social clubs and other organizations that exist to bring together a niche community.

☐ Stage Three—Military and law enforcement agencies.

☐ Stage Two—Prisons and other aspects of the justice system (where the mission is to help *Twos* climb to Stage Three) ... Crime organizations.

☐ Stage One—Nursing homes, hospitals, charities.

Schools operate at the various stages (or a combination of them) as well:

☐ **Stage Seven—Focused on grand mission of preparing generations of students to take over and better their world** (in addition to Stage Six below).

☐ **Stage Six—Encourages students to find and maximize unique talents ... "Open" classrooms ... Their main priority is hiring the highest quality of teaching professionals available, along with an ongoing evaluation process of teachers ... Focus never deviates from delivering the best possible education to each student.**

☐ Stage Five—Well run by highly competent staff for mainstream students; provides good curriculum and quality programs such as sports and other extra-curricular activities. Focus is more on the macro-school organization as an entity that serves many, than on what each student actually receives.

☐   Stage Four—Good at marketing and promotion ... Shows calculated "sensitivity" to parents and others who can affect or determine the extent of their existence or success (not quite as focused on the students as their carefully crafted image would indicate).

☐   Stage Three—Traditional schools that are run in an "old fashioned" or strict authoritarian manner.

☐   Stage Two—Specializes in various degrees of discipline for delinquents and those who act out. (Often part of a justice system.)

☐   Stage One—Provides various types of special education for non-delinquent, challenged, and special need students.

If there were seven **Travel Agencies,** each of which specialized in booking trips and vacations for its clients by the stages from which they wished to operate while away, a *tongue-in-cheek* summary of their specialties or mission statements could look something like this:

☐ **"Stage Seven Travels"—Sets up trips to places such as Africa, India, and/or other poverty-stricken Third World and disaster-ridden areas and countries to work for and contribute to various types of victimized and needy populations ... Doctors Without Borders, for example, other charitable missions, etc.**

☐ **"Stage Six Travels"—Books "Outward Bound"-type adventures, Shamanic trips to indigenous cultures for healing ... Tennis, baseball, football, or golf "camps" for adults, etc.**

☐ **"Stage Five Travels"—Specializes in bargain vacations and trips, cheap excursions to popular places that keep you very busy and use every minute to do as much as possible with what time you have to be away ... Main mission is to make sure you got more than your money's worth.**

☐ "Stage Four Travels"—Trips for singles and others whose mission is to meet people, make friendships and good impressions ... Vacations that encourage dressing to impress ... Cruises only on the ships or lines with the most prestige ... Vacations you would rather not even go on, but take to please someone else; such as a spouse, family member, group of friends, or someone you are visiting out of obligation.

☐   "Stage Three Travels"—Visiting the family "compound"… Highly predictable theme parks … Wherever there are no decisions to be made, only rules to follow, or highly structured programs to participate in.

☐   "Stage Two Travels"—Provides transportation to and from penitentiaries to which offender clients are sentenced as well as transportation and accommodations for their visitors … Books other vacations as well, but at a very high premium price or to non-existent locations … No bargains here, and the agency itself may not even exist by the time you actually leave for the trip.

☐   "Stage One Travels—Mindless vacations in which you can let yourself be totally taken care of and pampered, such as at an all-inclusive resort or spa where pure self-indulgence is the mission and the norm.

WORKSHEET

Use this reproducible worksheet to Make Your Own *Stage Climbing* Calibration for Any Area of Life, Problem, or Issue You Are Working On [Use calibrations in this section as appropriate for guidelines and reference. For additional help or to download this worksheet, visit *www.Stage-Climbing.com/worksheets* (Password: MyStageClimb)].

☐ **Stage Seven**

☐ **Stage Six**

☐ **Stage Five**

☐ Stage Four

☐ Stage Three

☐ Stage Two

☐ Stage One

CHAPTER 14

STAGE CLIMBING IN ACTION

Reach Your Target Stage in Any Chosen Area of Your Life and Much More with These Breakthrough Strategies

Making your default stage evolve to your target stage is both the *Stage Climbing* definition of optimal maturity and the key for reaching your highest potential with that part of your life.

This chapter provides you with step-by-step strategies that will help you to use the principles of *Stage Climbing* in the most straightforward way to integrate, navigate, and make the process work for you in the shortest time possible.

Specifically, the five strategies in this chapter will help you to:

Consider these strategies to be applications of the *Stage Climbing* principles that you can apply to any area of your life. You might also find it helpful to use these strategies in conjunction with those at the end of each chapter in Part I. All of the strategies, exercises, and worksheets in this chapter are in reproducible format. You can download them at your convenience. Just visit *www. StageClimbing.com/worksheets* (Password: MyStageClimb).

These first three strategies are expanded versions of that basic *Stage Climbing* Drill in the Quick-Start Guide on page 11.

BREAKTHROUGH STRATEGY #1

Make Your Default Stage Match Your Target Stage in any part of your life.

To change your default stage in a specific area of your life using the principles of *Stage Climbing*:

1) **Identify an *area* of your life in which you are *not* functioning optimally.** Examples include how you view yourself; how you function in your job or career, your marriage, or love relationship; how you parent or relate to your own parents; how you view spirituality, experience sex, become motivated, have fun, or choose to enjoy your leisure time.

   Please choose only one life area to work on at a time:

   _____

   _____

   Note: Do this exercise separately for each part of your life that you would like to address. You can download and reproduce the worksheet for this entire exercise at *StageClimbing.com/worksheets* (Password: MyStage-Climb).. Use additional paper if necessary.

2) **Identify your *present* default stage in this aspect of your life.** This is the stage—*that you recognize*—from which you **now** normally operate in this life area:

   Stage 1_____2_____3_____4_____5_____6_____7_____

3)   **Choose the target stage that would be ideal** for this part of your life. Consider this to be your goal. If you are unclear about your target stage, it may be helpful for you to find the calibration(s) in Part II closest to the life area you are now working on. In most cases, you will find yourself choosing Stages Six or Seven as your target stage (or sometimes Stage Five—the most neutral of the seven stages).

Stage 1_____2_____3_____4_____5_____6_____7_____

4)   **When you look at this aspect of your life through the lens of your *chosen target stage*, how do you now see things differently?**

_____

_____

_____

_____

_____

5)   **With this aspect of your life in mind, define what operating out of your chosen target stage would look like or mean for you. Focus on what's in it for you** immediately, next month, next year, in five years, 10 years, 20 years, or ultimately? That is, focus on whatever time frame(s) is relevant:

_____

_____

_____

_____

_____

Confirm that this is the target stage that you want:

It is_____ It is not_____

If it is, proceed with the next steps. If not, go back a few steps and do this again with another target stage. **Your commitment to reaping the *benefits* of your new target stage is what fuels your motivation to get and stay there.**

6) By using both the calibrations that appear in Part II of this book and any variations of those that you can customize to your own unique situation, **identify the attitudes, beliefs, and behaviors that characterize your *chosen target stage*** in the life area you are committed to change. **Include the action steps you are willing to take.** (Use additional paper, if necessary.)

_____

_____

_____

_____

_____

_____

_____

_____

7) The final step is to remember to adopt your new target stage as your own. **Whenever you can in that area of your life*, act as if* you are in the target stage, whether or not it comes naturally.** And chances are that at the beginning and until it gets hardwired into your brain **it may require effort**, even if that only means remembering that this is your **chosen** default stage, and that you are consciously walking the walk that it requires. **This is the most powerful step in hardwiring your new target stage as your default.**

Even if this target stage is completely new to you, when you *act as if* it were your default stage, you are there as powerfully as if you had been there all your life. Once you are used to operating out of your new target stage, it will surely become as automatic and second nature to you as the old one has been. In case you're wondering why this is so, it's based on a simple principle of reinforcement. **The higher stages tend to trigger such an ongoing sense of *internal* fulfillment, that they are constantly and perpetually reinforcing themselves. Soon they become hardwired into your brain, much the way any strong habit is.**

Therefore, as you live by and act on the beliefs and attitudes you have chosen, as a reward they will become an indelible part of you, or in *Stage Climbing* terms, your new default stage in that part of your life.

This breakthrough can be a life changer. And the best news of all is that it's available to you in any part of your life in which you are willing to pursue it!

Note: In many situations, that's all you need to do. However, below are some additional strategies for you to use as needed to reinforce and enhance this exercise:

Make a calibration to categorize the major areas of your life (e.g., relationships, career, hobbies, spirituality, friendships, etc.) **by what you see as their default stages. This can be especially helpful if you have a part of your life in which the default stage is unclear, to see where it fits into the bigger picture.** For example, you could be operating out of Stage Six in your career and Seven with respect to your volunteer work. Your involvement with your church or synagogue could be at Stage Five in that it provides some needed community involvement. At the same time, you might be recognizing your marital default at Stage Four, if it is characterized by various insecurities, while your parenting reflects a Stage Three attitude of adherence to rules. Of course, all of this is possible with a Stage Six sex life and spirituality, etc. Refer to the calibrations in Part II that most apply to you for examples. (Use additional paper, if necessary.)

☐ **Stage Seven—**

☐ **Stage Six—**

☐ **Stage Five—**

☐ Stage Four—

☐ Stage Three—

☐ Stage Two—

☐ Stage One—

Make a calibration below for any part of your life that you are working on. Start with your present stage, as you have identified it in (2), and fill in the blanks, including your chosen target stages. (Use additional paper, if necessary.)

☐ **Stage Seven—**

☐ **Stage Six—**

☐ **Stage Five—**

☐ Stage Four—

☐ Stage Three—

☐ Stage Two—

☐ Stage One—

You may also find it helpful to consult the section on "Making the Climb" as well as the strategies at the end of the chapter in Part I that are dedicated to your present stage. In fact, you may even want to reread the entire chapter on any stage you are committed to leaving behind as your default in this area of your life.

What else might you need to believe/tell yourself to be at your chosen target stage in this part of your life? Write out any belief or whatever else occurs to you that would put you in lockstep with someone solidly in that target stage. **Commit yourself to using these affirmations, and refer to them at least daily, but as often as necessary:**

_____

_____

_____

_____

_____

_____

_____

What other action steps are you now willing to take or commit to in order to get from where you are now to where you want to be (your chosen target stage)? Consider this a "How do I get there?" roadmap. Identify and apply whatever strategies and action steps may be needed to lock in your target stage (e.g., those that speak to you, which can be found at the end of each relevant chapter in Part I).

_____

_____

_____

_____

_____

_____

_____

_____

_____

_____

_____

_____

_____

_____

_____

_____

_____

This breakthrough strategy cannot fail as long as you are committed to staying with it until you achieve the results you want!

BREAKTHROUGH STRATEGY #2

Manage or Remove a Hook By Using the Principles of *Stage Climbing*

Your hooks are your thoughts, feelings, and/or behaviors that are characteristic of stages other than your default stage in a given life area. For you to be fully in charge of your life, you need to manage them, so they do not lead to or become stifling hang-ups. This means to identify, understand and bring your hooks firmly under your control. **In order for you to function** *optimally*, **the goal is to neutralize the ones that in any way make your life problematic by causing negative emotions or** *bringing you down* **to a lower stage than would be optimal at any given time.** *Once you are able to manage your hooks, they simply represent more choices for you.* In other words, they go away when you don't want them and are available for when you do. Each time you do this with a hook, you have taken another major step toward being fully and consciously in control of your life.

To manage or remove a hook:

1)   **Identify the hook** (or the issue related to one) **that you would like to work on.** However, please remember the one most important thing— *Stage Climbing* **can only help you to make changes** *within yourself*. This means changing an attitude, belief, or behavior that is driving a self-defeating pattern or negative emotion. *Changing another person or some set of circumstances outside of yourself is not an option* **or within the realm of possibilities available to you with this exercise.**

Please choose only one hook to work on at a time:

_____

_____

_____

_____

Note: Please do this exercise separately for each hook that you want to address. You can download and reproduce this worksheet at StageClimbing.com/worksheets (Password: MyStageClimb).

2) **Identify the Stage(s) that typifies the hook you are working on.** What follows are the seven stages along with a sampling of the **most common** or universal attitudes and beliefs that would underlie **a problematic hook at each stage**. Underline or highlight those that apply to your hook. In the space provided, using additional paper if necessary, fill in your customized version of the belief(s) or attitude(s) that you recognize at each stage as driving/powering your own unique hook:

STAGE ONE HOOKS—e.g., "I can't do it" ... "It's too hard" ... "I am Inadequate"... "I must be taken care of"... "I am incapable of change or taking the initiative to better my life"... "I must be certain that some (or any) decision I make be the right one or I will not be able to decide (and/or handle the consequences)"... "What's happened to me in the past (e.g., my childhood, etc.) makes it impossible for me now to live a happy and fulfilling life that I can take charge of."

My version: _____

_____

STAGE TWO HOOKS--e.g., "I must have and do whatever I want, regardless of the effect I (or my actions) have on anyone else (or even regardless of the *long-term* consequences I cause to myself)"; "I don't want to change"; "I will be/ do / say whatever I have to in order to get what I want at any given moment"; "Life, and especially any aspect of it that I am concerned with should/must be easy"; "I must always be treated well; and anyone who doesn't is just asking for revenge."

My version: _____

_____

STAGE THREE HOOKS--e.g., "I should/must or should not/must not (insert a rule or dictum that doesn't serve you, but you feel compelled to obey, though you are not required to by any authority outside of yourself) _____"; "I must fit in by doing only what I should do and by being what I should be—that which is expected of me—or some dire consequence will result"; "Others should/must do (and even believe) things my way"; "I can't stand it when things don't go my way."

My version: _____

_____

STAGE FOUR HOOKS---e.g., "What (some other person or people that in the grand scheme of things don't really matter) thinks of me is crucially important"; "Rejection by someone else is unbearable and even a reason to reject myself"; "I must be loved or approved of by others (specific person or people in general) and meet their expectations"; "I can only accept myself to the degree that I am accepted by others"; "I must do well at everything I do. Anything less than perfect is totally unacceptable"; "Failing at something (e.g., a relationship, a job, an exam, a sexual performance, or to meet a goal) makes me a total failure (to myself, in the eyes of others, or both)"; "_____, (fill in the name of someone specific) must love me in the exact way that I require or our relationship is unfulfilling and perhaps even untenable."

My version: _____

_____

STAGE FIVE HOOKS—e.g., "I can't (or I don't want to) handle (fill in the blank_____) in my life right now—I am overwhelmed"; "I feel trapped with no way out"; "I must keep it all together and step up to the plate with respect to all of my roles and obligations (e.g., spouse, parent, breadwinner, manager, etc.), regardless of whether or not those roles are working or provide me feelings of satisfaction or gratification "; "I 'have it all', but still feel unfulfilled."

My version: _____

_____

STAGE SIX HOOKS—e.g., "Not only should I have passion for, but I should also feel personally gratified by everything I do"; "Changing the world that is larger than me or making the time to help someone else is not my mission, problem or concern right now."

My version: _____

_____

STAGE SEVEN HOOKS—e.g., "I must save the world, some person, or a subset of the world." It should be noted that even though they might sometimes present a minor conflict, genuine hooks in Stage Seven will rarely be problematic to you, once you identify them (or they are probably lower stage hooks in disguise).

My version: _____

_____

Now ask yourself some questions:

Are any of the beliefs I have identified above and written down completely true?

Yes_____No_____

Does the attitude or belief behind this problematic hook serve any purpose that would make me want to keep that attitude or belief?

Yes_____No_____

Am I open to adopting a new attitude(s) or belief(s) regarding this hook?

Yes_____No_____

Assuming you answered "No" to the first two questions and "Yes" to the third, **take a minute to write down how this hook and the attitudes and beliefs that underlie it might be affecting you. Note how things in your life would be different without the attitudes and beliefs you noted above and *if this hook were no longer problematic for you*** (use additional paper, if necessary)**:**

_____

_____

_____

_____

_____

Hold on to what you've just written concerning the effect of this hook now and how your life **could be** once the hook is benign and no longer has any power over you. **Refer to it whenever you need a little motivation in removing this or any other problematic hook**.

Next, use this list below as a selection or sampling, by the stages, of some new attitudes and beliefs that you can choose as *healthy alternatives or affirmations* to the problematic ones you have just identified. Underline or highlight those that apply to your hook.

  Important: *To the extent that you choose to live by these attitudes and beliefs, your hook is no longer problematic*:

Stage One—"I can do it/handle it and *I will*"; "I am tired of being dependent and relying on others. I now want to and will begin taking charge of my own life"; "Certainty does *not* exist, therefore I *choose* to become comfortable with uncertainty"; "'Too hard' implies impossible, which it isn't. 'Difficult' is merely a challenge I can handle"; "I choose to be free of my past, wherever it limits me."

Stage Two—"Being excessively self-absorbed has thus far not gotten me what I thought/hoped it would, what I truly wanted or satisfaction around what I have gotten", "Nobody has *everything* they want"; "I can't always control how people treat me, only my reaction to them"; "Life is not always easy and I choose to accept that"; "There are long-term benefits *to me* in treating others as I would like to be treated."

Stage Three—"I am ready to start examining the unquestioned rules I have lived by (and/or that I have demanded others live by), and to consider being more flexible and open to new ideas that are now a better fit for me and my life"; "Fitting in is only one of many choices that are available to me"; "Other people have the same wide array of choices regarding how to live their lives as I do."

Stage Four—"People who won't accept me for who I am are no longer worth my time and attention"; "There is much more to life than putting boundless energy into fitting in and/or the hope of getting others to admire and/or envy, love and/or approve of me"; "Love and approval from certain people may be nice, but not as essential as I have told myself it is"; "I give *myself* unconditional acceptance regardless of who else does"; "I can only do my best, and I hereby let go of all versions of that impossible standard called perfection"; "Failing at something does not make me a failure"; "I can handle things even when I don't like them"; "How anyone else feels about me is out of my control."

Stage Five—"I want to be doing what I love and to feel rewarded internally (as well as externally)"; "I can handle being overwhelmed, and resolve to use those times when I *feel* overwhelmed as learning experiences that can act as insight to draw upon when deciding whether to take things on"; "Satisfaction and gratification are nice to have, but I realize and accept that there are many things I choose to have in my life that don't provide them to the extent I wish they would"; "I now take responsibility for putting into my life that which will fulfill me."

Stage Six—"Life is good; but there is something more to life than my own gratification. It's time to focus on the world that's larger than me."

Stage Seven—"On to the next (perhaps even a bigger or more challenging) mission!"

Using the above list (especially those you have underlined) **as a frame of reference, write out** *new affirmations* (attitudes and beliefs) **that represent how you** *choose* **to think and feel about** *this* **problematic hook** (use additional paper, if necessary and make your list of new affirmations as comprehensive as possible)**:**

_____

_____

_____

_____

_____

_____

_____

_____

Now ask yourself these questions:

Are my new affirmations regarding this hook *completely* true for me?

Yes_____No_____

Do my new affirmation(s) above remove or neutralize this problematic hook?

Yes_____No_____

(If you answered yes to both questions, go on to (3). **Most importantly, commit yourself to living by your** *new* **affirmations; and** *refer to them as often as necessary until they become a hardwired part of you*!

However, if either question got a "no" answer, keep tweaking your affirmation(s) until you can answer "yes" to both questions. If you are stuck, it will also be helpful for you to revisit the chapter on the relevant stage in Part I, especially the "Making the Climb" section, strategies and action steps as well as Part II for calibrations related to this hook.

3) **Choose your target stage** (consider this your goal) **from which you would prefer or choose to be operating, whenever you are up against this hook.**

Stage 1_____2_____3_____4_____5_____6_____7_____

4) **When you now look at this hook through the lens of your *chosen* target stage, how do you see it?** How is your attitude or perhaps even your life different? Is there anything else do you need to do, to believe or to tell yourself when necessary, so that you are never undermined or held back by this hook again? **What other *action steps* are you now willing to take to move beyond *this* problematic hook?** Make note of your answers to these important questions here (use additional paper, if necessary) and refer to your affirmations and action steps whenever any version of this hook challenges you again.

_____

_____

_____

_____

_____

_____

_____

_____

In most situations, what you have done with this exercise is all you need to do, along with religiously remembering to live by, behave according to, **refer to *and* defer to your newly chosen beliefs and attitudes regarding this hook.** With your strong persistence, **they will soon become second nature— a hardwired part of you.**

BREAKTHROUGH STRATEGY #3

Resolve a Specific Issue, Problem, or
Dilemma by Using the Principles of *Stage Climbing*

This strategy is quite similar to the previous exercise except that this one is especially designed to help you to **use the *Stage Climbing* drill as a way of problem solving as well as thinking about any issue that is *within* your power to resolve**. Since this strategy is designed to address a broad range of issues, parts of it may not apply to yours. Therefore, please feel free to customize it in any way that meets your needs.

To resolve a specific issue, problem or dilemma:

1) **Identify the issue, problem, or dilemma that you would like to resolve.** Once again, please remember that *Stage Climbing* **can only help you to make changes *within yourself*.** This means changing an attitude, belief, or behavior that is driving a self-defeating pattern, a negative emotion, or serving to push you in the wrong direction. **Changing another person or circumstances *outside of yourself is not an option* with this exercise.**

   Please choose only one issue, problem or dilemma to work on at a time:

   _____

   _____

   _____

   _____

   _____

   _____

   _____

   Do this separately for each issue that you want to address. (Note: You can download and reproduce this worksheet at *StageClimbing.com/worksheets* (Password: MyStageClimb).

2) **Identify the Stage(s) that typifies the issue, problem or dilemma you are working on.** This is the lens through which you are **now** seeing the situation.

Stage 1_____2_____3_____4_____5_____6_____7_____

If this stage is unclear to you, please revisit step 2 in the previous exercise on managing hooks (Breakthrough Strategy #2) where this step is explained in much more detail.

3) **Choose the target stage that would be ideal for you, to be able to resolve or obliterate this issue, problem, or dilemma optimally.** This stage is the one from which you would most like to be operating as you address or resolve this issue. If you are not sure, please use the calibrations in Part II closest to your issue for reference. If you are still in doubt, start from Stage Five—the most neutral of the seven stages.

Stage 1_____2_____3_____4_____5_____6_____7_____

4) **What would be the situation** (how would things be different or how would your life be different) *if* **the issue, problem or dilemma that you are working on were completely resolved?** Use additional paper, if necessary:

_____

_____

_____

_____

_____

_____

5) **Make a calibration for your issue** below. Start with the present stage, which is where you now see yourself with respect to this issue that you have identified in (2). Then answer some questions regarding your target stage (3): **What would you be doing or doing differently *if* you were operating out of the target stage you have chosen with respect to this issue? What would you believe differently about it?**

For each stage, fill in anything that occurs to you that may be relevant to your issue. **This includes any aspects of how you may be operating at the lower stages when addressing it**. (Use additional paper, if necessary)**:**

☐ **Stage Seven—**

☐ **Stage Six—**

☐ **Stage Five—**

☐ Stage Four—

☐ Stage Three—

☐ Stage Two—

☐ Stage One—

Review your calibration. If you've done it completely, **you can see a difference between how you were looking at this issue before and how you can see it now through the lens of your chosen target stage**. Take a minute to fill in anything that can make this perspective even more complete.

6) **Assume the point of view and posture of your chosen target stage. How do you now view this issue, problem or dilemma,**

presumably through the eyes of a *Six* or *Seven* (or a *Five*, if that is the target stage in this case that you've chosen)**?** (Use additional paper, if necessary.)

_____

_____

_____

_____

_____

If you were operating at your highest potential (and solidly at your target stage) **in this part of your life, what advice would you have for someone else** (whom you cared about) **who was struggling with this issue?** (Consider this "source of advice" and wisdom to be a great resource that is always available to you.)

_____

_____

_____

_____

_____

What action steps are you now willing to take or commit to toward resolving this issue, problem or dilemma? What support, if any, do you need, and how do you intend to get it? (Use additional paper, if necessary.)

_____

_____

_____

_____

_____

What else is left to do or to believe/tell yourself at your chosen target stage in order to *obliterate* this issue, problem or dilemma *in a permanent way*? For example, are you putting yourself down by telling yourself that you are not capable of resolving this? Or that you can't stand the pain or discomfort of change? Or that change is impossible? That you don't have the information, support, or other resources to pull this off? **You know how you sabotage yourself! Now is the time to commit to changing all of that and start focusing *a little bit less on the problem and a lot more on the solution*.**

Write out any additional new beliefs or attitudes as affirmations (the way you have done previously), and refer to them as often as necessary until this issue no longer exists. Also, include any additional perspectives, insights, and/or action steps necessary to reach the resolution you are seeking:

_____

_____

_____

_____

_____

_____

_____

_____

_____

_____

_____

_____

_____

Use additional paper, if necessary.

BREAKTHROUGH STRATEGY #4

Make a Decision Using a Three-Step *Stage Climbing* Strategy

This simple exercise can be applied to almost any decision for which a direction is unclear, including relationship, career. and/or lifestyle issues.

1)   **The decision I am trying to make concerns the following:**

_____

_____

_____

_____

_____

Use additional paper, if necessary.

2)   **Do a calibration that answers the following question: What would be the direction that someone operating *at each of the seven stages* would most likely take?** (Consult the calibrations in Part II and use additional paper, as necessary.)

☐ **Stage Seven—**

☐ **Stage Six—**

☐ **Stage Five—**

☐ Stage Four—

☐ Stage Three—

☐ Stage Two—

☐ Stage One—

3) **Based on the above calibration, choose the view that is most consistent with your long-term interest;** and note the stage that is speaking the most sense to you regarding your decision:

Stage 1_____2_____3_____4_____5_____6_____7_____

If you are unable to identify the best stage, keep refining your views and insights at each stage of your calibration until the right decision becomes clear to you.

Finally, write out your decision and any related action plan that comes to you through the voice of you at your target stage or the stage that most resonates for you regarding this decision:

_____

_____

_____

_____

_____

_____

_____

_____

_____

_____

Can I say that based on what I know now, this is the right direction and action plan to take regarding this decision?

Yes_____No_____

Answer "yes" if you are satisfied with your decision. If you answered "no," carefully go back over the steps and refine your responses until you are satisfied and can answer "yes."

BREAKTHROUGH STRATEGY #5

Define *"Yourself,"* by the Stages

Some fun lists to make to help any aspect of your stage climb: (Use additional paper, wherever necessary.)

☐ **Stage Seven**—The person(s) I admire the most or my favorite mentor(s)—real or imagined—in the area I would most like to make my best contribution(s) are:

_____

_____

_____

_____

_____

_____

_____

They have my admiration as a role model(s), because they inspire me to do the following:

_____

_____

_____

_____

_____

_____

_____

_____

☐ **Stage Six**— I love:

_____

_____

_____

_____

_____

_____

_____

I am passionate about:

_____

_____

_____

_____

_____

_____

(Note: Make these lists as long as possible.)

☐ **Stage Five**—The roles in my life that I am committed to are:

_____

_____

_____

_____

_____

_____

_____

☐ **Stage Five, continued ...** If I were to take complete control of my life, I would change (add, delete, or modify) these roles (list and explain how):

_____

_____

_____

_____

_____

_____

☐ **Stage Four**—If I had absolutely no fears, anxieties, or needs for blanket approval I would:

_____

_____

_____

_____

_____

_____

☐ **Stage Three**—If I were making and living exclusively by my own rules, I would:

_____

_____

_____

_____

_____

_____

☐   **Stage Two**—If I stopped sabotaging myself by thinking and /or behaving as if I can always have whatever I want I would:

_____

_____

_____

_____

_____

_____

☐   **Stage One**—If I were taking the initiative to completely and unquestionably take charge of my life, I would:

_____

_____

_____

_____

_____

_____

Remember to visit *www.StageClimbing.com* (Password: MyStageClimb)
anytime for additional strategies, help with your custom calibrations, and down-
loadable forms and worksheets containing all of the strategies and exercises in
this chapter. **Most importantly, revisit this chapter often and *be relentless*
in using these strategies anytime you become aware of another problematic hook or a new challenge to address!**

EPILOG
EMBRACING YOUR SEVEN STAGES

*"To laugh often and much, to win the respect of intelligent
people and the affection of children, to earn the appreciation of
honest critiques and endure the betrayal of false friends, to
appreciate beauty, to find the best in others ... to leave the world
a bit better, whether by a healthy child or a garden patch ... to know
that even one life has breathed easier because you
have lived. This is to have succeeded!"*

—Ralph Waldo Emerson

As you *stage climb*, **your life choices dramatically increase.** Remember, it is the nature of humankind to have hooks in all seven stages. Hooks are problematic only when they hold you back and become your hang-ups. Once you are in control of them, those hooks can be thought of as simply more choices at your disposal for whenever you need them. Sources of fulfillment at one stage may no longer work for you at the next. This reckoning with yourself as well as the people, places, and things around you is also an ongoing and organic, lifelong process.

You now know that you are free to operate out of any chosen stage—higher or lower—at any time. That is a great definition of living at your highest potential. You also know what motivates you at each stage. Whenever you function at the lower stages, even if it is rarely, you can now do it with deliberate consciousness.

If you believe that, all things considered, we are each doing our best at any given time, please accept *Stage Climbing* as simply one tool to make your best even better. You have *arrived,* to the extent that your life is as you want it to be. *Stage Climbing* is a process that continues as long as you are alive. It will help you continue to hit that moving target. I urge you to use every means possible to maximize *your* process so that your life can be one that is lived and enjoyed to the fullest.

I wrote *Stage Climbing* with one very important intention: that you, my reader, will keep it close to you and refer to it often. In addition, our Web site: *StageClimbing.com*—like *Stage Climbing* and life itself—is a work in process. We are constantly adding new strategies to it, resources, and sources of help for you and all aspects of your *Stage Climbing* process. On *StageClimbing.com* we will continue to offer many types of support: one-to-one coaching, workshops, seminars, teleseminars, blogs, articles, audios, videos, and many new applications that you can apply to your life. So I invite you to stay in touch through *StageClimbing.com*, email, snail mail, our social media sites (e.g., become a fan on Facebook and a follower on Twitter), or by coming to one of our events. Please let us know how you are doing, how *Stage Climbing* has had an impact on your life, and how we can be of further help to you.

I hope that you will consider this not the end, but only the beginning of our relationship. Feel free to get in touch at any time that we can be of help or support. I wish you much happiness, success, and fulfillment.

May you reach your highest potential in every part of your life!

Michael S. Broder, Ph.D.

REFERENCES

Beck, Aaron T. 1976. *Cognitive Therapy and the Emotional Disorders.* New York, NY: International Universities Press.

Broder, Michael. 1989. *The Art of Living Single.* New York, NY: Avon.

Broder, Michael.1993. *The Art of Staying Together*: New York, NY: Avon.

Broder, Michael. 2002. *Can Your Relationship be Saved? How to Know Whether to Stay or Go.* New York, NY: Impact Publishers.

Broder, Michael, & Goldman, Arlene. 2004. *Secrets of Sexual Ecstasy*. New York, NY: Penguin Group.

Deci, E. L., & Ryan, R. M. 2008. Facilitating Optimal Motivation and Psychological Well-being Across Life's Domains. *Canadian Psychology 49*, 14–23.

Ellis, Albert. 1994. *Reason and Emotion in Psychotherapy: A Comprehensive Method of Treating Human Disturbances*. Yucca Valley, CA: Citadel.

Ellis, Albert. 1975. A *New Guide to Rational Living*. Chatsworth, CA: Wilshire Book Co.

Erikson, Erik. 1963. *Childhood and Society*. New York, NY: Norton.

Kohlberg, Lawrence. 1987. *Child Psychology and Childhood Education; A Cognitive Developmental View*. United Kingdom Longman Group.

Lazarus, Arnold A. 1981. *The Practice of Multimodal Therapy.* New York, NY: McGraw-Hill.

Maslow, Abraham. 1987. *Motivation and Personality.* New York, NY: Harper Collins.

Maslow, Abraham. 1998. *Toward a Psychology of Being,* Hoboken, NJ: Wiley.

Orwell, George. 1949. **Nineteen Eighty-Four. A Novel**. New York, NY: Harcourt, Brace & Co.

Peck, M. Scott. 2003.*The Road Less Traveled*, New York, NY: Touchstone.

Strachey, Ed. J., with Freud, Anna. 1953–1964. *The Standard Edition of the Complete Psychological Works of Sigmund Freud,* 24 Volumes. London.

Sullivan, C., Grant, M., & Grant, J. D. 1957. *The Development of Interpersonal Maturity: Psychiatry Journal for the Study of Interpersonal Processes* 20: 373–385.

NOTES

NOTES

NOTES

SELECTED BOOKS AND AUDIO PROGRAMS BY DR. MICHAEL BRODER

Books

The Art of Living Single

The Art of Staying Together.

Can Your Relationship Be Saved? How to Know Whether to Stay or Go

Secrets of Sexual Ecstasy

Audio Programs

Positive Attitude Training

Self Actualization: Reaching Your Full Potential

Help Yourself Audiotherapy Series©:

- *Can Your Relationship Be Saved?*
- *How to Develop Self-Confidence and a Positive Self-image*
- *How to Develop the Ingredients for Staying Together*
- *How to Enhance Passion and Sexual Satisfaction*
- *How to Find A New Love Relationship That Will Work for You*
- *How to Manage Stress and Make It Work for You*
- *Letting Go of Your Ended Love Relationship*
- *Making Crucial Choices and Major Life Changes*
- *Overcoming Your Anger: In the Shortest Possible Period of Time*

- *Overcoming Your Anxiety: In the Shortest Possible Period of Time*

- *Overcoming Your Depression: In the Shortest Possible Period of Time*

- *The Single Life: How to Love It With or Without a Relationship*

**All available at *DrMichaelBroder.com*
or by calling 1-800-434-8255.**

Please visit StageClimbing.com (Password: MyStageClimb) for additional resources, downloads and worksheets or to sign up to receive our *Stage Climbing* newsletter **containing new tips, applications, and strategies as well as events—virtual and otherwise—that you can attend.**

Have Dr. Michael Broder speak at your next event. He is available for keynote presentations, half- and full-day seminars. For more information about Dr. Michael Broder's professional services, continuing education seminars for mental health professionals, talks and workshops tailored to the needs of your group or organization or Dr. Broder's media appearances, please go to **DrMichaelBroder.com.**

To contact Michael Broder:

Email: *MB@MichaelBroder.com*
Phone: 215-545-7000
Address: 255 South 17th Street, Suite 2900, Philadelphia, PA 19103.

ABOUT THE AUTHOR

Michael S. Broder, Ph.D. is a renowned psychologist, executive coach, bestselling author, continuing education seminar leader, and popular speaker. He is an acclaimed expert in cognitive behavioral therapy, specializing in high achievers and relationship issues. His work centers on bringing about major change in the shortest time possible.

A sought-after media guest, he has appeared on *Oprah* and *The Today Show* as well as making more than a thousand other TV and radio appearances. For many years, Dr. Broder also hosted the radio program *Psychologically Speaking with Dr Michael Broder*. He has been featured in the *New York Times*, the *Wall Street Journal*, *Time*, *Newsweek*, and hundreds of other publications.

Dr. Broder's previous books include *The Art of Living Single, The Art of Staying Together: A Couple's Guide to Intimacy and Respect,* and *Can Your Relationship Be Saved? How To Know Whether To Stay Or Go.* His audio programs include *Positive Attitude Training, Self Actualization: Reaching Your Full Potential,* and *The Help Yourself Audiotherapy Series*, which are used frequently by mental health professionals and coaches with their clients.

Dr. Broder earned his Ph.D. at Temple University. He conducts seminars, talks, and presentations to professional as well as lay audiences worldwide, and has trained many thousands of psychiatrists, psychologists, and other mental health professionals. Please visit DrMichaelBroder.com for more information.